D0146269

Janet M. Wright, PhD

Lesbian Step Families
An Ethnography of Love

The Haworth Press, Inc.

Lesbian Step Families
An Ethnography of Love

HAWORTH Innovations in Feminist Studies
Esther Rothblum, PhD and Ellen Cole, PhD
Senior Co-Editors

New, Recent, and Forthcoming Titles:

Prisoners of Ritual: An Odyssey into Female Genital Circumcision in Africa
by Hanny Lightfoot-Klein

Foundations for a Feminist Restructuring of the Academic Disciplines
edited by Michele Paludi and Gertrude A. Steuernagel

Hippocrates' Handmaidens: Women Married to Physicians by Esther Nitzberg

Waiting: A Diary of Loss and Hope in Pregnancy by Ellen Judith Reich

God's Country: A Case Against Theocracy by Sandy Rapp

Women and Aging: Celebrating Ourselves by Ruth Raymond Thone

Women's Conflicts About Eating and Sexuality: The Relationship Between Food and Sex
by Rosalyn M. Meadow and Lillie Weiss

A Woman's Odyssey into Africa: Tracks Across a Life by Hanny Lightfoot-Klein

Anorexia Nervosa and Recovery: A Hunger for Meaning by Karen Way

Women Murdered by the Men They Loved by Constance A. Bean

Reproductive Hazards in the Workplace: Mending Jobs, Managing Pregnancies
by Regina Kenen

Our Choices: Women's Personal Decisions About Abortion by Sumi Hoshiko

Tending Inner Gardens: The Healing Art of Feminist Psychotherapy
by Lesley Irene Shore

The Way of the Woman Writer by Janet Lynn Roseman

Racism in the Lives of Women: Testimony, Theory, and Guides to Anti-Racist Practice
by Jeanne Adleman and Gloria Enguídanos

Advocating for Self: Women's Decisions Concerning Contraception by Peggy Matteson

Feminist Visions of Gender Similarities and Differences by Meredith M. Kimball

Experiencing Abortion: A Weaving of Women's Words by Eve Kushner

Menopause, Me and You: The Sound of Women Pausing by Ann M. Voda

Fat—A Fate Worse Than Death?: Women, Weight, and Appearance by Ruth Raymond Thone

Feminist Theories and Feminist Psychotherapies: Origins, Themes, and Variations
by Carolyn Zerbe Enns

Celebrating the Lives of Jewish Women: Patterns in a Feminist Sampler edited by Rachel
Josefowitz Siegel and Ellen Cole

Women and AIDS: Negotiating Safer Practices, Care, and Representation edited by Nancy
L. Roth and Linda K. Fuller

A Menopausal Memoir: Letters from Another Climate by Anne Herrmann

Women in the Antarctic edited by Esther D. Rothblum, Jacqueline S. Weinstock,
and Jessica F. Morris

Breasts: The Women's Perspective on an American Obsession by Carolyn Latteier

Lesbian Step Families: An Ethnography of Love by Janet M. Wright

Women, Families, and Feminist Politics: A Global Exploration by Kate Conway-Turner
and Suzanne Cherrin

Women's Work: A Survey of Scholarship By and About Women by Donna Musialowski Ashcraft

Lesbian Step Families
An Ethnography of Love

Janet M. Wright, PhD

The Haworth Press
New York • London

The Haworth Press, Inc., 10 Alice Street, Binghamton, NY 13904-1580

Cover design by Marylouise E. Doyle.

Library of Congress Cataloging-in-Publication Data

Wright, Janet M.
  Lesbian step families : an ethnography of love / Janet M. Wright.
      p.   cm.
  Includes bibliographical references and index.
  ISBN 0-7890-0436-4 (alk. paper)
  1. Lesbian mothers. 2. Lesbian couples—Family relationships. 3. Step mothers. 4. Step families. I. Title.
HQ75.53.W75   1998
306.87—dc21   97-46157
                                                                                    CIP

To the participant families, who generously gave so much of themselves;

To my partner, Lael Greenfield, who jumped into deep water with both feet and who hangs in there with love, support, and generosity;

To my mother, Marion Marcus Wright, and my late father, Hollis Garrett Wright, who love me for who I am, and who taught me to want to be good, honest, and loving;

And to my awesome children—Luc and Isaac Nadeau, Brady Nelle Wright, and Jamie and Micah Wright Maples.

ABOUT THE AUTHOR

Janet M. Wright, PhD, is Assistant Professor and Chair of the Department of Social Work at the University of Wisconsin–Whitewater. She is a licensed clinical social worker and a member of the National Association of Social Workers, the Council on Social Work Education, the National Women's Studies Association, and the National Council on Family Relations. Dr. Wright and her partner are the lesbian co-parents of five young adults and children, ages nine to twenty-five.

CONTENTS

Foreword

This book is exhilarating. By putting down one honest word after another, Janet Wright captures and celebrates the everyday lives of lesbian step families. Wright's work makes us see in new ways: richer, more complex, questioning what we thought we knew about mothering, families, gender, homophobia.

A thread runs through the book, a tension between the things all families hold in common and what makes step families unique. Wright takes us along to tae kwon do class and church. We glimpse families laying linoleum and sipping lemonade. We listen to parents squabble about how strict they ought to be with their son. Drawn into family life, we forget, for a moment, that the families are headed by two women.

But we cannot forget entirely. Wright shows us how a family with two mothers struggles, day after day, to be recognized as a family. Their children harbor fears that someday others will strike out at them because they are different. "It's an angry world out there, you know," says seven-year-old Pauli.

In the fissure between being like other families and being different, lesbian step families carry on their lives in creative ways. Wright speaks of the possibilities and challenges of living between the spaces. For instance: What does parenting look like when neither parent can claim male privilege? Never shying away from complexity, Wright chronicles where lesbian families fumble and where they take flight.

At the center of Wright's book is a chapter that portrays the "heart and passion" of each of the five families. Each family finds its own way. Each family lives on in my memory: Terry, Tanya, and Kevin; Lori, Cady, and Molly. In their everyday lives, without strident politics, they bear witness to who they are. And so does Janet Wright. "My family is a lesbian step family," she tells readers. She speaks of "we" and "our children" and there's never a doubt about whose side she's on. Wright stands with lesbian families.

Janet Wright is a social worker, a researcher, a scholar, a teacher, a lesbian partner, and a parent. She brings all her knowledge and wisdom to bear in her writing. Her work is a touchstone for those of us who strive for compassionate, respectful research and service. Through Wright's book, all of us come to see lesbian step families. They are visible to us, collectively and one at a time. And, perhaps even more important, lesbian step families can see themselves. They can draw pride and power and parenting strategies from the stories of women and children making families in a space where society says there ought not to be families. This heartening vision is the true gift of Wright's book.

Linda Thompson, PhD
(former) Professor of Child and Family Studies
University of Wisconsin at Madison

Acknowledgments

It has been a long and anxious process to complete this book. Fortunately, I have had much support and encouragement along the way.

First and foremost, I thank the families who participated in this study. They were all incredibly generous, opening their homes and their hearts to me and to all those who read this book. I have tremendous admiration for their courage and their generosity. I have the deepest respect for the originality expressed in creating their families.

I am grateful to my dissertation committee members for their patience and endurance, and encouragement throughout the years. Linda Thompson has been especially helpful, critiquing my work with compassion and honesty and respect. My dissertation advisor, Diane Kravetz, has been a guide and support through the bureaucratic maze, encouraging me to keep at it even when the hoops through which I had to jump seemed endless. My other committee members—Joan Robertson, Mary Ann Test, and Mariamne Whatley—have encouraged me to finish and have always let me know they believed I could do it—even when I had serious doubts.

I have had other academic mentors along the way. Margaret Crosbie-Burnett was the first person who really affirmed my work and my topic and encouraged me to actively pursue it. She also served on my dissertation committee for a year before she left for warmer climates.

There were four special colleagues who read all of my work and offered ongoing critiques and challenges. Bill Powell provided the English teacher's perspective, giving me valuable editing feedback. Penny Engebose and Sharon Hayes read from their perspectives as lesbian step family members, adding their heartfelt, sometimes painful, and sometimes joyous confirmations. Sunshine Jones offered a supportive and critical analytical perspective, challenging me to delve deeper. I am grateful for their contributions, which so enrich the final product.

My fellow department members at the University of Wisconsin–Whitewater have supported me and encouraged me to complete my PhD, not only with words but also by sometimes "picking up the slack" so that I could concentrate on my degree work. I am especially indebted to Vicki Vogel, who not only transcribed all of the interviews and typed the final paper, but also added her insight and perceptiveness. It has been such a pleasure working with Vicki because she always comes through.

My friends have managed to continuously show interest in my project. I especially thank Steffi Greene, Gail Cyrkiel, Crystal Hyslop, Janice Czyscon, Carmen Hyslop, and Miranda Hyslop-Garza for maintaining interest over the long run. But many others have encouraged me to keep going and I thank you all.

Finally, I acknowledge my family. My partner, Lael Greenfield, read every word, heard every complaint, saw every tear, survived my distraction and my compulsion and she still loves me—who could ask for more? My mother, Marion Marcus Wright, supported me emotionally and with timely monetary gifts. She and Lael believed in me, even when I didn't believe in myself. My brother, Gary Wright, and sister, Judy Burtner, have always supported and loved me. Special thanks go to my "in-laws," Alverta and Lawrence Greenfield, who have accepted me as a daughter-in-law and who have helped make it possible for me to live in the country where my spirit thrives.

It has been a pleasure to have my older sons, Luc and Isaac Nadeau, begin to take a genuine interest in my work. It is an interesting stage of life—being a parent to adults. I mostly enjoy it. I am always learning from my children. Luc and Isaac, as well as Brady Nelle Wright and Jamie and Micah Maples, remind me of what is truly important in life. They keep me humble.

Chapter 1

Complexity and Opportunity

BEGINNING

This book began over fifteen years ago out of pain—like many good ideas. My first experience in a lesbian step family, although it held the possibility (and even at times the actuality) of much good, was ultimately more painful than healthy. It was in the midst of this experience that I returned to school to get my PhD in social welfare. From the beginning, my concern about my own family's welfare, and my concern for the many lesbian step family members that I knew who were also in pain, fueled my desire to learn about and share information about lesbian step families. I could find no information on the topic, which only increased my desire to understand.

My original step family no longer exists. However, the creativity that it spawned has continued in the writing of this book. My present step family, with all of its ongoing struggles, successfully nourishes enduring love.

Family has been the most compelling interest of my life. As a child growing up in a stable, loving, nuclear family, the idea that I might one day be part of a step family never even entered my realm of possibilities—the fact that it would be a lesbian step family would have been unthinkable, nonexistent fiction. And yet, there I was at age thirty-one, coming out, madly in love, and the mother of three children ages seven, five, and two. In my initial coming out euphoria, I believed that my partner and I and my children would be a family instantly and that, because we were two ardently feminist women, we would somehow be an even better family than the traditional heterosexual family.

I was disabused of this belief rather quickly as my partner's and my very different parenting styles, my children's grief at their parents' divorce, personal problems, and the absence of anywhere to turn for help took their toll. But my partner and I persisted in pursuing the family dream. I became pregnant through alternative insemination from a donor and gave birth in 1983 to another son. Five years later, my partner also gave birth to a son, after alternative insemination from a friend's sperm, thus increasing our family size to seven. These mutual children seemed to strengthen our family connections—initially.

It wasn't until I entered graduate school seven years later that it occurred to me that the literature on heterosexual step families might be helpful for our family too. Throwing myself into research on step families, however, did little to alleviate the crumbling and ultimately the breakup of my own step family. But, in the midst of my own personal darkness, it did give me hope—the hope that is afforded by knowledge. There *were* skills that could be learned to nurture a more positive step family! If some heterosexual step families could be successful, then so could some lesbian step families— given adequate knowledge *and* support. My greatest hope is that this book will provide some of that knowledge and support for lesbian step family members, their allies, and their counselors.

This book, then, originated as a dissertation for my PhD in social welfare. It is an ethnographic study of what actually occurs within five different lesbian step families and in their interactions with the outside world, as well as how the members of those families interpret or define their family experiences. The book provides an in-depth description of how these couples share (or do not share) parenting tasks, how the family members negotiate their relationships with each other, as well as the strategies they use to cope with bigotry and invisibility. It also examines how each family member interprets her/his family experience.

These are not perfect families. They struggle with the challenges that life presents, sometimes successfully, sometimes less so. I admire these families not because they are ideal but rather because they face their challenges with courage and tenacity, and ongoing love for each other.

I searched with these families for some of the answers to such broad questions as:

1. How do two women (one who is a legal parent and one who is in an unprescribed role as a kind of step mother) negotiate parenting?
2. What effects does this structure of a mother and step mother parenting together have on the children's definitions of male and female and their understandings of coupling?
3. What strategies do family members use to define and cope with oppression and what are the effects of that oppression on families?

This book focuses on lesbian step families—how they define and negotiate their family lives in a world that is at best, tolerating and at worst, bigoted and destructive toward their existence. For the purposes of this study, lesbian step families are defined as two women who self-define as lesbians, at least one of whom brings a child or children from a former relationship with her into the present family situation. The terms lesbian and step are used as adjectives to clarify the type of family being studied. I reject the use of the word "stepfamily," which implies that this structure is something other than "family."

There are many different types and structures of families, each with special strengths and unique challenges. Research on families other than the nuclear family has been distorted by the "deficit model" perspective—the assumption that no other family type can be as healthy or as nurturing for its members. Pasley (1988) writes about this problem in step family research:

> A consistent recommendation for researchers of remarriage and step parenting is to avoid the use of the deficit family model. This model implies that differences found between intact first-marriage families and all other structurally unique families (e.g., single parent, remarried) are interpreted such that the latter are less good, more dysfunctional, or deficient in some way. The nuclear family is, thus, used as the standard by which all other families are judged. A consistent argument made by clinicians and researchers is that reliance on the deficit comparison results in research that ignores the heterogeneity of step families, emphasizes step family weaknesses, and fails to consider the possibility that relationships between step

family members (e.g., step parent-step child) may be qualitatively different from relationships in intact, first-marriage families. (pp. 452-453)

The families described in this book represent, in my opinion,
some of the best characteristics of family—they love and nurture
each other, care for each other in sickness and health, tolerate and
even accept each others' weaknesses, and trust each other to be
there in the long run. The fact that they are lesbian families and step
families does not change the most basic underlying commitment
that they have to each other as, simply, family members.

THEORETICAL PERSPECTIVES

This book is about five functional lesbian step families, yet it also
provides food for feminist theoretical thought. Lesbian step families
are a fertile ground for examining and contributing to theories
because they represent a unique standpoint. A major discourse
within feminist theory has been the issue of "rethinking" the family
and particularly the role of motherhood. Feminists are concerned
with how sexism is perpetuated and recreated within the family. In
addition, feminists have questioned the role of "mother" as a possible causal factor of women's oppression. An important theme is
the debate of how to reconcile the needs of children to be dependent
and nurtured with the needs of women to be active participants in
all aspects of our society.

Interpretations of the impact of the family on women's rights and
equality are widely variant, even within the paradigm of feminist
theories. Early radical feminist writing emphasized the nuclear family
as a root to women's oppression and advocated for its eradication
(Firestone, 1972). Other theorists have developed this theme, exploring
the limitations not only in the nuclear family, but in any kind of
"home," which by its very nature is exclusionary (Allen, 1986; Martin
and Mohanty, 1988).

At the other end of the continuum are several feminist writers who
emphasize the importance of family, and, for some, the importance of
the nuclear family as it has been traditionally defined (Elshtain, 1981;
Friedan, 1981; Greer, 1984). This school affirms gender differentiation,

celebrates traditional feminine qualities, and urges a discontinuation of the struggle against male domination in the family as a detractor from more important feminist struggles.

Most of the feminist theorists have grounded their doctrines by examining and studying traditional nuclear family forms. This study suggests that some of these questions might be addressed by studying different family forms—in this case, lesbian step families. These families offer a unique perspective from which to view the perpetuation of sexism and women's oppression for three major reasons.

There Is a Mother and a Step Mother in the Same Family Household, Providing an Interesting Perspective on Shared Mothering

Lesbian step families house a mother and an "unmother" in the same family, blurring this duality and challenging the Western European concept of parental ownership of children. Mothering has recently been defined by that culture as the private responsibility of one mother for her children. This privatization of the child nurturing responsibility has created a sharp distinction between mothers and "unmothers," and a greater dependency between mother and child (Schaffer, 1977).

Nuclear families, and particularly the institution of motherhood, have been built on the cornerstone of parental possession of children. In some manner, possession is seen to precede and predicate the kind of unconditional love which child development experts have deemed necessary for the development of self-esteem. Lesbian families challenge the myth of exclusivity of motherhood. Some lesbians are creating new combinations of motherhood and adulthood.

Embedded in the definitions of possession are two key concepts. One is the idea of having power over something—to have as property, to hold or to occupy, to have belonging to one. This control over one's children and wife has been a crucial factor in the patriarchal nuclear family. In addition, the capitalist ethic encourages individuals to amass possessions as power and control. In a world where women often feel powerless, this concept of possession of (power and control over) children is difficult to relinquish. And yet, as with all relationships based on the concept of domination and control, it creates an unhealthy dependence between the controller and the controlled.

Within the lesbian step family, in order to share mothering, the biological mother must also share her mother power with the step mother. A second, different meaning of possess may illuminate how this can be done. Possession means also "to have knowledge of, to familiarize" (Random House Dictionary, 1987). As the step mother becomes more intimately familiar with the child, the biological mother may also become able or willing to share mothering.

If we redefine power, as many feminists (Ferguson, 1989; hooks, 1984; Rich, 1980; and others) suggest, as not power *over* someone or something (power = dominance), but as the ability to act, energy, strength, and effective interaction (Hartsock, 1981), we see an overlapping function with the second definition of possess. That is, we have power with specific children (or people) because of our ability to interact effectively with them, based on our knowledge of them, our familiarity with them. Thus, possession of a child becomes reliant on one's commitment to spend consistent time with the child and one's quality of interactions and caretaking abilities. As an adult takes more responsibility for a child, she/he also gains more power with the child.

Some child development experts insist that children need a strong bond with one parent (usually described as the mother) for the first several years of life (Fraiberg, 1977; Miller, 1983). However, many groups outside the white, middle-class family norm have maintained larger or different family structures that have provided financial and emotional security for their members. Martin and Martin (1978) found that the black extended family has played a major sustaining role for African Americans. According to McAdoo (1983), although in white families the male and female roles have traditionally been rigidly defined, in African-American families, "Both parents share the task of earning a living and share the domestic and childrearing tasks as well" (p. 186).

Native Americans have traditionally supported interdependence of the tribe and cooperation among their members. Witt (1980) quotes the protest of Bernice Appleton, an officer of the Native American Children's Protective Council, against white-imposed restrictions on foster homes:

These agencies are going into Indian homes and telling them their homes are unfit because they have two children, or three children, sleeping in one bed. . . . It isn't necessary for Indian children to have one bed apiece. I don't even think it is good for children to sleep apart. Our children learn sharing right from the start. (p. 26)

Witt continues, "Such requirements can force the breakup of families in a culture in which, traditionally, there was no such thing as an orphan or an illegitimate child" (p. 26). Clunis and Green (1988) write that minorities are more likely to grow up feeling part of a group, while whites grow up with the philosophy of "rugged individualism."

Mothers cannot let go of their overwhelming responsibility for their children until "unmothers," or other women and men, accept some loving responsibility for children. It is in this sense that the oppression of women and the oppression of children are interdependent systems. As Chodorow and Contratto (1982) point out, feminist theories of motherhood have not been able to move further because "they are trapped in the dominant cultural assumptions and fantasies about mothering, which in turn rest on fantasized and unexamined notions of child development" (p. 70). They go on to call for a feminist interpretation of and research on child development.

The study of lesbian step families provides one perspective on the issues of possessiveness and bonding. Lesbian step families, like nuclear heterosexual families, generally encompass only two adults living with children, although lesbian families, like other "minority" families, may also rely on friends and community for help with children. However, they also embody a mother and "unmother" as parents, and this unique quality may help to unravel some of the issues surrounding motherhood, possessiveness, and ownership of children.

The Structure of Two Female Parents Challenges the Traditional Male Power Base of the Family and Presents Opportunities to Further Examine the Role of Family Structurein Perpetuating Sexism in Children

Structurally, the lesbian step family is different from the heterosexual step family because two women are parenting. Some feminist theorists (Chodorow, 1978; Dinnerstein, 1976) propose that it is the structure of the heterosexual nuclear family—with father less involved with the children but still holding the power, and mother providing for (or not providing for) all the children's needs—which systematically recreates the subordination of women. But neither of these theorists discuss lesbian families. When two women parent there are at least two major differences: (1) family power is held by a female or females, and (2) the children experience a female upbringing since both parents were socialized as women.

Certainly power within the family would have to be identified with one or both female figures. Lorde (1984) questions the impact on her son, who was growing up in a household with two female parents and a strong older sister, by asking how this experience will impact on his relationships with women as an adult? On his view of power and gender.

Copper (1987) writes on this issue of power and female children:

> How does the female child raised in a heterosexual household learn to cede space, body integrity, or verbal prerogative to males, even before she is five years old? It seems clear that the daughter of a lesbian who has the opportunity to watch women exchange power, attention, and trust—preferably between as many different kinds of women as possible—will learn new ways of being a woman in the world. (p. 239)

Johnson (1988) challenges Chodrow's (1978) notion that it is the mothering role which perpetuates male dominance. She contends that it is the wife role and the father role that enforce sex role stereotypes, not the mother role. The wife role creates a juvenilization of women, economically and in coping with the world outside of the home. It is the wife role that defines the female as submissive to and less important than the husband.

In addition, fathers are more likely than mothers to reinforce passivity, dependence, and attractiveness in their daughters (Johnson, 1988). In EuroAmerican families, fathers tend to see girls and boys as more different than mothers do and act accordingly as parents. Girls grow up expecting and hoping to marry a superior mate to front for them in the hard, competitive world. It is this husband superiority that tends to reproduce in female offspring the feelings of psychological dependence on men that can prove incapacitating as adults. It also produces in sons a feeling of superiority to women, a sense of male privilege.

African-American feminist theorists have long recognized the power of Mother. Joseph's (1981) study of black mothers and daughters concluded that a "decisive 94.5 percent expressed respect for their mothers in terms of strength, honesty, ability to overcome difficulties, and ability to survive" (p. 79). Johnson (1988) postulates that this vision of the powerful mother exists in white American cultures as well, and that this powerful image does not create male dominance but serves instead to mitigate it:

> It seems to me that if we take the view that neither girls nor boys know their mother is inferior (or heterosexual) in their earliest relationship to her, it is quite possible to imagine that at first a child does not identify with her inferiority but with her active caretaking. (Johnson, 1988, p. 198)

Thus Johnson (1988) believes that mother influence may foster less gender-typed attitudes in children. Hite's (1994) interviews with family members support this thesis. Boys who were raised by single mothers or lesbian mothers had more respect for women in general. If it is the wife role and the traditional father role that perpetuate male dominance, then lesbian mothers could be in a unique position to redefine and reinterpret power.

Another impact of two women parenting emerging from the female socialization of both parents. Gilligan (1982) has illuminated differences in Western EuroAmerican male and female voices on morality. The male voice typically embraces the role of separation as it defines and empowers the self. The female voice, on the other hand, defines herself in the ongoing process of attachment. A lesbian couple, therefore, may have "two partners who tend to be relationship focused and who have the emotional skills necessary to nurture the couple" (Green, 1990, p. 98).

Two women as parents may also provide a unique family atmosphere because of what Ruddick (1989) calls "maternal thinking." That is, it may not be only how two women interact in a relationship that is a difference for their children, but also how those women relate to children and how that relating creates a maternal outlook on life. Maternal thinking requires strategizing how to protect, nurture, and train children. Ruddick (1989) does not attempt to idealize mothering so much as to examine it as a particular way of knowing—a way of knowing which has been discounted and silenced. Like any other long-term "job," the vocation of mothering requires the development of certain skills and a particular outlook on the task at hand. This, in turn, influences how one relates to the rest of the world. Although both Ruddick and Gilligan have been accused of essentialist thinking, both assert that the differences they illuminate originate not in biology but in socialization. If maternal thinking is a socialized/learned construct, then it can be accomplished by men as well as women, and by nonbiological parents. Mothering becomes degendered and is removed from any biological imperative.

Children who are raised in a home with two women as parents might, therefore, be expected to manifest some differences from children of heterosexual families. Because both parents have been socialized as women and both are perhaps engaged in the task of mothering which creates maternal thinking, their children are likely to be presented with different models of coupling and parenting than the children of heterosexuals.

The Peculiar Nature of Oppression Against Lesbian Families Locates These Families as Both Inside and Outside of Society

This location provides insight on the nature of oppression and its effects on families. Lesbian step families live outside of the familial norm at the intersection of sexism and homophobia, and for lesbians of color—racism. This allows for an almost anthropological perspective on the "traditional" family, as well as, in some cases, an increased freedom to experiment with alternatives.

Radical lesbian feminists assert that lesbianism is the greatest threat that exists to male supremacy (Kitzinger, 1987). Being a lesbian sets a woman outside of the possibility of participating in a traditional nuclear family (unless, of course she lives a lie). This is not true for other oppressed peoples. For example, research by Longres (1990) shows that racial and cultural "minorities" attempt to pattern their families after the norm and the longer immigrants stay in this country, the more their families come to resemble the white, middle-class norm. The cultural push toward this end is strong. But lesbians, perhaps more than any other oppressed group outside of gay men, have less stake in the familial norm—and less to lose by altering it. Pollack and Vaughn (1990) question what makes lesbian parenting special. If lesbians are consciously outside of the norm, if they are aware of and attempting to practice a feminist political consciousness and lifestyle, then they have a special opportunity to develop and maintain environments in which having and raising children is a revolutionary experience.

By experiencing family life outside of the norm, some lesbians and their children may be freer to challenge and/or ignore that norm. As lesbians grow more self-confident and less tolerant of lesbian hating, they are able to engage in more experimentation. The increasing number of published stories of lesbian lives (such as Alpert, 1988; Arnup, 1995; Hanscombe and Forster, 1981; Pollack and Vaughn, 1987; Schulenburg, 1985) can leave no doubt—there is a richness of diversity among lesbian family lifestyles. There is experimentation with sexuality, monogamy and nonmonogamy, mothers and "unmothers," parenting by groups of biological and/or fictive kins, living in separate households and coparenting, etc. It is out of this rich diversity that new questions are formed and new answers are found.

More lesbians and gay men are beginning to understand that they have a particular standpoint resulting from their queerness and that this unique perspective can be used to enrich theory and practice. Brown (1989) identifies three elements of being lesbian or gay male that are common to all. The first is biculturalism—lesbians and gay men are always simultaneously participants in both heterosexual experience (because we "pass") and lesbian and gay experiences. "The bicultural perspective of lesbians and gay men facilitates an understanding of the rules by which the mainstream culture operates, while simultaneously being able to envision new forms by which the same tasks might be accomplished" (Brown, 1989, p. 450).

The second element is marginality—the experience of existential "otherness." Feminist writers (Daly, 1973; Harding, 1986) have long been aware of the value of being outside the system—in being able to see differently, know differently, and ask different questions.

The final common element to gay men and lesbians is called "normative creativity" by Brown (1989, p. 451). Because we have lacked clear rules about how to be gay and lesbian (or lesbian step families) in this world, we have made up the rules as we go along. It is important to examine how lesbian step families have created themselves. What seems to be working? What are the challenges?

While difference may make one more creative, the danger of an oppressed status is the temptation to become as much like the oppressor as possible in order to be accepted Freire (1989) writes, "The oppressed, have internalized the image of the oppressor and adopted his guidelines, are fearful of freedom. Freedom would require them to eject this image and replace it with autonomy and responsibility" (p. 31).

What we have named internalized homophobia or internalized racism is not so much a problem of low self-esteem or self-hatred (although they may also plague the oppressed), but a problem of embracing the oppressor's basic worldview. A major act of resistance, as hooks (1984) reminds us, is that we reject the powerful's definition of ourselves—the oppressor's definition of the oppressed.

The act of defining or redefining oneself, then, is a key to empowerment. Freire (1989) makes this happen through "conscientizacao" or a consciousness-raising technique that refers to learning to perceive social, political, and economic contradictions, and to take action against the oppressive elements of reality.

Another way of conceptualizing the importance of positive self-definition is through the lens of family stress theory. Family stress theory helps define the elements necessary in coping with and overcoming stress—and oppression can be defined as an overriding, unending source of stress. Chester Pierce (McAdoo, 1986), an African-American psychiatrist, compared the stress on African Americans to the stress on those who live in extreme climates. He called this racist climate a "mundane extreme" environment—because the extreme difficulties that white society impose on African-American peoples are not unusual or extraordinary but mundane daily pressures for African Americans. Lesbians also experience this mundane extreme environmental stress.

Family stress theory as first conceptualized by Hill (1949) and extended by McCubbin and Figley (1983), examines the question, why do some families cope with a stressor while others crumble. According to the model, whether or not a family adapts successfully or poorly to the crisis depends on the mediating factors of (1) the resources available to the family and (2) the family's perception or interpretation of the stressor event. Stressed families can even avoid crisis altogether by managing to hold the degree of stress to a tolerable level—a process called coping.

Resources include socioeconomic resources—such as jobs, education, and skills, as well as social support and family support. For lesbian families, community support can be a stress-mediating resource. "However, involvement in the lesbian community may have particular implications for lesbian mothers, whose fear of societal discrimination often precludes such involvement" (Levy, 1989, p. 43). The double bind is that involvement in the lesbian community may jeopardize a lesbian mother's custody rights, and yet this involvement may be one of the most important ways to support the mother's psychological health.

A sense of control over the stressful situation appears to be an important precedent to an act to change the situation. For lesbian mothers, a positive lesbian identity or a feminist perspective (Ettorre, 1980) can serve as a belief system that gives meaning to stressful events related to societal homophobia. "For example, if lesbians cannot change their troubled person-environment relationship, they can use their feminist belief system to understand the environment and regulate their emotional distress" (Levy, 1989, p. 44). An approach that seems to facilitate coping and adaptation is family effort to reframe or redefine the situation as a challenge, an opportunity for growth, or to endow the crisis with a special meaning (McCubbin and Patterson, 1983).

In an oppressive situation such as lesbian families face, redefining their lesbian family as a positive strong family model instead of a deficit model may lessen the impact of homophobia. Freire (1989) writes:

> Self-depreciation is another characteristic of the oppressed, which derives from their internalization of the opinion the oppressor hold of them. So often do they hear that they are good for nothing, know nothing and are incapable of learning anything—that they are sick, lazy, and unproductive—that in the end they become convinced of their own unfitness. . . . As

long as their ambiguity persists, the oppressed are reluctant to resist, and totally lack confidence in themselves. They have a diffuse, magical belief in the invulnerability and power of the oppressor. (p. 49)

In stress theory, Freire's (1989) process of consciousness raising is reinterpreted as changing a fatalistic belief system into one of mastery. For lesbian families, an understanding of their oppression as something outside the family, something that can be changed, could lessen stress and increase family cohesion.

However, the family's internal interpretation of their oppression is only one part of the perception factor in the stress model. The community perception also impacts the family's ability to cope. As Lazarus and Folkman (1984) explain, coping failures do not necessarily reflect the shortcomings of individuals; in a real sense they may represent the failure of social systems in which the individuals are enmeshed. If the threat of violence is high, lesbians, and particularly lesbians with children to protect, will more likely feel coerced into following more normative family patterns. In an atmosphere of tolerance, lesbian family experimentation would be encouraged to flourish. Instead of worrying that lesbians choosing motherhood will threaten the radical potential of the lesbian community (Herman, 1988), lesbian feminists might be considering ways of supporting lesbian mothers to increase and maintain their radicalism. Indeed, Burke (1993) documents how the act of becoming a mother actually pushed her into radical action:

When my lesbian partner had a child through assisted conception, I could no longer pass for straight. I was propelled into a world where every act, no matter how everyday, became political, whether I wanted it to be or not. Everything from taking our child to the doctor for a checkup to enrolling him in nursery school, brought with it a kind of visibility I had always avoided, and an unnerving vulnerability to the attacks of the radical right. My life became a crash course in "the personal is political." (p. xi)

The ability to "pass" as heterosexual creates a unique form of stress for lesbian families. Simmel (1950) long ago identified some of the advantages and disadvantages of belonging to a secret society. One advantage is that it provides reciprocal confidence and protection. "Of all protective measures, the most radical is to make oneself invisible" (p. 345). The secret society reinforces interdependency among its members, but takes its toll in isolation and exclusion from the rest of the world.

Children are often confused and suffer from the secrecy aspect of their families. At some point, lesbian parents must explain to their children that their families may not be generally acceptable. This can be quite stressful for children, to feel there is something about their family that cannot be discussed (Riddle and Arguelles, 1981). The secret isolates the child from seeking the help and confidence of other children, adults, and/or counselors. Lewis (1980) describes, "The younger children focused on the need for secrecy and the isolation a secret imposed on them, separating them from their peers" (p. 199). Secrecy, then, is a daily and overriding issue for lesbian families—one of the factors in their own form of mundane extreme environmental stress.

Based on the stress model, one might predict that lesbian step families would cope better with the stress of oppression if they have a supportive community, a strong interpretation of lesbian families as a healthy alternative to traditional nuclear families, and a greater visibility (being "out") as lesbians. This book examines these factors in the lives of lesbian step family members.

The postmodern era has forced a recognition of different kinds of families. The majority of families do not fit the modernist prototype. Some of them do not even aspire to emulate the prototype—they reject its claim to moral superiority. The ensuing chaos has led to a struggle among those who would go back to the moral supremacy of the prototype, those who vehemently fight against it, and those caught unwittingly or ambivalently between. Irrespective of those who desire to go back to a time when there was clearly one right kind of family, many families refuse to be erased or discounted any longer. Once something is finally seen, it becomes difficult to ignore, especially if it demands a place in one's paradigm.

Lesbian step families are one of these different family types who have long been erased. This book concentrates on bringing them into view. It is estimated that there are between three and eight million gay and lesbian parents in the United States who are raising between six and fourteen million children (Martin, 1993). It is likely that a large proportion of those children are being raised in lesbian step family situations. In spite of the fact that this represents a significant minority group, there has been little information available on lesbian step families to date. Baptiste (1987) has attempted to define some of the particular dynamics of gay step parent families, noting that the step issues are ignored in most research on gay and lesbian families and "the step parenting role of the partner as well as the step family structure of the family is unrecognized and de-emphasized even though the family's living arrangement is reported to include children and two same-sex adults in a committed step family relationship" (p. 113). Baptiste's (1987) information, although an important first step to understanding lesbian and gay step families, is based on clinical observations, not research.

There is a small but growing body of anecdotal/life history information that includes lesbian step families (see Arnup, 1995; Maglin and Schniedewind, 1989; Pollack and Vaughn, 1987). Although providing some rich and much-needed voices on the topic, these accounts are not intended as research material. Quality research on lesbian step families has simply not yet been available. This book addresses that gap.

METHOD: THE COMPLEX RELATIONSHIP
OF RESEARCHER TO RESEARCHED

Why include a section on methods? First, this story is not only about five families. It is the story of my relationship with and perceptions, insights, and understandings of those families. It seems somehow dishonorable to attempt to tell their stories without acknowledging and describing for the reader my own challenges and decisions as a researcher. By allowing the reader to understand my process with the research, I hope to privilege the reader to make his/her own informed interpretations of my analysis. I acknowledge that this book is a combination of lenses or standpoints—those of the five families and their members, my own as a researcher, and ultimately the reader's interpretation of it all.

Second, I share my research process in the hopes of encouraging others to do research. Research is about searching, seeking information. Each one of us is a researcher—it does not belong in the academic domain exclusively.

And finally, as a feminist, I believe it is important to share our struggles, challenges, and insights with the task of attempting to do research in a respectful and empowering manner.

Although I had read extensively about feminist research, nothing prepared me for the complexity of actually trying to accomplish it. Feminist research created a climate of continuous anxiety because it focused my attention on ethics above everything else. What was supposed to be an academic and scientific pursuit for a degree was fraught with concerns for the participants, as well as for lesbians and their children in general. These concerns can be organized into three categories: the concern with honoring the participants, the concern that the research would be *for* the participants, and the concern with acknowledging my influence on the research as the researcher.

Honor connotes respect, fairness, honesty, and a sense of privilege in being involved with someone. Feminist methodologies insist on honoring the participants as experts on their own lives. The researcher is not the only "knower," and instead acknowledges that the participants possess personal knowledge and expertise (DuBois, 1983).

Although the issues raised in this study were often (but not always) mine, the dialogue that ensued was a collaborative search to get to the bottom of issues—to reach a deeper and broader understanding. As Devault (1990) writes:

> It is the interviewer's investment in finding the answer, her own concern with the questions she asks and her ability to show that concern, that serves to recruit her respondents as partners in the search: the things said are responses to the words of this particular researcher. The researcher is actively involved with respondents, so that together they are constructing fuller answers to questions that cannot always be asked in simple, straightforward ways. (p. 100)

Research, after all, is a search—a search for reality or truth, as it is experienced by the participants. It is a kind of problem-solving activity—and problem solving, as social workers know, is best done with the fullest possible collaboration of those experiencing the problem.

STUDY DESIGN

Ethnography is the study of groups and people in their natural setting as they go about their everyday lives. It involves not only seeing how others react to various events in their lives, but examining one's own reactions. The ethnographer uses him or herself as a research tool to deepen his or her understanding of the participants and their lives.

I studied five lesbian step families and used intensive interviewing of each family member, a limited number of observations of each family, and an analysis of documents: structured journals kept by family members. With each family, I began with a short meeting with the entire family, explaining the process and the research topic, as well as issues of confidentiality and potential problems. At that time, if the family elected to continue with the project, we arranged as many of the interview and observation times as we could. I always began with the first interview of the couple. After that, schedules for interviews and observations were based on the family's needs, although I generally tried to do most of the interviewing before I did the observations.

I conducted a series of intensive and extensive interviews: two interviews (approximately 1½ to 2 hours each) with the adult couple and one interview (1 to 2 hours) with each family member individually (including each adult partner). All of these interviews were audiotaped and were transcribed by a paid transcriber.

Although I had clear guidelines for each interview, I allowed myself to add questions and to follow tangents as they surfaced. The atmosphere was structured; participants knew I had a list of questions to ask. But it was also informal because we would often pursue tangents or delve more deeply into the original questions.

The interview questions were centered around the three themes of this inquiry: (1) how the family members define and live the step roles; (2) how the two parents divide tasks and parent together; and (3) how the family copes with the system of heterosexual supremacy in this society. A list of the various questions that were pursued is in Appendix A.

In addition to the interviews, I completed at least four observations on each family (two to four hours each)—including an initial entry observation. My plan was to spend a dinner and evening, to go outside of the home, and to spend time during a ritual or celebration with each family. The family dinner and bedtime observation would allow me to observe how the family members interact with each other, what the rules were and how they were enforced, how the chores and parenting tasks were divided, and how the step mother role was actually lived. By accompanying the family on an outing, I was able to observe the family as they interacted with the world outside of the private realm. And finally, by observing a family celebration or ritual, I could see how the family created and participated in an act of family solidification and nurturance. I could see how the family interacted within this context and how the step mother participated in this process.

During the observations, I assumed the role of participant observer, joining in family activities such as meals, games, and work around the home. The observations were not taped, nor did I take notes during them. I wanted to be able to feel and experience what it was like being with the families, without the intrusion of the research tools. Most of the time I was treated as a guest, although as I got familiar with the families, the guest role evolved into more of a friend of the family. One family and I had a standing joke that I was Auntie Janet, since it felt as if I was somehow a part of the family because I was with them so often. After these visits, within twenty-four hours, I would record my observations as well as my thoughts and feelings about the visit.

As a shy person by nature, I found the prospect of asking to simply "hang out" with the families somewhat daunting. Although ethnographies are by their very nature intrusive, family ethnographies seem particularly voyeuristic. The researcher is invading the most private institution in our society and this invasion is likely to leave the family changed in some aspects, for better or for worse.

As Stacey (1990) writes in her acknowledgments:

> My heart, much more than my hands, has been engaged with the people portrayed in this book who so generously agreed to subject their family lives to my impertinent sociological scrutiny. To them I owe my first and greatest debt, as well as my apologies for whatever "domestic upheavals" my intrusive study introduced into their lives. (p. ix)

This intrusion is perhaps even greater for lesbian families, who feel completely safe so few places in this world. Truly our homes are our havens—where we can go about living our lives as if we were the most normal and accepted type of family. To invade that one arena of safety seemed almost too much to ask. And yet, the participants were remarkably open and welcoming. Several participants let me know that they enjoyed my visits and felt they, too, were gaining something valuable from the study.

Finally, each individual was asked to keep a structured journal for one week at any point during the study. The adult journals asked participants to identify and explain any issues that had occurred that day concerning being a step family, parenting with a partner, and the impact of homophobia on the family. The children's journals asked what they did with their mom that day, what they did with their step mom, and if anything happened that made them feel sad or happy about being in a lesbian family (see Appendix C). Thirteen of the seventeen participants kept a journal for at least some days and most wrote daily for an entire week. This task, as I suspected, was particularly onerous for some folks—because it smacked of "homework" and because it required writing. Others seemed especially pleased to have the opportunity to write their thoughts.

Observations allowed me to see the family actually at the business of being a family. Interviewing explored their meanings and interpretations, as well as reports of unobserved behavior. Interviewing also allowed for more collaboration with the participants. Journals enabled me to explore the life and meanings of participants as they were lived and reflected on daily. These methods combined to create a solid basis of inquiry.

THE PARTICIPANT FAMILIES

Although finding families who fit the sampling criterion was not hard, getting families to commit to participating turned out to be much more difficult that I had anticipated. When I originally conducted a pilot study for this project in 1991, I had several families express interest and, although I did not need them for the pilot study, I had hoped they would be available for the dissertation study. However, several problems interfered with my ability to secure participant families.

The major obstacle identified by potential participants was the time involved. This study required a large commitment of time and many family members were unwilling to make that commitment. Although time was the most frequently stated reason for refusal, I suspect that the invasiveness of the project also discouraged some people. The participants in this project probably must feel confident in the health and cohesion of their families in order to subject themselves to this kind of close scrutiny. Therefore, this is a sample of relatively functional, healthy families.

A second problem often cited as a reason for refusal was the unwillingness of the child to participate. There were at least three families that I contacted in which the adults reported a willingness to participate, but said that the child was unwilling. All of these unwilling children were adolescents. With one family, we were in the entry meeting before the child decided not to participate. In at least two families, the children did not want to participate because they disapproved of the mothers' lesbianism.

A third reason for refusal was the impingements of various unexpected crises or problems for the family. One family that I actually began interviewing dropped out of the study when the child decided to go live with the father. Death in the extended family, the stress of a new job, or difficult shift work hours were cited as other reasons for being unable to participate.

Although I did not specifically seek out healthy lesbian step families, some of my sampling criteria my have eliminated families who were less functional. For example, the families had to have lived together for at least one year which required some minimal stability. In addition to the sampling criteria, the intrusiveness of the study may have led to self-selection by relatively functional families. Whatever the reasons, this appears to be a group of people who are functioning rather well as families.

There were a total of seventeen participants in this study. The ten mothers and step mothers range in age from thirty-one to forty-seven. The "children" range in age from seven to twenty, with two clusters at either end of the range. The children included two boys and five girls/young women.

This is a middle-class sample, with annual family incomes of $45,000 to $140,000. Individual adult incomes range from $15,000 to $90,000. Four of the five families own their homes. The education level of the adults includes four high school graduates, one college graduate with additional training, four master's degrees, and one PhD.

Three of the participants identify themselves as mixed race. One is Asian/African American/Caucasian; one is African American/Caucasian; and one is one-quarter American Indian and Caucasian. One person identifies herself as one-eighth Jewish. Three children are partially Hispanic, including two who are one-half Hispanic, and one child who is one-fourth Hispanic. Other ethnicities that participants identified as part of their heritages were German, Danish, Norwegian, Swedish, English, Welsh, Spanish, Scottish, Hungarian, and Polish.

The adult partners have been in their present relationships for an average of 7.4 years. The relationships range from four plus to more than fifteen years in duration. The children in the study were between ages one and seven when their moms got involved in the present relationships. One family had a child who was thirteen when the parents became involved, but she was not interviewed because she was not living at home at the time of the study. Four of the biological mothers were married to men before the present relationships and their children are products of those marriages. Of those four marriages, one lasted three years, one four years, and two marriages lasted fourteen years Only one step mother was previously married—for a year and a half. One biological mother had her children by alternative insemination by donor in the context of a nine-year lesbian relationship.

Only one family regularly attends and maintains membership in a church—United Methodist. However, several other adults define themselves as spiritual and some read and think about spiritual issues and/or attend various spiritual/religious ceremonies or events. Chapter 3 includes a more in-depth portrait of each family.

DATA ANALYSIS

I followed the manner of analysis suggested by Emerson, Fretz, and Shaw (1995). The first step consisted of coding the data line by line, thought by thought. In the left margin, I wrote a word or several words which contained the kernel of what was said or done. I did this with the entire corpus of data from each family, in chronological order. In this way, I put out of my mind any preconceived themes and tried to simply get the gist of each idea, event, action, or behavior.

Next, I immersed myself in the data of one family at a time. I began by creating charts and lists from the data, based on four of Lofland and Lofland's (1984) "thinking units": meanings, practices, roles, and relationships. This allowed me to turn my focus away from the themes I had preconceived and forced me to examine the data from a different perspective. In addition to these four Lofland themes, I created a file of key issues. These were the special issues that these particular family members emphasized as important in their lives together.

Only after this method of organizing and examining the data, did I reorganize the data into the broad themes of my original inquiry. I tried to compare and contrast these themes within the family database. How did the different family members talk about or act on certain topics? How were they similar? How were they dissimilar? I also looked for meta-meetings from the individual family data—what is it like to be in this family? What are major methods of coping and surviving? What topics or ideas seem most prevalent in each person's data? What does that mean for this family?

The next step of the analysis consisted of a careful comparison of themes across all five families. I pursued this part of the analysis through an elaborate system of charting and combining of files. For example, I created a chart titled, "Factors affecting the definition of step mother" and I searched the database from each family to examine this issue.

This stage also included a detailed search for contradictions and disconfirming evidence. For example, whereas one family heavily emphasized the parenting the adults had received as children as a determining factor in how they they parented their children, another couple felt strongly that they had overcome their own history of being poorly parented and were able to create themselves as much more positive parents. These contradictions between families became important sources of additional scrutiny.

Finally, I began the process of writing, which was actually another layer of analysis. The writing forced me to reconsider all of the data, pick and choose, and organize, As I wrote and the participants, the outsider consultants, and my committee read and reacted, the data were recycled and the analysis continued in layers of writing and rewriting.

VALIDITY

Lather (1986) recognizes the need to build confidence in the trustworthiness of qualitative data. She recommends that the following accountability measures be built into all qualitative research designs:

- triangulation of methods, data sources, and theories;
- reflexive subjectivity (some documentation of how the researcher's assumptions have been affected by the logic of the data);
- face validity (established by recycling categories, emerging analysis, and conclusions back through at least a subsample of respondents);
- catalytic validity (some documentation that the research process has led to insight and ideally, activism, on the part of the respondents). (pp. 77-78)

Although I believe Lather's concept of catalytic validity is important for researchers to address, and the participants in this research have expressed that the research process has given them new insight, I have not included it as one of my checks for validity. This would have required another stage of the research project in which I would have returned to the families at a later date to see what impact the research had on them. Time constraints made that impossible for this project. Instead, I have added to Lather's (1986) first three accountability measures, a fourth one recommended by several qualitative researchers (e.g., Emerson, Fretz, and Shaw, 1995; Erikson, 1990), a search for disconfirming evidence. The next sections address these four measures of validity.

Triangulation

Triangulation is based on the belief that reliance on a single piece of data may lead to error. However, if diverse data all lead to the same conclusion, the researcher can be more confident (Hammersley and Atkinson, 1983). I used a variety of methods and sources. I interviewed the couple together, as well as each individual separately. This allowed for different emphasis to emerge and gave me the opportunity to see how the couple negotiated their responses and storytelling. For example, when asked to talk about how their child(ren) handled a homophobic situation, the mother and the step mother, in separate interviews, would often choose the same example to discuss. This not only provided an opportunity to examine consistency, but also provided a window to view how the two mothers may have interpreted the same event differently.

In addition to the interviewing, I observed the entire family together on four different occasions. These observations were then used to enrich, collaborate, and challenge the data from the interviews. Finally, I conducted an analysis of the journals. The journals were particularly helpful in understanding those individuals who express themselves more clearly in writing than in speech. They also provided a daily log of family life—examining day-by-day activities and thinking, as opposed to the broader and more historical thinking that is usually explored in interviews. The close scrutiny of multiple families allowed me to see definite similarities, as well as clear differences in style and behavior and speech.

Triangulation is also useful in analysis. If there is more that one researcher involved in the project, their differing perspectives can enrich the analysis. Even if there is only one researcher, he/she can obtain assistance in the analysis by using consultants, or outsider checks (Briggs, 1986). In addition to my dissertation committee members, I asked four nonparticipants to read the first draft of the chapters and give feedback.

These outsider checks were extremely helpful. They provided a chance to dialogue with others about the wording, the analysis, and the interpretations. These outsiders included two members of a lesbian step family that was not part of the study, a lesbian mother not in a step family, and a male colleague in a heterosexual step family. They read the first draft of each chapter as I wrote it and gave me both written and verbal feedback. These outsider checks became one of the great strengths of my data analysis. At times they changed the course of my thinking. They challenged my assumption, and they enriched my understanding. These four people were my collaborators in the analysis of the data.

Reflexive Subjectivity

Allen and Walker (1992) note that ". . . this is what is unique about feminist scholarship and practice: Who the researchers are as people is relevant to the research process, yet hardly ever discussed in most positivist and naturalistic research reports" (p. 203). With that in mind, I have attempted in this research project to not only scrutinize who I am as a person, but to consciously examine and analyze who I was as a researcher and who I was as a lesbian mother in a step family during this research process. I did this in two ways. First, I kept an ongoing journal of my own family experiences during the research year. Second, I coded and analyzed my own speech, reactions, and actions when involved with the participants. In a sense, my family has become another participant family and I have become a participant in my own research.

Reflexive subjectivity is the act of recognizing that oneself, as the researcher, is a part of the world one is studying (Hammersley and Atkinson, 1982; Stacey, 1990; Stack, 1974). The people we are studying are reacting to our presence. We fact the difficulty of a director who acts in her own play. The key is to recreate this problem into a research strength. "How people respond to the presence of the researcher may be as informative as how they react to other situation" (Hammersley and Atkinson, 1983, p. 15).

As an ethnographer I am a subject of my own research. Reflexive subjectivity requires that I show how my preconceived ideas have been changed by the data. This shows an openness toward the data and a willingness to see what I did not see previously. In the findings, I acknowledge my surprise at various factors. For example, I did not expect the magnitude of the fears expressed by the children as a result of heterosexual supremacy. And, although I resisted throughout my entire first written draft of the findings, I finally conceded that an additional theme, besides the three that I began with, had indeed emerged from the data—the issue of normality. I had to make a place for it in my analysis. When the researcher clearly shows that the data have changed her thinking, she exhibits that the data, rather than merely her own subjective thinking, have directly supported the findings.

Face Validity

Face validity is explored by soliciting feedback from the participants. This is also called member checking, recycling the data, respondent validation, or various other terms (Hammersley and Atkinson, 1983; Lather, 1986; Stake, 1995). Member checking allows participants to offer additional information, as well as to validate or critique the materials. Member checks are also consistent with feminist research models of involving the participants as colleagues in the research (Mies, 1983).

As I began to compile the analysis, I sent the first draft of each chapter to the study participants, asking for feedback (see Appendix D). Chapter 3, which initially describes each family, generated the most feedback from participants. They had concerns about possibly being recognized through some of the identifying information, as well as some desires to clarify what they had meant in various interviews. Although I gave first drafts of the other chapters to participants, I received minimal feedback beyond praise. This is, apparently, a common phenomenon. Stake (1995) writes that he frequently gets no response when he attempts member checking of his research materials.

Member checks also represent another kind of triangulation in the analysis phase. The member checks used in this study allowed participants access to each other's information as well as their own,

which gives the opportunity for increased depth to the data analysis
(Hammersley and Atkinson, 1983).

Disconfirming Evidence

The search for disconfirming and conflicting evidence was ongoing
throughout the data analysis. I looked at conflicting evidence within
families as a particular point of interest. In general, these conflicts did
not appear to be evidence of misrepresentation on someone's part but
rather a fascinating view of differing perceptions or differing
emphases. For example, when one teenaged daughter discussed the
reasons she had been in therapy, she emphasized her struggle with
drug misuse. Her parents, on the other hand, emphasized a perhaps
broader scope of dependency, particularly what they perceived as an
unhealthy relationship with a boyfriend. Thus, the differences within
family reports often gave me a broader and more in-depth understanding of the issues.

The differences between families were vast, giving me opportunity
to carefully examine each theme—and to often find exceptions to the
majority patterns. For example, there were major differences in the
parents' verbal commitments to feminism. Several women flatly stated
that they were not feminists. Others were heavily involved in feminist political action. Yet all the parents worked hard to discourage
sexism in their children and to teach their children to value the
equality of the genders. This illuminated how differently various
participants interpreted the word "feminist." Although I identify
themes and patterns in the findings, I recognize family life as an
amazingly complex system. This study only adds a piece to that
puzzle.

ETHICAL CONSIDERATIONS

I had four major ethical concerns in the pursuit of this study. The
first was the issue of confidentiality—how to disguise the participants. Although it was easy to change names and identifying
information, it was obvious that many lesbians and perhaps others
in the communities that were studied would be able to guess who

the participants were. I was very clear with the participants from the beginning that this was a probability, so that participants could make a knowledgeable decision. Participants, including the children, signed informed consent forms (see Appendix A). Confidentiality was also protected by using initials or pseudonyms in all notes and transcriptions.

A second ethical issue emerged as the study progressed: how or if to present material, particularly material from the children, that might hurt a parent or even potentially disrupt the family. Children do not have the same ability to screen such material from the researcher and therefore, I felt it was part of my responsibility as the researcher to do that screening for them. In a situation, for example where a child berated the step mother, my dilemma was to decide whether that was information crucial to understanding this family or a theme and, if so, how could it be presented so as to minimize any disruption to the family, any retributions to the child, and any overwhelming discouragement to the parents. This was one of my major challenges and was addressed on an instance-by-instance basis. It required some guessing on my part, both as to motive of the participants and their possible reactions. It also required a thorough examination of the importance of a piece of data to my account.

In an ethnographic study, only a fraction of the data are actually used in the final write-up. My challenge was to maintain the integrity of the data presented while at the same time maintaining my ethical and protective stance toward the participants. I gained a more insightful respect for other kinds of methodologies which do not require the same vulnerability from the participants. In the end, I believe I have achieved this balance of reporting realities, while protecting and respecting the participants.

The third ethical dilemma concerned the fear prevalent in perhaps all "minority" groups—that the results might somehow be misconstrued or misinterpreted in a manner that would increase prejudice or oppression. By opening these families to public scrutiny, the public will see that we are not perfect, that we have struggles, that we make mistakes. If one assumes that there is one family structure that is ideal, one that is "normal" and "natural," then won't every flaw, every challenge identified in a lesbian step family be blamed on that alternative family structure?

I have attempted to provide a context for understanding some of these problems. Our society's insistence on and saturation with heterosexual supremacy presents enormous problems for these families to address on a daily basis. It tears at our stability and at our self-esteem. It affects our abilities to financially provide for our families. It forces outsider status on ourselves and our children. Of course, it will sometimes be reflected in our ability to function in a healthy manner. In addition, step families in general have challenges that are well documented in the literature on heterosexual step families. These challenges may be even greater for lesbian step families, when layered within the context of homophobia and the complete lack of role acknowledgment for the step mother. By presenting this information clearly within context, I have attempted to minimize the potential harmful effects that it could have in bigoted arguments.

Finally, there was the ethical issue of collaboration and the researcher stance. Qualitative researchers differ on attitudes about the nature of the relationship should be between the researcher and the researched. Some argue against becoming too close. Many traditional field researchers felt/feel that, in order to clearly understand a group of subjects, one must maintain or even create distance. Hammersley and Atkinson (1983) write, "Even where he or she is researching a familiar group or setting, the participant observer is required to treat it as 'anthropologically strange' in an effort to make explicit the assumptions he or she takes for granted as a culture member" (p. 8). This illuminates the importance of not taking the familiar for granted—the need to make oneself scrutinize even what seems natural, normal, or unimportant.

McCracken (1988) identifies three arguments against taking a more collaborative stance with participants. First, if the participant understands the objectives of the research, he/she may not give spontaneous responses. Second, if the researcher becomes overinvolved with the participant, he/she may not be able to ask the tough questions or undertake the delicate analysis. Third, he believes greater anonymity provides a better climate for candor.

On the other hand, some researchers believe that an intimate relationship with the participants is more respectful, less hierarchical, and can still allow for accurate information gathering (McMahon, 1995; Stacey, 1990; Stack, 1974). Stacey (1990, pp. 32-33) writes that the field method she employed was "to enter gradually into a set of personal relationships" with her participants. Stack (1972) insists that all social science researchers are defined by participants as outsiders, "even if he or she has close attachment and commitment to the community" (p. xiv). She continues that the researcher must come to an "intimate point of contact in the study whereby he becomes both an actor and a subject whose learned definitions can themselves be analyzed" (p. xv).

I chose to take a more intimate stance with the participants because it felt more honest and respectful of them, within the context of an ethnographic methodology. Above all, my style as a researcher was to be authentic and genuine. This approach allowed me to validate, to probe, to present my side or alternative view, to joke, and to be genuinely who I was at the moment. The research proceeded through intimate and honest dialogue, by developing personal relationships and talking together openly.

Distance creates perspective, but that perspective is colored heavily by the lens of the observer/researcher. Intimacy, on the other hand, may perpetuate the biases of the participants. Both approaches have drawbacks in the search for validity. Both require some adjustments based on the types of threats to validity they present. I relied on outsider checks, my intense and extensive exposure to the data, and the differences between the families to enhance the honesty and accuracy of my data analysis.

I kept an ongoing journal to document my personal reactions and thoughts, my mistakes, my hunches, and my questions. This journal became part of the data to be analyzed. I coded it line by line, idea by idea, just as the other data were coded. It, therefore, became a source of information as well as a check on my own biases. In addition, I coded my own speech and interactions in the interviews and observations. Through this careful analysis, I found that my role as researcher was much more complex than can be illustrated by terms such as "outsider versus insider."

After coding and examining my actions, thoughts, and speech as a researcher, I identified four major roles. These roles are overlapping and at times simultaneous. Some of the traits are the same across roles. And yet, they seemed to be clearly discreet based on purpose, if not always on technique.

The first two roles developed as a result of the collaborative stance I took with the participants. They were a friendship role and a colleague role. There are at least three important aspects to friendship: a sense of liking and enjoying each other, a sense of connection or attachment, and generally a reciprocal, or two-way relationship. I could identify these aspects continually throughout my analysis of my researcher role in the data.

The third and fourth roles were those of social worker and researcher. These roles required a different stance—acknowledging that I was responsible for the project, that I had a greater investment and more control over the final product.

The social work role grew out of an ethical standard that demanded I become responsible at times for protecting and caring for participants; the researcher role was different in that I was also responsible for this particular project. I had more control over both the content and the process of our meetings—at least in the interview situations. I thought of the questions and decided when and how to ask them. I spent time explaining the research project to the participants so that they would understand the inquiry. I changed the subject when I thought it was time to do so and I made an effort, at times, to keep us on task.

These four roles overlapped and were not always clearly separate from each other, yet each was distinctly a part of who I was as I participated in this research project. The roles worked together to create a learning and exploring atmosphere—an atmosphere of collaboration in which each of us at times was both teacher and learner balanced with a clear understanding that I was still ultimately responsible for the research project. The process was in some ways analogous to a play with a director who learns from and changes the direction of the play based on the actors' talents and feedback, yet the director remains the director.

Ethical considerations were a strong focus in this research. There were rarely any clear answers for me. I cannot say whether I always made the right choices, but I can at least say that I engaged in the struggles.

Davis (1986) makes a case for supporting new qualitative methods in social work research:

Social work is a female profession led primarily by men. As the profession has been incorporated into the university, the male leaders increasingly have sought the respect of their academic peers. To counteract the perception of social work as a profession of soft-hearted and soft-minded women who rely on caring and intuition, social work academicians have firmly adopted the male research model . . . the next step is to adopt methodologies that reflect how women experience their world. (p. 44)

However, I believe that the focus on methods is misplaced. The challenges that feminist researchers have brought to the traditional scientific approach are embedded in ethical concerns. Feminists reject thinking and behavior rooted in oppressive ideology. Feminist research is not, therefore, determined by method but rather by values. Those values require a thoughtful scrutiny of, as well as action to resist, ideologies and behaviors that support domination by one group over another.

This study employed a feminist research strategy—examining women's and children's meanings and behaviors through an ethical and passionate search. It also employed a qualitative scientific methodology. My hope is that the following results provide a beginning understanding of lesbian step families for other such families, as well as for the helping professions. Chapter 2 introduces the five participant families. I have tried to highlight some of the key issues in each family that constitute that family's unique culture. Chapter 3 addresses a theme that was continually discussed and developed by the participants—the idea that their families are "normal." These family members insisted that they would be accepted by mainstream society if society could just see clearly how "normal" lesbian families really are. The chapter discusses the similarities lesbian step families have with other couples and families and examines what "normal" means to these participants.

When two women parent together, how does that affect the children, the couple, the family as a whole? Chapter 4 investigates the issue of gender and the transmission of sexism and male privilege. It also examines how gender may influence coupling and its resulting impact on the children.

Chapter 5 focuses on the issue of creating and maintaining the step mother role—bringing the outsider in. It examines the various relationship that the nonbiological mothers have with the children and identifies three distinct step mother stances that have been created by these family members.

Chapter 6 examines the ways in which heterosexual supremacy in society affects family members. Heterosexual supremacy is defined as the belief that heterosexuality is spiritually, morally, emotionally, and physically superior to homosexuality. The chapter scrutinizes both positive and negative effects on participants and identifies the ways these family members cope with homophobia and heterosexism. It also demonstrates how the covert side of heterosexual supremacy creates fear in family members and ways which this might be exposed and challenged.

The conclusion, Chapter 7, summarizes the findings and addresses the implications of those findings. It acknowledges the need for additional research and continuing dialogue concerning the theoretical issues about mothering and family, as well as the concrete realities for lesbian step families. Seven guidelines are offered for those who are working with or creating for themselves lesbian step families.

BACK TO THE BEGINNING

Seven years ago when my present partner walked into my life (and I into hers), I already had five children. My oldest son was on his way to college, my second son in high school, my daughter an emotional thirteen-year-old, my third son beginning grade school, and my fourth son still a toddler in diapers. Neither of us could afford to take lightly the decision to create a new family.

It is difficult to discuss my present family because I am immersed in it. I am afraid that if I say we are very happy, I will somehow jinx the happiness thus leading to its demise. What if my partner and I break up in the years to come? Will I look back and see that I was simply delusional in my happiness?

Certainly, the struggles, the crises, the anger, the hardships of life continue. But something has evolved over the seven years of this relationship that is different in my experience. There is a growing trust and belief that, regardless of the challenges that we may face, my partner and I, and to a somewhat lesser extent, the children, will stand united and eventually solve problems together. Our problems no longer seem to be cracks in the walls of our relationship that could eventually crumble the whole. Rather they seem to be a part of life that the two of us—or the seven of us—will face and address. And somehow they now work to strengthen, rather than diminish, our relationship. Much of the literature on heterosexual step families suggests that it may take six or more years for a step family to create itself as Family (see Sager et al., 1983; Visher and Visher, 1990). Time spent together has been a blessing for our family. Now one of the children will say, "Remember when we went to Mexico and we played cards until 2 a.m.?" or "Remember when our canoe tipped over on Crystal River and we lost our shirts down the river?" We have a history together now. Memories of togetherness become additional cement in our family gestalt. Something has grown in our family, slowly and imperceptively, so that I have only recently recognized it myself. I see it in the changes of my journals. The crises, rather than threatening our relationship, have beome challenges to be faced together. We *are* family.

Chapter 2

The Family Gestalt

DESCRIPTION OF THE PARTICIPANT FAMILIES

1. *Norden/Westby/Engleking Family*—a middle-class, multiracial family

   Tanya Norden—biological mother, white
   Terry Westby—co-mother, multiracial
   Kevin Engleking—son, nine years old, biracial

2. *Iliff/Dubrovsky/Iliff-Hernandez Family*—a middle-class, white, and Hispanic Family

   Delia Iliff—biological mother, white
   Kathy Dubrovsky—nonbiological mother, white
   Diana Iliff—daughter, twenty years old, white and Hispanic
   Natalia Iliff-Hernandez—daughter, seventeen years old, white and Hispanic

3. *Uphoff/Dillard Family*—a middle-class, white family

   Nisi Uphoff—biological mother, white, pregnant
   Florence Dillard—co-mother, white
   Frannie Uphoff—daughter, eight years old, white
   Dale Uphoff—son, eight years old, white

4. *Peterson/Timms/Taylor Family*—an upper-middle-class, white family

   Cady Peterson—biological mother, white
   Lori Timms—co-mother, white

Molly Taylor—daughter, fifteen years old, white
Nell Taylor—daughter, nineteen years old, white
(not interviewed for this study)

5. *Stark Family*—a working-class, white, Hispanic Family

Dory Stark—biological mother, white
Becky Stark—step mother, white
Pauli Stark—daughter, seven years old, white and Hispanic

INTRODUCTION

Healthy families may provide their members with similar benefits: nurturance and love, safety and protection; food and shelter. And yet, each family is unique in emphasis and style, each has a special ambiance. This chapter introduces the five families that participated in this study. Although I asked similar demographic questions of each family, I found that they differed in terms of key issues. Key issues were ideas and acts that were emphasized in a particular family. They were the heart and passion of the family members—the glue that held the family together.

I know that my limited time with each family does not allow me to understand their whole story or to describe fully how they live. However, my interest in their stories enabled, as Lightburn (1992) describes, "a gestalt to develop, a gestalt that was a construction of each family's history and beliefs, representing one version of the family's life." In the following pages, I introduce each family and their key issues. Originally I thought I would use only one last name to designate each family-to make it easier for the reader. However, I realized that that would fail to communicate one of the numerous complexities of our lives as lesbian step families.

THE NORDEN/WESTBY/ENGLEKING FAMILY

Janet: What is the best thing about your family? What are some of the high points?

Terry: I think everyday life. I can't think of anything that sticks out because I think a high point is that I come home and

I have two people that love me and come up and kiss me and I share my life with, so that is kind of a high point.

Tanya: I think when we've taken trips together.

Kevin: Um . . . everything! Like . . . ah . . . we all like *Star Trek!*

This family includes Terry Westby—the step mother, Tanya Norden—the biological mother, and Kevin Engleking—their son. Terry and Tanya are in their late thirties and early forties and Kevin is nine years old. They have been together as a family for four and a half years. They are a multiracial family with African-American, Asian, and Caucasian heritages. Terry is multiracial, Tanya is Caucasian, and Kevin is biracial. Race is an important issue in this family and is a factor in decisions such as where to live (and where not to live), toys, books, and schools. However, it is one factor which they take into consideration and is not always the overriding factor. For example, these mothers consciously chose to promote the TV show and movies of *Star Trek* to their son because it portrayed peoples of various races in powerful positions and because it is a show that places value on diversity. Race is also an important concern for Terry in the activism she pursues in the community. This family is united in their stance against racism.

Time and money are two of the big challenges these parents identify. They own their home in a middle-class neighborhood. There is a parochial school nearby and Terry and Tanya laugh about how they didn't realize until after they bought the house that they were moving into "The" Catholic neighborhood. They are a middle-class family with a combined income of $45,000-48,000. Terry works full time in criminal justice and is presently working the night shift (11 p.m. to 7 a.m.). Terry is also in school, trying to finish her bachelor's degree in criminal justice. This additional degree will lead to a pay increase, however, at present it creates a stressful time for the family. Terry has less time to spend with Kevin and Tanya, and her night job creates an ongoing and chronic fatigue.

Tanya works thirty hours per week as a paraprofessional, but is looking for a professional job. She has her master's degree in library science. Kevin attends public school in an open classroom program and is in the third grade. Generally, Tanya is able to be home from work before Kevin gets off the bus from school. However, on Mondays, when school gets out early, Terry is responsible for Kevin after school.

Tanya and Terry pool their salaries and make decisions on expenditures together. They do have separate retirement funds from their jobs; the rest of their money is shared. Although they may have to negotiate on large purchases, this negotiation does not seem to create any major problems for them.

Tanya was previously married to Kevin's father for fourteen years. That relationship ended when Kevin's father died of heart disease. Kevin was two and a half years old. His father had been ill throughout his life, so, in many ways, Tanya was a single parent from the beginning of Kevin's life, with the additional burden of caring for a sick spouse. Terry and Tanya and Kevin met shortly after Kevin's father died. Terry had recently moved in next door to them. Kevin initiated their meeting by conversing with Terry as she sat on her front porch smoking. (She has since given up smoking.) Terry, whose father had recently died, says that it was death that was their initial bond.

> It wasn't until that Easter when you came over from the Easter egg party that we sat down and really talked, and that's when we found a common bond, which was death, actually—taking care of somebody who was dying.

Although death may have created one initial bond, it is clear that Kevin was a factor in their attraction. Terry enjoys children and was charmed by Kevin's approach in getting to know her. He is an outgoing child who sought Terry's attention easily—asking to sit on her motorcycle or showing her his teddy bear. Terry admits that she fell in love with Kevin and he drew her to Tanya.

Tanya had not been in any previous lesbian relationships before meeting Terry, although it had crossed her mind.

> I think when Kevin's dad was—he was pretty—I don't know, I would describe it as kind of an effeminate man, very gentle and not aggressive in any way, more intellectual, more . . . and

I just remember thinking if I wasn't with him I would be with a woman.

Although Terry's process of coming out took several years, Terry feels that identity was clear from a very early age. Terry had other lesbian relationships before pairing with Tanya, but her relationship with Tanya has been qualitatively different, mainly because of Kevin's presence.

My problem was I didn't want to get involved in a relationship with a kid if I wasn't sure about it. I just couldn't do that to the kid, so I kept being wishy-washy in a sense. But then I decided for sure that was what I wanted; then I felt that I was more comfortable with someone with a kid.

Tanya was raised in a large Catholic family in the Midwest. Tanya maintains contact with her family and her family accepts Terry as part of Tanya's life, but they don't talk about her being a lesbian. Tanya and Terry and Kevin do spend time with Tanya's family, since they live in the same state. For example, they like to visit for Tanya's parents' birthdays. However, Tanya's parents are certainly not part of their major support system.

Terry, on the other hand, was raised in two step family situations. Her father, who came out as a gay man before she was born, moved out of the family when Terry was only two years old. He soon entered a long-term relationship with a man, Carl, who still refers to himself as Terry's "step mother." Terry's mother remarried, so Terry also had a step father during her growing-up years. At one point, when Terry was a preteen, her two families engaged in a court battle.

Visitation with her father was restricted; however, Terry recounts that she was old enough at that point to ride her bike to see her father whenever she wanted to—so the court battle had little effect on her relationship with her father.

Terry's father and step father have both died. Terry feels that her family, at this point, is very accepting of her lesbianism and of her chosen family. Her family of origin includes Kevin and Tanya in their Christmas and birthday gift giving and in all family events. Terry regrets that her family, which is so supportive of them, lives half-way across the country. Terry's experiences of growing up in both a step family situation and a gay family have provided her with models, some positive and some more negative, which guide her ideas about family now.

Terry and Tanya and Kevin are a "nuclear" family in the sense that Kevin lives full time in the home, with Tanya and Terry as his only parents.

Kevin is a very bright, energetic little boy and Terry and Tanya work hard at keeping his energy and giftedness channeled into positive activities. Tanya, because she is with Kevin more than Terry, is involved in driving Kevin to his tae kwon do classes several nights per week (where he is working toward a black belt) and several other sports activities. In addition, Kevin takes piano lessons and Terry and Tanya enforce a daily practicing schedule. Kevin does well in school, and excels in "practically everything he tries." He enjoys playing with several friends. Presently, then, Kevin presents no major challenges in parenting, outside of his high energy level.

Summary

The Norden/Westby/Engleking family is a step family; however, Kevin does not live in another home. His father is deceased. He does have pictures of his father and the family talks about him easily. Terry is the major breadwinner at present, making almost twice as much as Tanya. Although Tanya is looking for a better job, she is happy that her work allows her to spend time with Kevin when he gets home from school. Tanya is presently more of the homemaker in this family. Terry enjoys Kevin and likes to spend time with him when she can. She worries about having to spend so much time away from home.

These parents believe in providing a structured home environment for their child. Kevin is involved in several structured activities, including piano, soccer, tae kwon do, and camp. His parents agree that these activities help him to channel his high energy into constructive activities. But they also add to the busy schedules of his parents and the resulting stress relating to lack of time for everything.

As a multiracial family, they are very concerned with actively working toward multicultural awareness and acceptance within the family, as well as in the community.

THE ILIFF/DUBROVSKY/ILIFF-HERNANDEZ FAMILY

Janet: What is the best thing about your family? What are some of the high points?

Delia: I think we do birthdays the best. Holidays. It doesn't matter what holiday. You can tell that Kathy grew up in a family where she had two doting aunts, as well as a mom. And arts and crafts were something. I mean they were forever making—to this day, they make their own centerpieces—that kind of thing. . . . We always go to an opera or to a play and then to dinner. And then, presents at home. And she has got every event, from the first tooth to graduation now, on video-tape. And we've got these family tapes which are really—I never thought I'd say it, because we all kind of go—"No, not the camera!" But we must have this for history!

Kathy: I don't know if it's true of all lesbian households, arents and kids, but that was the thing around here—we tried to be very democratic. . . . We might get the last word or get to make the decision, but [the kids] had a voice, and they had ears that would listen [to them] for as long as they needed to talk . . . We often did take votes—how do you feel about this? I don't know, that's what I like about our family—we value each other and we all work hard to connect. . . . As a lesbian household, we also have the benefit of alternative perspectives.

Diana ("Deeana," 20): Well, we went on all these vacations, because Mom and Kathy really like camping. And me and Natalia really don't like it, but we like traveling—so we would go.

Natalia ("Talia," 17): We always do stuff. I mean like we go to the [Shakespearean] Theater just about once a year. And we see plays. And we go to operas—because Kathy and Diana like operas—me and my Mom don't know why—we can't stand them. But we go to operas, we go to plays, and we go to concerts. . . . I don't know—[we have] the strengths of any normal functioning family. I guess I mean, we're not abusive toward each other and we don't try to hurt each other. I don't know.

This family includes Kathy Dubrovsky—the co-mom, ("I don't consider myself a step mother, nor do Delia, Diana, and Talia. I am a parent and totally immersed in parenting.") Delia Iliff (the biological mother), Diana Iliff (twenty years old)—the oldest daughter, and Natalia (Talia) Iliff-Hernandez (seventeen years old)—the youngest daughter. In order to differentiate the generations, I will sometimes refer to the daughters as "girls" or "children," however, I am well aware that they are young women. Kathy and Delia are in their early forties.

Kathy identifies as having a Polish heritage and Delia has a Scottish ethnic background. Diana and Talia's father is Hispanic, however they are both quick to say that they don't really feel Hispanic or identify much with the culture.

> **Talia:** [Dad] was born in Chicago, and my grandfather, I guess, was born in Texas, like really close to the border. I think everybody before him must have been from Mexico, I don't really know. But Dad's probably all our lives tried to push being Mexican down our throats. We never really accepted it too much. I mean, we don't really look Mexican, you know. It's like we've never experienced racism, like people being racist to us and stuff like that, so—I know that I'm Hispanic, but I don't really consider myself a minority, simply because I'm never judged by my heritage.

Delia and Kathy have a combined annual income of approximately $60,000. Both are college educated. Delia has an additional degree as a paralegal and Kathy has a master's degree. They own a three-bedroom home in a middle-class neighborhood. They pool all of their money and make financial decisions together and say that money has not been a problematic issue in their relationship.

Delia and Kathy have been together for fifteen years, since the girls were only two and four years old. They couldn't remember exactly how they chose their anniversary day, but they do celebrate their anniversary each year and are proud of their longevity as a couple. When I asked how they had managed to stay together for so long, they identified that having to deal with the girls' father was the most difficult part of their relationship in the past. "As I often reflect, you know, having relationships and families is difficult, but having this father in the picture was the most difficult part" (Kathy). However, the problems with the father may also have acted as a kind of cement for the relationship, as they were able to unite around a common enemy.

> **Kathy:** Well, you know it was, because I think what helped was the things we fought about always were instigated from the outside. And that the two of us never really had, not that I could remember, a real issue with one another—like you are doing something that I don't like. It was the outside forces that got us going. And if anything we didn't agree on, how to resolve the problem, what approach to take, or who did what or who said what, or . . . When we would really sit down and realize—are we going to let that divide us and make us end our relationship? . . . Are we going to let him do this to us?

So Delia's ex-husband unwittingly played a part in strengthening the relationship between Delia and Kathy, even as he attempted to isolate and stigmatize Kathy as the problem.

> **Delia:** Yeah, that was when [the kids] were with him and he was feeding them that crap. Like, "You don't have to listen to Kathy. She's not your mother. You have one mother."

Instead of allowing this to drive a wedge between them, Delia and Kathy simply increased their determination and efforts to insist on Kathy's status as a full parent.

Delia was married to Diana and Talia's father for four and a half years. The divorce stipulation gave them joint custody of the kids, with the kids going back and forth between their homes on a weekly basis, until about five years ago. At that point, Diana decided she didn't want to live with her dad anymore. Three years ago, when their father relocated to a nearby city, Talia was given a choice about who to live with and she stayed with her moms in Newville. Diana no longer has contact with her father, but Talia sees him occasionally. Diana has also dropped her father's name from her last name, so that she is Diana Iliff now instead of Diana Iliff-Hernandez.

Delia is clear that she only opted for joint custody because of her fear about her lesbianism becoming an issue in court. Had she not been a lesbian, she would have fought for full custody of the girls. However, her lawyer advised against that.

> **Delia:** At that time you didn't come out and say on the table that this was an issue. So I had in my file a sealed envelope that he had signed that acknowledges that he will at no time now or in the future be able to raise this [issue] as an unfit parent. And that's what [the lawyer] said we had to have him sign something to guarantee it, but we won't bring it up in court, because, why get into that talk. So, at that time, that is how you dealt with it—seal it up.

The fact that Delia wanted to share her children was "a gift," according to Kathy, who has always loved children. However, the children did force serious contemplation and discussion between Delia and Kathy very early in their relationship.

> **Delia:** I said, look, if we get into this, this is a package deal. The kids are coming with me. You are going to be a parent. It's all or nothing. Now, if that's not something you want to do—I mean, she is still in diapers. It's going to be work for a while— you are going to get up at night when they are crying, just like me. And she looked at me and said, "Well, I'll have to think about it." Now she doesn't remember saying that, but she did. And I felt that's fine. I want to hear an honest thing here. If this is going to be too much, we can see each other, but keep our lives separate. Now I don't remember how long—I don't think it was very long. And then you decided it was worth it.

It is crucial to understanding how this family has developed to perceive the complementary stances these mothers took and take toward the children. Delia was willing and able to let go of some of her power with the children and wanted to really share parenting with Kathy. Kathy, for her part, took the risk of truly loving the children, as well as taking on at least half of the responsibilities for them. Indeed, in the childrens' early years, Kathy's job allowed her to spend more time with them than Delia's work allowed. So, together, they have created a virtually equal parenting relationship.

Connection with family members is very important to this family. Delia's family of origin is not supportive of her relationship with Kathy, although, over the years, they have become more accepting. Unfortunately, her father died before anything was really resolved on the issue and Delia still feels the pain of this unfinished business. However, after her father died, her mother, and even her two sisters, have allowed themselves to be more accepting and to even establish a pleasant, if not close, relationship with Kathy. This distance between Delia and her parents even extended to her children; her mother once told Diana and Talia that their mother was "abnormal." Delia's father's inability to love and accept her children was particularly pain-ful to her, especially when she saw the contrast with how he treated his other grandchildren. In spite of her pain, Delia has made efforts to retain connection with her family of origin and she does see signs of her mother and sisters' attempts at acceptance and understanding—for example, her younger sister and her husband, her mother, and her grandmother came to Diana's high school graduation.

Kathy's family of origin has been somewhat more accepting of her lesbian family. She believes that her family for the most part doesn't see her lesbianism as morally wrong (with the exception, perhaps, of her born-again Christian brother), but simply as "it's too bad you can't be normal." Kathy's father died before she actually came out to him and she regrets that she never got to have that conversation, since she thinks he might have been even more understanding and accepting. However, she has maintained close contact with her mother, two aunts, and her two brothers. Recently they had a family reunion with Kathy's whole family. Although there were some problems related to homo-phobia, and Kathy felt very hurt about how her mother and aunt treated Delia, Diana, and Talia, the commitment to maintain and even create deeper family ties remains. This commitment to family connec-tion is very evident in the way this family lives together. It is very important to these parents to remain aware of and involved with their children's lives, even though their daughters are young adults.

Diana is a second-year college student who lives at home and attends the local technical college. She is vivacious and easy to talk to and enjoys joking, teasing, and kidding her friends and family. She is unsure of the career(s) she may pursue, but enjoys attending her school. Her interests include traveling, movies ("I love movies. I'm addicted to movies. Movies are my life!"), and computers. She thinks she may get married some day, and maybe even have a child, but she enjoys and takes pride in her independent thinking and would not want give that up.

Talia is a senior in an alternative high school. She struggled with drug abuse and skipped school during her late middle school and early high school years. But, with the help of some counseling, her moms' eagle eyes ("I mean there was no way I was doing drugs again-not with my moms. They watched me like a hawk."), the alternative school, and her own courage—she was able to turn her life around. She is proud to be graduating this year. Talia enjoys photography, but is unsure of what she will do after high school. "I just want a job that doesn't run my life—to be able to do other things."

Summary

The Iliff/Dubrovsky/Iliff-Hernandez family is a family with strong political beliefs. Kathy and Delia met when they were both serving on a committee to pass the ERA. They have openly and actively supported feminist causes and gay/lesbian rights. They openly acknowledge their lesbianism in most situations and their daughters are also very open about their parents' sexual orientations.

This is a family that places a high value on maintaining and nurturing connection. They make an effort to spend quality time together, work hard at talking out their disagreements, and clearly enjoy joking with each other. There are many family insider jokes.

They have been particularly challenged by the joint custody agreement that they had with the father. Although the issues have diminished as the girls have matured, they have not dissipated altogether.

Finally, this couple has negotiated a co-parenting stance which is unique in this sample by its equal sharing of both responsibility for and power with the children.

THE UPHOFF/DILLARD FAMILY

Janet: What is the best thing about your family? What are some of the high points?

Florence: Oh, gosh. There are so many. Well, I think the baby is a real heartrending experience for everybody. You know, it's like we were camping Memorial [Day] weekend, and Nisi was resting up against the back of the van. She kind of had pulled down the front of her pants and was rubbing her tummy. And it was kind of spontaneous—all three of us just walked over and put our hands on her tummy, and that was just . . . oh, yeah!

Nisi: Hum. As far as high moments, I think there's high moments every day. I think just daily interactions that to me feel warm and close and cohesive, or where I see growth. Those everyday kind of experiences are my high moments. . . . Well, they are so mundane, they don't sound like anything. Just hugging the kids good night. Just when they make a meal for us—just because it is growth and its new territory.

Frannie (8): Well, we are a loving family. They—that's a hard question to answer, too! . . . Once I beat [my moms] both in triple yahtzee, and once we went to a water park. But I like doing activities with [my family]—going to baseball games, and . . . trips, yeah, I love going on trips.

Dale (8): Oh boy, everything. Let's see. They are not mean at all. They, when something gets broken, they always fix it for us—they are real good about that. . . . They have enough time for me usually. . . . They are not a yelling family. . . . We play games, like Chinese checkers. Two nights ago we played Crib-bage. We watch TV shows. . . . .We go camping. We hug a lot.

There are four people in the Uphoff/Dillard family right now, but there will soon be another. Denise ("Nisi") Uphoff, who is in her late thirties and the biological mother of twins, Dale (eight-year-old boy), and Frannie (eight-year-old-girl) Uphoff, is pregnant again with a girl. Florence Dillard, who is in her early forties, is the step mother to Dale and Frannie and co-mother of the unborn baby. Although these family members identify themselves as white, Florence is also proud of her one-quarter American Indian heritage.

They are a middle-class family with a combined income of about $58,000, depending on how much overtime Florence works. They own a two-flat home and live in the lower flat, which is a two-bedroom converted to a three-bedroom apartment. They are currently doing some remodeling, including adding a hallway and a second bathroom. They rent the upstairs flat to a single mother and her daughter.

Florence has a high school education. She works days at a factory. She leaves home about 4 a.m. and commutes to work, works for about ten hours, and returns home about 5 p.m., working five days each week. Nisi, who has a master's degree, works for the school district. She works four days per week during the school year and has summers off. Nisi and Florence, who earn roughly the same amount of money annually, keep their money separate and each contributes to a joint household account. Nisi believes that this eliminates a whole level of conflict that some people have and Florence agrees. "Well, what she would consider important enough to spend money on, I wouldn't. And vice versa, and that way we wouldn't have to ask, unless it's to do with the house."

Frannie and Dale are in the third grade, in separate classrooms. Their school is part of a paired school system, so they attended the close neighborhood school in grades K through 2 and now they bus to a school in another district for grades 3 through 5. This seems to be an enjoyable education experience for them.

Nisi and Florence have been together for five and a half years. Their commitment to each other has definitely grown over those years. In the early stages of their relationship, they agreed to stay together only as long as it was good. Now that they are parenting together and having a baby together, Nisi says that they are "in it to stay together." Still, Nisi feels strongly that she would not hang onto the relationship if it got bad and stayed bad—"nobody benefits in that kind of situation." On the other hand, she wouldn't want to give up on the relationship too easily. They agree that they will get help if the relationship is not going well. They have gone to see a therapist to work out problems between them. Nisi says that it is a priority for them to stay in tune with the relationship, to be kind and considerate, to maintain a friendship and a sexual relationship, to communicate, and to parent as a team.

Before getting together with Florence, Nisi was with another woman, Kitty, for nine years. It was in the context of that relationship that she gave birth to Frannie and Dale by doctor-assisted alternative insemination. The children's donor is unknown, although they have some basic information about him. Nisi and Florence were able to use the same donor for their present pregnancy.

When Frannie and Dale were three years old, Nisi broke up with Kitty. At the time of their breakup, Kitty and Nisi had an agreement to do joint parenting, including sharing financial responsibility for the children. However, this agreement never seemed to function smoothly for Nisi.

Nisi: Yes, they went over there for three days a week. They went over there Tuesdays, Thursdays, and one weekend day. But she wouldn't . . . she just . . . I didn't feel like she was responsible and living up to her end of parenting at all. She wouldn't contribute to the cost of day care. She wouldn't make sure they had baths or brushed their teeth, or . . .

Florence: Ate right.

Nisi: Yeah, ate decent meals. And I battled with her with it and went to therapy with her about it—struggled over two years. And she was not going to change and there didn't seem any hope for her changing. And so, I didn't feel like it was really good for me or the kids. It was making me crazy. And so, I just finally said, that you are not going to have this kind of access to them anymore. That's it. And I figured that twice a month was kind of like a minimum that the kids would need, because she is very important to them. They love her very much and they think of her as a mom, I'm sure.

In the present arrangement, the kids go to Kitty's house about every other Sunday, from 8:30 a.m. to 5:30 p.m. They also go on a summer vacation with Kitty for a week or a week and a half each year.

> **Nisi:** You know, it was my initial feeling that it was a joint parenting situation and that she said she wanted to keep on with it. And I believed her. And I was real committed to make . . . to continue with that. It would be like a divorce and we'd both have substantial contact with the kids. I feel like I tried.

Florence was in a relationship with two women before she became involved with Nisi. She was with one of the women for sixteen years. The other woman was with them for the last six years of their relationship. Florence was also married very briefly when she was twenty to a man who "turned out to be gay."

Florence's family of origin includes two older sisters, a younger half-sister, and two younger half-brothers. Florence was raised as a "strict" Pentecostal. Her parents divorced when she was about three years old and she grew up with her mom and step father. She has only recently made contact with her father again. Her relationships with the members of her family of origin are somewhat mixed.

> **Florence:** Unfortunately, most of my relatives, I don't stay in contact with. There's very few that I feel close to, and, or that accept me. And there's some that tolerate me, and love me, but don't really accept it. And it makes a big difference. Whereas Nisi's family seem very accepting, very loving, supportive, happy for her.

Florence's older sister hunted for and found their father a few years ago. Now Florence enjoys maintaining contact with her father and her step mother, who is "a little sweetheart." When I asked if she was out to them, she replied,

> Oh, they know, yeah. [My step mother] is fine with it, real fine with it. My dad, of course, he's kind of—it's OK, you know, he's not going to slam the door in my face. But I'm sure he'd much prefer it be the normal, for him. It's easier to deal with.

Nisi is the baby in her family of origin—the fifth child, the only girl, born nine years after her next older brother. Nisi is out to her whole family and they are all very supportive of her and her family. Although her brothers are spread out around the country, they try to visit often and always make a point of spending time with Frannie and Dale. Nisi's parents live in town and are very involved with her family. Her father helps with their remodeling projects, gardening, car maintenance, etc. Her mother is "getting pretty thrilled" about Nisi's current pregnancy. She also baby-sits for the children sometimes. They get a lot of support for their family from Nisi's family of origin.

Frannie and Dale are twins who spend much of their time together with remarkably little fighting. However, both Florence and Nisi are quick to point out that there is competition between them. Both children are very bright and they enjoy school, as well as athletics. Dale, however, has the challenge of attention deficit disorder. He takes Ritalin several times a day to control the disorder and this has helped him with his schooling as well as improved his behavior at home. Although he ends up getting more time-outs at home for his behavior than Frannie does, Nisi is clear that "so much of what he does wrong is out of his control." This has been hard for Dale and has had a negative impact on his self-esteem—something that Nisi and Florence are hoping he can overcome. He has become more self-confident after going on the medication in first grade.

Summary

Florence and Nisi are committed to teaching the children various skills that foster their independence and competence. The children are expected to help with the family work and generally seem to enjoy it. The children are also involved in many activities, such as baseball, scouting, gymnastics, and soccer. Nisi has made an effort to encourage the children's individuality, rather than emphasizing their twin status.

The Uphoff/Dillard family has several challenges. Dale struggles with his attention deficit disorder and the problems it presents in school, with his own self-esteem, and with family relationships at home. Florence has worked very hard to overcome the example of poor parenting that was modeled in her family of origin, but this continues to be an issue in this family. In addition, Florence's long work and commuting hours and the physical toll they take make it difficult for her to parent. Finally, the relationship with the children's other parent, Kitty, has been contentious. Although the parents seem to have reached an agreeable compromise, the children acknowledge feeling pain and sadness about this issue.

This is a family that truly enjoys working and playing together. They have fun together—playing games, going camping, taking trips, and doing building and maintenance projects. The children have embraced Florence as a parent and an important person in their lives. They are all good friends.

THE PETERSON/TIMMS/TAYLOR FAMILY

Janet: What is the best thing about your family? What are some of the high points?

Loretta: ("Lori—I would like to use my real name but people say it sounds too snooty or something.") I think one of the nicest times for all four of us—those have been kind of rare— when we were all on the same wavelength, or whatever, is usually our Christmases. But we have a time when we read these stories. They have some old Norman Rockwell Christmas book of Cady's, and we have these rare moments where Cady is reading them a story, or Nell reads the story, you know, and we just all are kind of on the same wavelength. And they have always, especially Nell, with all her anger, has always gone way out of her way to give us each wonderful gifts, and several of them. They are really tailored to our personalities, which, I've never been able to figure this out, considering all her feelings, you know. And so those are always just kind of nice times for us.

Cady: Probably now, really. With Nell just dropping in, and the four of us being able to sit down and have a conversation together. I'm really excited that Nell wants to go on vacation with Lori and me. That's really going to be fun.

Molly (15): ("I wish you'd call me Magnolia in your book!")
My sister. . . . We didn't get along when we were younger, but
now we . . . we've grown together within the past two or three
years.

Although there are four people in this family, the older daughter,
Nell Taylor, who is nineteen and a sophomore in the local university, is no longer living at home and therefore I did not interview her
for this study. However, Nell continues to be an important part of
this family. The other family members include Loretta Timms, the
step mother, Cady Peterson, the biological mother, and Molly Taylor, who is fifteen and a sophomore in high school. Loretta (Lori) is
in her early forties, while Cady is in her upper forties.

This is a middle- to upper- middle-class family with a combined
income of about $140,000. They own a home in a rural subdivision
near Newville. Lori has her PhD and works full time as an adminis-
trator. Lori earns about twice as much as Cady, who is in management. She has her master's degree. They maintain a household
account, to which they each contribute to equally, for such goods as
utilities and food. They have a system for paying the mortgage
which is based on the equity they each have in the house, since
Cady contributed a larger down payment. The rest of the money is
kept is their own separate accounts.

Spirituality is a very important part of Cady's and Lori's lives.
Although Cady was raised Protestant and Lori was raised Catholic
and even spent time in a convent as a young adult, they have been
unable to find a church home where they feel comfortable and
accepted.

Lori: That's something we've both talked about—we would
really like to have somewhere where we felt like we had a
common faith life that would be a place that was tolerant of
our lifestyle. And I don't think I feel like anything is intoler-
ant—it's just too big and too impersonal.

Cady: And actually I think that, at least for me, my spiritual
life has changed a lot since I was divorced, because I did more
of the traditional, I really felt it was an important part of my
growing up to go to church regularly. And it was a positive

experience and it was throughout the time that I had small children and was married. So, when I left my marriage, I really felt I didn't belong anywhere. It was really weird. And I still kind of grieve that.

Lori: I think that really one of the things that really attracted us to each other was our spirituality, and . . .

Cady: Yes, I do, too.

Lori: I'm real interested in Buddhism and Eastern religions and to me, Cady is really just a grounded Buddhist, you know. I'm into the theory, but she walks it.

Cady and Lori have been together for eight years, and the family has been living together, in their present house, for six and a half years. So Nell was thirteen and Molly was nine when they moved in together. Cady had been divorced from a fourteen-year marriage and was living alone with the children for a year before she and Lori began their relationship, and it was an additional year and a half before they moved in together.

They have had some conflict over whether or not to have a commitment ceremony of some sort. Although they compromised on a private ceremony during a weekend alone together, Lori is disappointed that they didn't have a ceremony with friends.

Lori: I have a big thing about this. I would like to have some giant, huge ceremony, with all our friends, that had some religious overtone. But Cady doesn't. Cady thinks that's too much like heterosexual marriage. And I think it's essential to really knowing you are committed. But I've gotten over that with much time, I think you know. I know we are committed now, but we had our own private ceremony. . . . I just like that kind of thing. But at bottom it's because I believe, there has to be a spiritual component to this. Now there is a spiritual component to our relationship, and that's wonderful. I look at it differently now than I did in the beginning because Cady kept saying to me "That ceremony isn't going to make you secure." And I said, "Yes, it will!" And the thing is, I wasn't secure, and I'm secure now.

Cady: And see, I had some feelings from a relationship—and you've heard me say this—where I felt all of the ceremony was a farce.

After Cady's divorce, she and her ex-husband agreed on joint custody of the two girls; however, Cady was always the custodial parent. The father, Sam, lives in the same city, so the kids have had a lot of freedom to see both parents. Sam abused alcohol during the time that Cady was married to him. Although he is recovering now, Cady and Lori feel that he is still unwilling to really make a commitment to consistently spend specific times with the girls—"that is too much of an infringement of his freedom." On the other hand, he hasn't caused many covert problems for their family.

Cady: He doesn't have that kind of concern [to fight for custody]. He's pretty casual about that. But he's been extremely cooperative. He's never, ever given me a hard time about being a lesbian. He's never fought to change the custody or the financial support.

Cady says that she has always felt that she had to somehow make up to the kids for their dad's indifference and unwillingness to give up any of his adult independence for them.

Lori had a five-year relationship with a woman that ended a couple of years before she and Cady met. She also had several shorter relationships with women, but was never in a relationship with a woman who had children until Cady. Although she has had physical attractions to men, she has not been in any committed relationships with men.

When asked how this relationship was different from former relationships they have had, Lori's first response was that Cady was a "grown-up." Cady is "really kind of the first person I've been involved with who is whole." Cady emphasized the mutuality and equality and respect in their relationship. "There's no doubt in my mind that she wants me to do what I really love to do and be who I want to be."

Both Cady and Lori have practiced a kind of "don't ask, don't tell" policy on talking about their lesbianism with their families of origin. Lori is the oldest child and is six years older than her only sibling, a brother. Both of Lori's parents have died.

Although she didn't tell them that she was a lesbian, she feels that they were aware. Her mother said to her at one point that she knew that she would never get married, but that she hoped Lori would find someone to make her happy. When Lori's mother died, Cady and Lori had only been together for two months. Cady came to sit with Lori at the hospital on the day of her mother's death, which was an important moment for their relationship.

> **Lori:** So I was really sad that this was how Cady met [my mother]. But at one point, Cady was holding my mother's hand and you could kind of feel like some little communication was going on. And I said to [Cady], "What are you doing?" You know. And she said, "I'm telling your mother [who was in a coma] that I'm the one who's going to make her daughter happy."

Lori's mother had been fighting cancer since Lori was only four years old, so Lori lived most of her childhood and her early adulthood with the overriding fear of her mother's death. She was alone with her mother—at Cady's insistence that she take some time alone—when her mother died. Lori feels blessed to have had that moment—"so I just always feel like that was something that Cady gave to me." Lori's father died several years later. She pointed out that her father, who was in construction, always let her tag along with him on his jobs—"I did everything, you know, so [my parents] left me with the sense there was nothing I couldn't do. And I told them I was going to go to [a boys' prep school] and then to Harvard. And they never pointed out to me that those were both, at the time, men-only schools."

Cady is out to her sister, who is also a lesbian, but she is not out to her father or brother, although they are aware that she lives with Lori. Cady is the middle child. Her mother died thirteen years ago. Cady says that her parents were unusual when she was growing up. Her mother worked full time in management. Her father owned a business and wasn't home a lot of the time. Of the two of them, he was probably more emotional. "I don't remember [my mother] ever saying that she loved me." Her father was raised by women and

Cady notes that "he has a great deal of respect for women." Cady said that when she married she was shocked to learn that some men thought that they were more important than women, simply because they were men! Cady never got this message from her parents.

Molly is a fifteen-year-old high school sophomore who is in a smaller-class track high school program. Although she has traditionally had difficulty with school and got into a pattern of truancy in middle school, she feels she has been doing better since she has switched to this program. Molly has held several part-time jobs, in part because of a family rule that kids pay their own car insurance. She is currently working at the public library.

Molly, like her older sister Nell, is very much into the Grateful Dead music and scene. She enjoys listening to music—that is one of her favorite activities. Molly is not dating at this point and does not often have friends out to the house. She used to get along well with Lori, but presently feels a lot of distance from her. Cady muses in her journal, "But I blame this 'drift' on adolescence first, and on being in a lesbian step family a very remote second." Molly, however, seems to see it as a personality clash.

Lori and Nell (the older daughter) have had a contested relationship from the beginning—"She literally locked me out of her mother's house once!" They have survived the teenage years by letting go and distancing. Nell moved in with her dad for her senior year in high school and first year of college. And Lori has "given up" some of her parenting—"My finally giving permission to myself not to keep trying to find a way to get these kids to love me every minute." Since Nell has been in college, her relationship with Lori has improved dramatically, much to Lori's relief. Although this very difficult relationship between Lori and Nell, and now between Lori and Molly, has been perhaps the hardest part of their family life, the struggles have also forged a clearer and stronger relationship between Cady and Lori.

Cady: I mean these kinds of struggles have always—even though they've been hard, with Lori feeling left out, and me feeling like I'm sort of in the middle—really have forced us to get clear about how we feel about each other. And I think it's really obvious to both of us that this is worth it. Our work is worth it, because we really love each other.

Summary

Lori and Cady's relationship has a deep spiritual base. It is this connection on the spiritual plane which has held the family together on the more turbulent plane of everyday living.

One of their major challenges as a family has been the contested relationship between Nell (the older daughter) and Lori. This has forced Lori to take a less active parenting role in the family than she would have liked. As the tension with Nell eases, Lori is now confronted with increasing rejection from Molly. The parents struggle with the question of whether this is a passing adolescent rebellion or something deeper and more lasting. It is important to remember that the children spent their early years in an alcoholic home, which has likely affected on their senses of trust and safety and their abilities to relate to their parents. In spite of these at times painful relationships with the children, Lori has persisted in her love for them and her attempts to connect with them. And Cady has also maintained an enduring love for them all.

Lori and Cady are strikingly different personalities. Lori is more demonstrative and emotional. Cady is active, never idle, always on the go, whereas Lori prefers to sit and read. Lori needs to socialize more with others. And yet, in spite of, or because of, their differences, they hold each other in great respect. They are proud to have given the children a good model of two people who love each other and who manage to work out their differences with respect.

THE STARK FAMILY

Janet: What is the best thing about your family? What are some of the high points?

Rebecca (Becky): Well, I get the kid I always wanted . . . Well, I guess probably right now [is one of the best times]. Because we are both working. We both have, you know, decent incomes coming in. We've got a nice, nice place now . . . not that the other one was awful or anything. But it makes it a lot easier on—with being all on one level—for Pauli and I. And with the garage, Pauli doesn't have to go out in the cold. . . . Pauli, with her school and everything—it's working out a lot better. In kindergarten, she spent most of her time in the [principal's] office. And now she spends all her time in class and, you know, learning. She's doing so much better. Physically, she is not doing real well, but at least Dory has insurance.

Dory: Well, from my perspective, I mean, I think we blend well together. I mean, I don't see having Pauli and not having Becky in my family. It works real well. And I don't think that would have been possible in a heterosexual—I'm just not cut out to be a mommy. . . . Probably our vacation was a really good time. Before that, like I said, we'd really been sort of— the survival mode. There wasn't a lot of highs. I would say that the vacation was real fun—going to the water park, watching the two of them play, where they were having fun.

Pauli (7): We went out to this place and it was these hot air balloons and they were all kinds of colors. . . . I love my whole family. But you know, the worst thing is that my grandma— both my grandmas—died.

The Stark family includes Rebecca Stark—the step mother, Dory Stark—the biological mother, and Pauli Stark—their seven-year-old daughter. Rebecca (Becky) chose to change her last name so that it would be the same as Dory and Pauli's name. She did it because she had already changed her last name once (she and a former partner had chosen a last name together) and because she felt it would be so much easier. For example, she says, "I don't have any kind of power of attorney over Pauli, but having the same last name gets me a lot."

Becky is in her late thirties and describes her ethnicity as German, Danish, Norwegian, and one-eighth Jewish. Dory, who is in her early thirties says that she is a "Heinz 57" in terms of ethnicity. Pauli's father is half Hispanic, "although you couldn't tell it by looking at her."

This family is particularly challenged with health problems. Pauli was diagnosed with juvenile rheumatoid arthritis when she was two years old and it has spread since then, presently affecting almost one whole side of her body. She is on two medications for this and needs some special services from the school, including riding in the bus for physically challenged children and requiring special therapy in the school swimming pool. She has difficulty with certain physical tasks such as climbing stairs and brushing her hair. Pauli is also affected ("98 percent") by attention deficit disorder (ADD), which was diagnosed about one and a half years ago. Pauli takes Ritalin to help her manage the effects of the ADD.

At the same time that Pauli was diagnosed with ADD, Dory recognized the symptoms in herself and had herself tested. She discovered that she also had ADD and now takes Ritalin as needed to help her control the symptoms. These diagnoses have helped the family to understand and cope with many of the problems that were plaguing them early in their relationship. As Becky says, "Winding up getting them both diagnosed (with ADD) really took a lot of the irritating factors away."

Becky also has arthritis in her knee as the result of a car accident, so she and Pauli connect regarding this issue.

> **Becky:** When she's in an arthritic flare, the only thing that . . . a little Tylenol helps . . . but nothing else she gets. She gets medication on a daily basis that they have to give her [at school]. The Tylenol reduces the fever. But the pain, when she is in a flare, there is not a lot we can do. . . . But, one of the radio stations here is doing this holiday wish thing. So I wrote up that I wanted a soft-sider [hot tub] for her. We'll see if they grant it.

Particularly because of these persistent health problems, finances have been problematic for this family at times. When they first moved to Stafford, a city of 75,000 about 100 miles from Newville, they were both unemployed and had to pay for medical expenses out of their own pockets. Presently, finances are better because they both have jobs. Becky has a full time job in electronics, with good benefits. She makes about $30,000 annually, with overtime. She commutes to work, leaving home at about 5 a.m. and returning between 3:30 and 5:30 p.m. She works Monday through Fridays, and some Saturdays. Becky loves her job, describing it as "like going to Disneyland every day!"

Unfortunately, Dory's job is less satisfactory, although it at least guarantees that she and Pauli have health insurance–and the hours allow her to spend time after school with Pauli. Dory is presently a supervisor for a security company and makes about $18,000 a year. Both Dory and Becky wish that Becky's insurance would cover the family so that Dory could either go back to school or look for a more fulfilling job. In fact, Becky even asked her company if she could cover Dory and Pauli.

> **Becky:** Yeah, I did [ask the company], because then it would make it even better, because then, if I could cover those two, then Dory could like actually get a job that means something to her. But the lady said, well, she would continue checking into it, but that she doubted that the corporation would go along with it. . . . What I told her, I said, if I don't ask, then I never know and I said, if we continue to be part of the wood-work, nothing will ever change.

The Starks rent a small three-bedroom home into which they recently moved. Their goal is to begin putting away some money for a down payment on a home of their own. They pool all of their money. When I asked if this was a problem, since Becky makes more money, they said that it wasn't, noting that at the beginning of their relationship it had been Dory who made more. However, Dory admitted that she has had some trouble accepting the fact that she makes less money right now.

Dory and Becky have been together for almost five years. They met at a twelve-step retreat for lesbians with various addictions. Becky is a recovering alcoholic who has been sober for fourteen years. Dory was dealing with an overeating problem. Becky had been in the military and Dory was still in another branch of the military. They decided from the beginning that they wanted to set some healthy ground rules for their relationship, so they went to couple counseling. It was important to Dory that she not have people "bouncing in and out" of Pauli's life. She wanted to be sure that this relationship would last. Becky was also ready for a long-term commitment, as she was tired of the stress of serial relationships.

The beginning of their relationship was fraught with chaos and stress. Pauli, who had been living with her grandparents for the past year while Dory was on duty, came to live with Becky and Dory one month after they got together. Dory's mother was having her arm amputated and could no longer care for Pauli. This meant that Becky became a full-time mother while Dory worked. Three months later, Dory left the military and the family moved to the Midwest. This move was prompted by the fact that Becky's family was in the Midwest. They felt it would be less expensive living in the Midwest and they would have a better chance of buying a home. They were also concerned about Pauli's paternal grandmother possibly pushing her son to battle for custody. When they arrived in Stafford, they were both unemployed and they struggled financially until they were able to get their present jobs. In addition, shortly after they moved to Stafford, Dory's mother became increasingly ill and eventually died. Two months after that, Becky's mother, to whom Pauli had become very attached, died suddenly and unexpectedly.

How did their relatively young relationship manage to survive all of this trauma? Dory and Becky attribute it to their strong faith and belief in a higher power. In discussing how they found their present house, Dory explains this faith. "It was a situation where we really needed to have something and something turned up. And that has been our pattern all the way through our relationship—is that the faith element has been there." Dory also explains that the level of commitment makes this relationship strong. What helped them pull through in these low moments?

> **Dory:** A strong commitment, I think. I don't think there was any. You get into a fight and I go, "Fine, then I'll leave." But there was never a point where we were serious about that. Along with that, you know, we had always been going to couple's counseling, and stuff, and I think that helped it a lot. We were doing the couple's counseling right after Becky got a job, which was helpful, because there was a place where we could at least go and communicate. . . . I can truthfully say that

this relationship was very much different to the ones we had before—the level of commitment is strong and the desire to make it work on both sides.

Religion has been an important part of their lives together. When they first moved to Stafford, they attended the Metropolitan Community Church (a gay and lesbian, nationwide, church) in a nearby larger city. However, the pastor was replaced with someone that they felt did not reach out to them. They give as an example of this the fact that the pastor never contacted them after their mothers died to offer sympathy and support. So now they attend a United Methodist church in Stafford—a church that Becky's cousin invited them to attend.

It is a mainstream church, but the pastor is aware of their relationship and is accepting and supportive. Although Becky's mother didn't want her to tell anyone else when Becky originally came out to her, she eventually came around to accepting Becky and her family. When Becky and Dory first moved to Stafford, Becky's mother and aunt used to spend every Saturday evening with them, playing cards. She also grew very close to Pauli, and accepted her as a grandchild. Becky did come out to her entire extended family by writing a letter, and she feels that most of them are accepting and supportive. She does not get along with her older brother, who abused her and her mother after her dad died when she was six. She describes him as an alcoholic and abusive man who "held my mother and I hostage" after her father died, until he left the house six years later. Becky's extended family gets together quite often for parties and dinners and Becky and Dory and Pauli are always invited.

Dory describes her family of origin as "very, very conservative." Although she originally came out at eighteen, her parents thought it was a stage, and they were ecstatic when she got married. However, the marriage didn't last. Although Dory used to pretend that her girlfriends were "just friends," she was unwilling to do that with her relationship with Becky. Her mother never really adjusted to the idea of Dory's lesbianism. Dory expresses a lot of hurt when she describes inviting her parents to the Holy Union Ceremony ("pretty much like a marriage") that she and Becky had when they were still living on the West Coast, and her parents refused to come. Since her mother's death, her father has "come a long way." Dory and Becky were proud to show the anniversary card that he sent them this year!

Dory got married when she was in the military, hoping to force herself to be heterosexual by living it. She almost immediately went overseas for fifteen months and says that she and Pauli's dad only actually lived together for about three months total, although they were married for three years. They separated before Pauli was born and Dory was in a lesbian relationship for about a year after Pauli's birth. Although Dory doesn't believe that Pauli's father would ever sue for custody on his own, she is concerned about his mother pushing him to do it. At present, he has visitation rights and he has visited once. He also calls occasionally, sends presents, and sporadically pays child support.

Pauli is an energetic and active seven-year-old girl who loves art and drama and dance. She took ballet lessons for a while, but had to stop because of her arthritis. She is, like most people with ADD, impulsive and distractible. She has a difficult time keeping on task, preferring to play with toys she finds, for example, rather than put them away as asked. She is bright and articulate. Since she began taking Ritalin, she has learned to read and is now doing average to above average work in her second grade classroom. Dory and Becky describe Pauli as a "frill." As Dory says, "But God's biggest joke on both myself and Becky is that Pauli is probably the most frilly little girl that ever existed. Dresses are like a godsend to her, and make up and this kind of stuff."

Pauli is a thin child, perhaps due to the medications and the arthritis. Dory and Becky have considerable trouble coaxing her to eat. In addition, she is conscious of her weight and is determined not to get fat. Both Becky and Dory are concerned about their own weights, frequently alluding to how "fat" they are and joking about it in everyday discourse. Weight consciousness is a family theme.

Pauli says that she likes her teacher in school this year and she loves to swim. She is also enjoying her first Brownie troop and she says the girls in the group are "nice to me." She attends a day care before school and is in a regular second grade classroom in a public school.

Summary

This couple's strong beliefs in a higher power have sustained them through the difficult first years of their relationship. It is a faith in God that connects these parents with each other and with their child.

They have had many challenges as a family. Pauli's arthritis and her attention deficit disorder have created a continuous stress on the family. Since Dory is also afflicted with ADD, Becky has had to assume the major burden of the caretaker role for the family. The combination of these stresses with the financial problems they were having created a kind of chaos from which they feel they are just beginning to emerge. This has made it difficult for them to develop any kind of structured and stable parenting approach. Other significant stresses have included the recent deaths of both women's mothers and the pervasive underlying threat of a custody battle with Pauli's father.

In spite of these very difficult early years in this family, the parents remain firmly committed to loving and nurturing Pauli and to their deep love for each other. Since the financial problems have eased somewhat, they are presently concerned with defining a more stable parenting and family system.

This concludes the introductions of the five participating families. Each family has unique challenges as well as strengths which cultivate their own special family gestalt. The following chapter addresses an issue that was emphasized by all of the participating families—the idea that they are just normal families.

Chapter 3

We Are (Normal) Family

INTRODUCTION

"Normal" is defined as conforming to the standard or common type; usual; not abnormal; regular; natural. The psychological and medical definitions also include the concepts of being sane, free from any mental disorder and being free from any infection or other form of disease or malformation. These definitions illustrate the inherent contradictions within the term. Must one be average, standard, common, and usual in order to be also defined as sane, natural, and healthy? These family members repeatedly insist that their families are "normal," and there is ample evidence presented here that families such as these can be adequately sane, natural, and healthy to sustain necessary family tasks, while also being different and unique.

The use of normality was not part of my original inquiry or plan. It originated in the persistent use of the word "normal" by the participants. There is clearly much frustration with the negative myths about lesbians which permeate society—colonizing and defaming our families. These participants believe that their lives together and their love for each other defy those negative myths.

The challenges faced by these couples and families and the strategies they used to address them are similar to those faced by any kind of couple and step family—they are the "normal" challenges families face. They are also the "normal" (but nonetheless heroic) responses to those family challenges. Berzon (1988) writes:

> Gay and lesbian people are not so psychologically different from our heterosexual counterparts. We, too, have the need to

affiliate, to have the continuity of companionship that brings true understanding and intimacy. We, too, have the need to be caretakers and to know that there is someone to take care of us if the need arises. We, too, need the stability and tranquillity that enables us to compose a life of meaningful activity from a home base that is secure. We have the need. We have the right. We have the personal resources. (p. 7)

These families, like heterosexual step families, sometimes struggled with the complex tasks involved in developing new family relationships among strangers (Kelley, 1995; Maglin and Schniedewind, 1989; Visher and Visher, 1990). Building the relationships necessary to integrate the family takes time—usually years. It takes time to bond.

Time builds familiarity. And familiarity, a term that originates from the Latin term connoting "of a household"—the same origin as the word "family" builds family. Because the child and step parent have not freely chosen each other as family (as the adult couple has), building this familiarity positively between the child and the step parent may be the most difficult task. It may also be the most important task in creating family happiness. Crosbie-Burnett (1984) found, in her multiple regression analysis of heterosexual step families, that "mutually suitable step relationships were more highly associated with family happiness than was the marital relationship" (p. 462).

Five major issues challenged these families in their quests to create new families. These issues have also been identified as problematic for heterosexual step families. They were: discipline disagreements, the other parent, the children's particular personalities and challenges, the impact of herstory from families of origin, and the stress of jobs. This chapter addresses those challenges and some of the strategies families used to overcome them.

DISCIPLINE DISAGREEMENTS

As in heterosexual step families (see Visher and Visher, 1990), discipline was an arena of conflict in four of these families. The complaint expressed most often was that the step parent was overly strict or harsh and, on the other side, that the bio parent was too lenient. As Lori, a nonbiological parent, describes this dilemma:

Well I think now we've learned to come to more compromise. I think Cady would say I'm stricter and not as tolerant as she is of letting certain things play out. And I would say, these kids really actually want a limit.

Some of the step parents felt that they were usually at fault in these discipline fights. Terry feels that she is overly strict, especially when she is tired and stressed out. Florence admits that her disciplining often comes out harsh and angry and even scary to the kids. "I don't do it well. I don't have a lot of knowledge on how to do it correctly, or wisely."

Biological moms often experience pain when they believe the children are being treated harshly. They may also get angry, especially if the step parent seems to be butting into an argument that the biological mom is having with the child.

> **Cady:** . . . one of the places that I don't want Lori getting involved is in discussions, like when the kids start something with me—she often feels that she needs to rescue me. And it drives me crazy. I don't want her rescuing me. And I think it really irritates, it makes [the kids] angry, too. . . . I feel like it gives the kids fuel to think she is a witch.

Children may also experience the step parent's entry into a discipline issue as interference. Molly described angrily how she often overheard her step parent talking to her mom in another room:

> **Molly:** I can hear her say things to my mom like, "Well, you had better punish her for that," or, "What do you plan on doing about this?"

Although the biological parent may experience this interference as criticism of her parenting, the step parent often interprets it as having higher expectations for the children.

> **Lori:** [Their dad] was an alcoholic and I felt like there wasn't a lot of expectations that the kids would be carrying any part of the load of family life. Also when Cady and I met, my mother died about two months after we got involved with each other

and I just had a real hard time with kids who aren't enormously respectful of their mothers. And so I think that has been another area for me of difficulty.

These different beliefs for what can be reasonably expected of the child lead to a frustrating position for the biological mother of feeling "in the middle." Cady describes being in the middle as akin to the concept of co-dependency—watching out for everyone else's needs but her own. The dilemma is that the biological mother cannot both protect the children and support her partner. So, as Dory says, "I lose all the way around."

> **Dory:** Pauli and Becky sometimes go head to head—which puts me into this role of trying to pick and choose who's right. We've tried to do it where I back up Becky 100 percent, whatever it is. That doesn't always work. I tried the other side where I get in the middle and I absolutely hate it. There was one point where I was saying, "You guys deal with it. You settle it. I don't want to be involved in it at all." And that doesn't work either.

The bio mom may try to walk a tightrope, finding a way to somehow support the child and the partner. Tanya discusses how she sometimes might handle being in the middle.

> **Tanya:** Oh, God. Well, I don't know—just Terry will tell Kevin to do something, or he has done something wrong and she has reprimanded him or whatever, and he'll get a long face. And I'll say, "Well, what happened?" And he'll tell me, "Terry made me do this" or "Terry yelled at me" or "Terry did this, this, and this." So then I kind of solve it for him—on the other hand, not go against what she's really said or expected.

Step parents agree that one of the worst things the biological mother can do is to question their authority, or not back them up, in front of the child. As Florence describes it, "When she does intervene in front of the kids, that bothers me. It bothers me the most." Step parents see this as one of the most damaging blows to their ability to establish credibility with the child as a parent.

Becky: See, and it all started back, within that first year after we got here. Dory thought I was too strict. I thought she was too lenient. Dory would change what I'd say. And we'd gone down to Family Service and done some couple's counseling and the guy there said, "No, you can't do that." So she tries, but sometimes she just forgets and sometimes, I think that the attention deficit is a really big deficit because she doesn't stop to think a lot of the time and she'll pop off with whatever she's thinking at the time instead of waiting until we are not within radar ears. So on one hand I understand it because she's afraid she's going to forget. But, carry a little damn piece of paper around and write on it! You know?

And in Dory and Becky's case, the fact that Dory did not back up Becky early in the relationship has had long-term consequences. Pauli continues to tell Becky that her mom will change whatever limits Becky has set for her. As Becky described it—"So I am the big ugly bugger."

However, the participants also had several strategies they used to ameliorate the discipline problems. Step parents found that they could apologize to children if they felt they had been overly harsh or critical. As Florence said, "I find myself apologizing a lot and that in itself is a big step." To apologize is to be vulnerable to the child—a scary step to take because it isn't the child's job to take care of the adult. The child might not be gentle in his/her response. On the other hand, it can be a powerful tool for bonding. As Lori said,

> **Lori:** I really hate being vulnerable to a younger person. I hate being vulnerable, but I hate being vulnerable to a younger person more. And usually when I do that its been really help-ful—if I will go out and do that.

Along with apologizing and making oneself vulnerable, these step parents also found it helpful to back off sometimes—to simply watch how the bio mom handles it, to let some things slide, to realize that not all infractions need to be confronted. Sometimes the step parent is surprised to see that the bio mom does indeed con-front the child.

Terry: It's interesting because there was one day when Kevin was just doing his thing. And normally I just say, "Stop it; cut it out. You are being obnoxious." Or whatever. But I wasn't saying a word and I was just doing my little thing, thinking, I'm not going to deal with this. And then Tanya started to be like I was or I am and finally said, "Kevin, you are getting to be" whatever. And I just had this smile because Tanya had to take this different role because I didn't do it. And so it kind of gave some perspective that, well, you are not just being [the overreactor].

And sometimes nothing will be done to correct the child's behavior. If nothing is done, the step parent may choose to talk about it with the biological mother at some later point. Or she may just decide to let it go.

Several strategies were used by the biological mothers to address discipline disagreements. One strategy is to get out of the middle by simply allowing the step parent to handle it her way. As Dory says, "that leaves Becky to make the decision as the parent as to what's going to happen with it, which to me is like backing her up because I'm not taking it away from her to make the decision."

Another strategy is for the bio mom to ask the step parent to go into another room with her so that they can discuss it and come to an agreement. This strategy of discussing the issue away from the children, Florence says, "doesn't bother me." However, it is important to be out of earshot of the children in order to truly present a united front.

Some biological mothers made an effort to include the step parent in daily decisions concerning the children, even if the children complained about it. For example, Cady would tell the children she needed to talk with Lori before deciding if they could have a sleepover. When the kids would complain about her not being able to make a decision on her own, she explained to them that this was about respect for the other adult in the household.

It has helped Florence and Nisi to understand that their arguments concerning discipline are not so much about Florence having unreasonable expectations for the children, but more about how Florence communicates with the children. Nisi has strong feelings about not yelling harshly or meanly at the children. It is important to define carefully what the disagreement is about in order to figure out a method for working toward a solution.

Nisi also has recognized the value of Florence's perspective—that her higher expectations of the children, such as that they are capable of picking up after themselves and being respectful, etc., have contributed to a better parenting strategy in the family. The biological mother can validate and respect the perspective that the step parent brings in as an outsider. For example, Becky, a step parent, pushed her partner to have the child tested for ADD. Dory resisted because of her fears of stigmatization. But Becky insisted—"something needs to be done." And this has resulted in a better quality of life for their family. Cady recognizes the importance of Lori's added perspective—"sometimes when I don't want to hear it." The children also are aware of this added perspective.

> **Molly (15):** Sometimes, though, Lori can see things my mom doesn't. Like with certain situations. It's weird.

And Cady admits:

> If I had it to do over, I'd have the wisdom to expect a lot more in terms of [the kids] pitching in and helping out more in the family.

Other strategies used by these parents included therapy (all five of these families have used a counselor or therapist at times), and specifically creating or allowing for times when the step parent is the "good guy." The step parent may buy treats for the child, or be more willing to run an errand for the child, or take the family out to eat, or allow an extra treat—some little act of kindness or indulgence that encourages the child to feel good about the step parent.

There was one couple who related significantly fewer problems with discipline—Kathy and Delia. They used all of the above strategies. In this family, Kathy (the nonbiological mom), tends to be the soft touch with the kids—bringing them little presents and apologizing and hugging after fights. She does have her own values, like following through on commitments (such as practicing piano) and she is major disciplinarian concerning those issues. However, what is most striking about how this couple handles discipline is that they almost always try to do it together as a team. They did have some fights early in their relationship over Delia not backing up Kathy in front of the kids, but these appeared to dissipate over time. Everyone in the family talked about how Delia and Kathy disciplined together, including both of the kids.

> **Diana (20):** Well, Kathy and my mother have always worked together like when disciplining us and stuff. They made sure they both said the same thing, so we could never (play one off against the other). . . . they are always together in their decisions.

When I asked Talia (16) about disciplining, she talked about parents sitting together at the table, waiting to talk with her when she got home.

> **Talia:** Oh yes, it drives me nuts, because you come home and they will be sitting at the table and you're like—oh God! Oh shit! What did I do this time? They called the school and they know I've been skipping. So, they don't let us get away with much at all.

This disciplining together is something they have worked at and improved over the years of their relationship. It appears to be a strategy that has paid off well for them. Certainly, there are fewer dissatisfactions expressed on discipline issues in this family.

THE OTHER PARENT

A second significant factor which influenced the integration of the family was the other parent. Four of these families have a parent living elsewhere to contend with. (Kevin's father died when he was three, so there is not another parent in the picture in that family.) This is also a common theme in heterosexual step families. Visher and Visher (1983) list creating a "parent coalition" as one of eight important steps to establishing a new family identity. This means developing and maintaining at least a civil relationship among all the adults who are involved in raising the children. However, this task has been very difficult for these families.

While Delia and Kathy had fewer problems with discipline, their relationship with the other parent, Diana's and Talia's dad, has created ongoing pain and outrage. Although this has diminished as the girls have gotten older, the effects are still evident. Delia's lawyer, at the time of her marriage break up in the early 1970s, urged her to avoid a custody battle and to accept joint custody. She feared that the fact that Delia was a lesbian would negatively affect her ability to win custody. So, Delia and her former husband had joint custody, "but it was never equal."

For years, the girls switched homes every week. Delia and Kathy were constantly worried about the girls when they were at their dad's house. They felt he didn't really want to parent. He was irresponsible—not brushing their hair or making them brush their teeth, letting them stay up late, keeping a dirty, messy house. Delia tells of a time when she totally lost it and he came home and found her in his house, cleaning his toilet, because she was so disgusted with the state of his house. Delia and Kathy believe that he didn't really care about parenting the children, he just wanted power and control over his situation.

This constant stress (he would sometimes call them twice a day) created tension between Delia and Kathy. Delia felt stupid for ever having been involved with him. She would sometimes not challenge him or back down. This led to fighting between Delia and Kathy.

To make matters worse, the girls' father has always seen Kathy as the corrupter and has criticized Kathy to the girls. This was confusing and painful.

Diana (20): He used to put down Kathy all the time and I didn't understand why, because I didn't see her as an evil person. But he always said, "She's so bitter. Don't be bitter like Kathy. Don't get a hard heart like Kathy. Be like your mom—she's so creative, she's so. . . ." And I'm like, excuse me, you don't know this woman. OK. You probably didn't know [Mom] when you were married to her and you don't know Kathy at all. And I would just . . . for a long time that really bothered me because then I'd come back and I'd be thinking, Dad said Kathy was nasty. And Kathy wouldn't do anything nasty to us, you know. Yes, she'd punish us when we'd do stupid stuff, but that's because she was our mom and she had a right to do that. That really [confused] and hurt me.

The crucial factor that kept Delia and Kathy together during the worst of these struggles was the fact that they wouldn't let an outsider pull them apart.

Although Delia and Kathy managed to keep their own relationship strong in spite of the challenge they faced with the girls' father, it took its toll. Diana presently has no relationship with her father and has even chosen to remove the hyphen and his name from her last name. She feels that her dad was abusive, irresponsible, and played "like he was one of us—he was like our kid friend."

> **Diana (20):** When we would get in trouble, he would hit us. And he would hit us for the stupidest reasons, like the sugar bowl was half empty and we forgot to fill it. And he would call us names and he'd tell me especially that I was lazy and that I was ugly and I was fat and that I never did anything right and that—but then he would always come back with, "Oh, I'm sorry, I didn't know what I was thinking," or something like that.

Diana, who decided not to spend every other week at her father's house when she was about fourteen years old, has no desire at this point to have a relationship with him or his family. She even wishes now that he had simply left when her parents were divorced. She is disgusted by what she sees as his "macho" behavior and values. At one point she described her father as only interested in his daughters so that he could "prance around and say this is the fruit of my loins."

Talia's ongoing relationship with her father is fraught with anxiety. Talia describes her father's attitude toward her mother's lesbianism as "ridiculous, absolutely ridiculous. I mean he really never comes right out and says it; he wouldn't be that dumb, but . . ." She continues later:

> **Talia (16):** So basically, he is really weird. Because both of them [moms] hate him with a passion. And he'll always talk about my mom like—oh, respect your mom and your mom is so wonderful, and blah, blah, blah. But then he will just hate

Kathy, with a passion. And I think he just basically can't bring himself to hate the mother of his children. I mean, he's Hispanic and he is all into the father is the head of the house and stuff like that. So I think he just can't bring himself to hate my mom because it was his wife, or whatever. And so he just takes everything out on Kathy. He has always hated Kathy, for as long as I can remember. And he always just spoke so highly of my mom all the time.

Still Talia wants to maintain a relationship, however minimal, with her dad. But when she does try to maintain that relationship, she feels disloyal to her moms. She writes about this in her journal:

> I come back from a trip to [nearby city] today. As usual, I was ignored when I came home. My mother asked a little about my visit; Kathy said nothing. This was because I saw my father in [nearby city].

This has been an extremely difficult situation for the whole family. Delia and Kathy worked hard to deal with the challenge as best they could. But damage was done. Diana wonders if she might be overly hostile toward men now—prejudiced—but points out with relief that there are some men she knows and respects. Talia clearly feels "in the middle" sometimes, in her efforts to maintain contact with her father. In addition, it seems that the complex interplay of their father's irresponsibility and, his "macho" attitude and behavior with his Hispanic heritage has left his daughters, at least temporarily, with a definite disinterest in their Hispanic background—and that is a loss for them.

This is not the only family that has had difficulty dealing with the other parent. Although Dory is out as a lesbian to her ex-husband (in fact, she was in a lesbian relationship when she met him) and she has sole custody of Pauli with her ex-husband having visitation, she is very fearful that his mother (Pauli's paternal grandmother) will pressure him to fight for custody.

Dory: His mother, I believe, would love to have custody of Pauli. [Pauli's] father is smart enough to know that he does not want that responsibility. He doesn't want that involvement, and he also knows that she is better off where she is, with us.

This fear was part of what led she and Becky to leave the West Coast. They have not given an address to Pauli's father, using a post office box number instead. And even when he came to town one summer to visit, bringing his mother along, they did not tell him where they lived, but met him elsewhere. Pauli has never really had a sustained relationship with him. Pauli (7) is aware of this loss, saying, "Yeah, I wish I could have seen him when I was a baby but I didn't get to. All I see is pictures of me and my dad together . . . [and] I wasn't sure that the pictures were real."

Florence and Nisi have had a contested relationship with Kitty, the children's other mother. Like Delia and Kathy, they had concerns about Kitty's lack of responsibility—both financially and as an inconsistent parent. Although they originally shared physical custody, with the children spending three days a week with Kitty, Nisi didn't feel that Kitty was responsible and living up to her end of the parenting. After two years of battling, Nisi decided to minimize the children's contact with Kitty. The children now see Kitty every other week for one day and they vacation with her for a week or two in the summer. Again, there is always a trade-off for the children. As Frannie said to me, teary eyed, "Yeah, its really hard for me because I really love someone that I don't get to see [very often]."

Since Nisi is the biological mom in this case there is little fear of reprisal from Kitty. But Nisi is aware of the trade-offs—as she says, even though she prefers not to think of Kitty as a mom, she knows that the children think of her as one of their moms.

Cady has joint custody with her ex-husband, although she has been the major custodial parent. Cady and Lori have had few problems relating to Cady's ex-husband. He pays child support regularly and is extremely cooperative. As Lori describes it, their relationship has been a "stunning nonevent." In fact, they were able to continue a cooperative relationship even when Nell (now twenty) elected to live with him during her senior year in high school and her freshman year of college.

However, he has refused to make an emotional commitment to the kids—e.g., to actually spend time at home doing things with them. When they went to therapy with him concerning this issue, according to Lori—"it came up point blank in the session that he could not commit to that—that was too much of an infringement of his freedom, even though Molly had asked and said that she really wanted it. And that was awful for her and really a sad thing. I mean there was no—the therapist basically realized there was no following up on that (except by working with Molly individually)."

Cady's response to this emotional abandonment by the father, which began probably when he was an active alcoholic, before the divorce, has been to be very protective of the children. As she says, "I've always felt the pressure to make up personally for that."

The strategies these couples have used to cope with problems with the other parent have included withdrawal and minimizing contact, seeking help from a counselor or therapist, engaging and fighting, and letting go. None of these couples has tried to completely cut off contact between the child and the other parent.

There are also advantages to having another parent involved in the children's lives. One of the major ones is that it gives the couple time to be a couple and build a couple relationship. Finding time to relate as a couple has been much more difficult for Terry and Tanya, who don't have another parent for Kevin, and for Dory and Becky, who don't live near Pauli's father. Since couple time is also crucial for the health of a family, this is not a small issue. The other parent then, by taking the children, allows the couple to have child-free time and to reconnect on what drew them to each other in the first place. If that other parent is an adequate and caring parent, that certainly increases his/her value to the parents and the children.

Clearly the other parent may present challenges to the step family over which they have little control. Lesbian families are particularly vulnerable if the other parent is a legal and/or biological parent, because of the threat of losing their children due to their lesbianism. While these families, in general, were able to maintain the primary homes for their children while not breaking contact with the children's other parents, the stress created in the children's and the adults' lives was clearly considerable.

THE CHILDREN AS ACTIVE AGENTS IN FAMILY CREATION

Children are also active participants in determining the creation and type of the step family. As parents of multiple children can attest to, some children are simply easier to parent than others. Children with special challenges, adolescents, and a child whose personality conflicts with the parent's personality (and vice versa) are some of the difficulties presented in this group of families. Two of the children in this sample are challenged by attention deficit disorder (ADD) and one of those children, Pauli, also has juvenile rheumatoid arthritis. People with attention deficit disorder (ADD) have varying degrees of problems with impulsiveness, hyperactivity, lessened ability to attend, and difficulty following rules (Ingersoll, 1988). The ADD child often doesn't perceive his/her impact on other people and yet tends to be overly sensitive to their impact on him/her. Dory makes an insightful analogy in describing how Pauli (7) gets caught up in a fight.

> **Dory:** Pauli doesn't get the focus that she is not going to win this, you know. And you . . . it's like driving down the freeway and there are a whole bunch of off ramps that Pauli could take—she takes none of them.

These traits can make it more difficult for a solid bond to develop, particularly with step parents, who didn't have the chance to bond during the child's infancy. Florence describes it as a personality conflict between herself and Dale (8), which makes the bonding more difficult.

It is particularly difficult for Becky who has to relate to a partner with ADD as well as the child. In the first place, Dory's ADD means that she forgets and can therefore be inconsistent in her parenting. Becky speaks about this.

> **Becky:** Dory does forget and then Pauli figures she can get away with anything. Which then causes a whole nother string of difficulties.

What happens then is that Becky provides the consistency in discipline and that places her in "the bad guy" role.

The fact that Dory and her daughter both have ADD has also created another basis for alliance in this family—leaving Becky on the outside. Dory describes it as she and Pauli being "buddies— because we'll hang out together and because we both have ADD.

We kind of understand each other a little bit, you know." This puts Becky in the awkward position of feeling at times like she has two children—Dory and Pauli.

> **Becky:** OK. Sometimes I feel like I'm really brought up short in it, because I hear a lot of "well, I've got ADD and I know what it is like. And this is what you have to do." And any thoughts I might have on it sometimes are discounted, like, "well, you don't know." And I don't think that is fair. Because although I may be on the outside looking in, there are some things that [give me perspective]. . . . Or if we are out shopping and "Oh, I want this." [and I say] nope. Sorry. Not this week. So yeah, sometimes it does feel like I've got two little kids.

The biological mother may react very protectively to her ADD child because she is aware of the numerous negative reactions the child gets from the outside world. Both Dory and Nisi were very reluctant to have their children labeled as ADD and are concerned about the negative stereotypes associated with the disorder. This desire to protect the child with difficulties may also be a factor in whether the step parent can form a positive bond with the child.

In Becky's case, there is also the added stress of Pauli's juvenile rheumatoid arthritis, which requires extra financial resources as well as time and energy. Pauli must be carefully monitored by several doctors, needs special physical therapy, and takes several medications. Although this has been an added source of stress for Becky, it has also served as a conduit for her to bond with Pauli. Since Becky has arthritis in her knee from a car accident, she also has a focus in common with Pauli and she has spent a lot of time with Pauli, taking her to various appointments. So this has not created a stumbling block for Becky's relationship with Pauli.

Adolescence is another factor which can drastically affect the step parent/child bond. The only couple (in this study) that had an adolescent child when they first got together was Lori and Cady. Nell was thirteen when they first moved into a house together and, according to Cady and Lori, she was angry from the beginning.

> **Lori:** She was angry that her life was disrupted and that she left the house she liked and most of all—angry, you know.

Janet: About the divorce?

Cady and Lori: No.

Lori: She had her mother alone and I think that (bond) was abundantly clear with both of them. And its the same way I would have felt if my parents were divorced.

Sager et al. (1983) discuss the high incidence of turmoil in remarried families with adolescents. However, it is important to remember that there is a high incidence of turmoil in any family with adolescents! The needs of the adolescent are to begin the process of separation and individuation from the family. Adolescents are rarely looking for another adult to parent them—they are trying to break away from parents. In addition, the oldest child often has more anger about a step parent coming into the family, particularly if he or she has lived alone with the biological parent for awhile (Sager et al., 1983). And there is some evidence that step families are more problematic for girls than for boys (Crosbie-Burnett, Skyles, and Becker-Haven, 1988). Also, Nell had spent some of her childhood years in an alcoholic family—not exactly a situation that nurtures a child to easily trust and reach out to others. So it is not surprising that Nell and Cady and Lori had difficulties. Cady and Lori's strategy was to validate the couple bond, while at the same time trying to remain open and there for Nell. That they have managed to maintain an open home and family for Nell, even when she chose to live with her father for two years, is a testament to the fact that, sometimes, just "hanging in there" can eventually work. When discussing how Cady has supported her, Lori said:

Well, for one thing, she's always encouraged me to keep up my relationship with her kids when I've been discouraged. She's reminded me that they each do have a relationship with me and that that is important to them, and especially to Molly—that she doesn't want me to give up on Molly, or give Molly any sense that I'm giving up on her. She is also patient with the times I do have a hard time with her kids. I think it causes her a lot of pain, but she is patient with that. And she has tried in every way, shape, and form to have us be a family.

And for instance we are going to New York—we've just planned this in the last couple of days—with her older daughter, Nell—for Thanksgiving. From the get go, we've talked about this in terms of the two of us taking Nell to New York—not just Nell and her mom. Just things where we keep trying to do this in whatever way we can.

These children, in spite of, and/or because of, their challenges offered the step parents positive growth and experiences and the step parents were aware of this. In their own words:

Becky: I guess [what I love about Pauli] is just seeing her grow up, and the different things she picks up as she goes. Because you'll be talking to her and she'll seem like a seven-year-old and all of a sudden she'll pop off with some statement or comment—you know how they look so much older and . . .

Florence: I think [Dale] is just an absolutely brilliant guy, but he has no common sense, whatsoever. But we have our moments. I would be outside on the picnic table, watching the birds and having my coffee. He would come out and say something so cute. How did he say that? "Let's have a bonding moment" or something like that, you know.

Lori: The fact of the matter is, I do love [Nell], and don't ask me why, but I do. . . . once her mother was bending over to put something in the dishwasher and I saw Nell. Nell is a woman who does not hug you ever, ever, ever. No physical contact with her mother that I've seen. Her mother will hug her, but she doesn't really hug back, you know, and it is just amazing. Well, this night I saw, out of the corner of my eye, Nell reach over and just tap her mother's back, and she did it and just quickly withdrew her hand. And Cady didn't even see it or feel it. But I did and it's something that I've kept in the back of my mind, when I've wanted to kill her, that there is some vulnerable spot in there and there is a woman in there who does have love.

These children illustrate several ways that children contribute to building connections with their step parents.

One important indication of the children's understanding of the step parent's role comes in the naming of that step parent. Although these children usually call the step parent by her first name, Diana, Talia, Pauli, Dale, Frannie, and Kevin all refer to their parents as "my moms" when they are discussing them to a nonfamily member. Sometimes they even call the step parent "mom."

> **Terry:** It does warm my little heart when he says mommy to me, which he does occasionally.

Most of the children also seem to experience the step parent as part of their family. For example, once when I was at her home, Pauli complained that she didn't get to put the lights on the Christmas tree. Becky explained that that was her job. She told Pauli that her [Becky's] mother did it for years and then she passed the job on to Becky. Pauli insisted that Becky should pass it down to her, then. Becky told her that she was only seven—she'd have to wait.

Children also reach out to connect with their step parent. Some of them try to connect physically, as Lori remembers.

> **Lori:** Molly was always, you know—crawl on your lap and try to snuggle with you in bed and blah, blah, blah. That's how she always was. Now it is different, but, yeah.
>
> **Janet:** Was she that way with you?
>
> **Lori:** Yeah, probably almost with me more than with her mom—just because I am more affectionate that way. So I can still get away with that sometimes with her.

Or they may try to connect emotionally—by being helpful. Florence explains how Dale reaches out to her, even though they have personality clashes.

> **Florence:** And like the other day, even if it is something that is totally bizarre—at least he thought of it—he tried to make that connection. He says, [we were working on the back porch], "Maybe this would be a good time to use your new toys—out in the van." New toys? Oh, you mean that new ratchet set I

got? "Yeah." Well, hon, those are different tools—they won't work on this. Those are for automobiles and stuff like that. "Oh." But, you know, keep them in mind for other things. But just little things like that. It's not so much, you know. I have felt someday working on cars together or going fishing or stuff like that [will help us connect].

Or they try to connect by giving thoughtful gifts; for instance, like Nell and Molly go out of their way to give Christmas gifts that Lori will like. And Diana writes about her sister's gifts in her journal.

> Yesterday my sister came home after her yoga class with presents for Mom and Kathy—two gay bar chocolates! Huge pink triangles of semisweet chocolate. Needless to say we were all excited.

Lori describes how Nell is coming around and making an effort to connect with her now—helping her to believe in the merits of hanging in there.

> **Lori:** . . . and [Nell] does stuff that I never thought she would. You know, she calls me in the room to look at the drapes she's making, and has whole conversations with me where she has eye contact—and I'm not kidding you—the whole time we lived together we hardly ever had eye contact. Neither one of us could deal with it.

The children often showed concern for their step parent. They do this by making an effort to be inclusive, as Kathy illustrates in her journal entry:

> Talia called me at work yesterday [and she called Delia today], so we think that she's calling us alternately.
> Diana called me at work to let me know she'd been practicing the hoola hoop and to ask me who made the gay bars (chocolate triangles) that Talia bought for Delia and me yesterday. Diana's crazy phone call just made me laugh. I laughed even harder when I came home and found her napping. She hoola-hooped herself into a deep sleep.

Younger children often showed their love for the step parent by expressing concern for their health. When I asked Florence if she thought their family was jelling more now, she told this story.

> **Florence:** Wow, I think it is—it seems like when I fell and broke my leg, laying there in the desert, and seeing how upset the kids were, and how helpful they wanted to be. They just wanted to do something. And I think that really—and [their uncle] dying—has made Dale, for whatever reasons, much more affectionate toward me.

And when I asked the children if there was anything they wished that they could change about their families, here were two of the responses.

> **Frannie:** Well, no . . . maybe not Florence having a broken leg.

> **Pauli:** That my grandma would be alive and Becky and me never had arthritis and we never had the [car] accident and that my grandmas were alive, and that I never had ADD and my mom didn't either. And my mom and I never had any of the other things—either of my moms.

It is important to understand that the children are active agents, both negatively and positively, in the family creation. They can also create connections simply by being children—who give us a fascinating look at ourselves and childhood. But when the child has special challenges, it helps if the step parent and the parent can maintain a loving and good-humored coalition to guide the child. This coalition must include the bio mom's respect for and willingness to compromise based on the step parent's more distanced perspective on the child. It must also include the nonbio mom's respect for and willingness to compromise based on the bio mom's insight and intuition gained from her close, intense, long-term relationship with the child. Otherwise, the parents may find themselves pitted against one another and everyone is the loser.

THE IMPACT OF HERSTORY—FAMILIES OF ORIGIN

This issue practically jumped out of the data, although I had not pursued it with any particular interest. This was a group of women who were very aware of the influence their upbringings had on them—probably because all of them had been in therapy at some points in their lives. There were several ways that these women felt their experiences with their families of origin had affected their present parenting. One typical response was to react against one's upbringing—I won't be like that! Florence probably talked the most about this issue. She feels that she was raised in an authoritarian household where children were treated meanly and with disrespect. Florence recognizes this and tries to rise above it, but, like the rest of us, sometimes is horrified to find her parents' style of parenting slip out of her mouth. Nisi has also reacted to something from her herstory. She felt that her own parents were not very nurturant and she has made an effort to be very nurturant with her children.

Kathy felt that her childhood was actually pretty good, but she was concerned that her parents were reactive—putting out fires instead of working to prevent them. Therefore, it has been important for Kathy to be an involved, proactive parent.

Cady's mother was a professional at a time when most children had mothers who were homemakers. She felt that her mother had overly high expectations for her children and Cady didn't want to repeat that.

On the other hand, sometimes these women consciously modeled the positive aspects of parenting they had received as children. Kathy had the model of two aunts who were involved in her parenting—so she saw how women who were not the mother could enrich a child's life. Terry had the successful model of her gay father and his long-term partner to guide her, as well as a fairly good experience with her mother and step father. Cady's father was raised by women and Cady felt that her father had a true respect for women. It was a shock to her to discover that some men don't have that same respect, feeling that they are more important than women. But her father was a model for her of respecting the equality of women.

There was generally a strong recognition of the profound impact that certain events which occurred during childhood had on one's personality. Lori's mother was diagnosed with cancer when Lori was only four years old. She spent her childhood with an underlying fear that her mother could die at any time. This fear of abandonment still haunts her adult life. She also had a father who, although he gave her every indication that being a woman was not a limitation at all, was not safe. He could be critical and demeaning. This has perhaps exacerbated her fears of making herself vulnerable, especially to children who have few restraints on their reactions.

Nisi's father was a workaholic and an alcoholic when she was growing up, which may have contributed to the fact that she likes to be in charge—to be in control. Perhaps the saddest story was that of Delia, who spoke of the impact of her mother's emotional illness on her childhood. She said that her mother was on Valium all of the time. Delia would come home from school and find her mother rocking on the couch, crying. Delia said that she had to take care of her younger sister and her mother from the time she was seven or eight years old. As an example, she told me that if her father was out of town and she and her mother came home at night, her mother would send her into the house alone to check to see if anyone was in there.

> **Delia:** I had parents who were very much dependent on me to carry the load—to the point that, now I know as an adult and how I deal with my own kids, that it was way out of line, the expectation. Just ridiculous. And unfortunately it has really formed kind of a bad personality for me. And I think that's why I really kind of keep to myself. It's not easy for me to share feelings. It's like, OK, I'm set to deal with this. And I always think I have to do things alone, because I think growing up the expectation was there that your parents aren't there for you—you're there for them.

What seems truly remarkable in light of her herstory is that Delia was able to share her parenting with Kathy and that the two of them worked so well as a parenting team.

A final herstorical issue was the way the parents' different upbringings led to conflicts with each other and sometimes with children. For example, Nisi hates yelling. She grew up with parents who fought a lot and she is very sensitive to it. Florence, who also grew up with yelling, but much of it directed at the children, finds that yelling, or talking harshly, sometimes comes too easily. This leads to conflict.

In a slightly different twist, Cady grew up in a family that was very restrained—no fighting, no open expression of feeling. Cady said that her mother never told her that she loved her. Lori, on the other hand, grew up in a family that yelled, got it out, and made up. There was much hugging and open affection with her mother. So to Lori, yelling leads to a resolution of the crisis, whereas to Cady, yelling creates or exacerbates the crisis.

Perhaps one of the most difficult conflicts between couples arises from Dory and Becky's very different childhood experiences. As an undiagnosed ADD child, Dory suffered a childhood of being labeled as bad, dumb, lazy, and immature. Understanding the devastating effects of this self-fulfilling prophecy, she is very protective of Pauli, determined that she not be labeled a bad kid. Becky, on the other hand, grew up in the shadow of the hostile big brother who literally "held my mother and me hostage" after her father died when she was six and her brother was twelve. "I mean there was a time when he tried to strangle me to death, and my mom, and I had gotten our winter coats on. We were leaving because he was on a tirade." Therefore, she is equally determined not to let Pauli become a tyrant who rules the house. Although this is a big conflict between Dory and Becky, Pauli is probably better off with a compromised stance, if they manage to come up with a consistent, united approach.

These women used several strategies to positively integrate their herstories into their adult lives. Many of them found therapy helpful in giving them insight into their issues and their partner's issues and in helping them to make some positive changes.

Many of the women found that as they understood their partners' herstories it softened their own attitudes and judgments. They learned to love each other in spite of their issues. Lori speaks to this:

> **Lori:** And when I think [Cady's] wrong, I challenge her about it, you know. There's nothing we don't talk about when we disagree. We try to resolve it, I guess. I mean, there are many times I have felt that's unfair, but I've also kind of come to the

point of seeing that this is a combination of things with Cady: One is the normal parent role; another is a woman who really hates conflict; and a third is a woman who's mother had one damned expectation after another and she's determined not to do that to her children. So she has gone to the other extreme and worries that I'm being like her mom.

And later, she adds:

> **Lori:** Because I've come to believe she's [Cady] really right. She's just a tolerant person and someone who doesn't have to go over there and try to control it. You know, I admire that. I can't do it as well.

And finally, these women learned to value what they brought to each other from their varied backgrounds. They acknowledged each other as teachers and as people who could fill in for each others' weaknesses. While Florence admires Nisi's ability to treat her children with respect, Nisi sees Florence as the "fabric that holds us together." She appreciates how Florence helps set the standards of behavior and makes sure that the kids carry out their responsibilities. Terry thinks Tanya is a wonderful nurturer. Tanya enjoys the way Terry plays with Kevin and is there to protect him. Cady appreciates Lori's ability to hang in there with the kids and learns from Lori's ease in expressing her feelings, and Lori learns from Cady to let go a little more. Delia thinks Kathy is incredibly nurturant; Delia helps Kathy loosen up—not be so rigid. Becky appreciates Dory's willingness to let her mother Pauli. Dory would be lost without Becky's organizational skills. And the list goes on. These partners realize that we all come into relationships with our issues from our families of origin. It helps to learn to tolerate each other's struggles with love and some humor, and to acknowledge how we benefit from our partner's strengths.

JOB STRESS

This final stumbling block emerged from the data more powerfully than I had expected. Our careers can impact both positively and negatively on our family and couple building processes. Visher and Visher (1983) found a positive correlation between socioeconomic status and step family success. Certainly the stress of not making enough money to live on overrides other parenting concerns. When Dory and Becky and Pauli first moved to the Midwest and neither Dory nor Becky had a job, the stress was overwhelming, especially considering Pauli's medical needs. In discussing her present job, which she is not thrilled about because she doesn't get to use her skills, Dory says,

> **Dory:** But the job is something that guarantees Pauli medical insurance, which is a primary. When I was doing the paralegal job we were going down the tubes fast. Because even though I was making it, we didn't have insurance and it just wasn't helping.

The fact that Becky now has an adequate-paying job that she loves and that Dory has a job which at least covers insurance has allowed them to begin thinking about how to establish a more consistent parenting plan.

> **Dory:** I mean before, since we've been so much on the survival mode, we've never been able to sit down to really set up tactics to deal with a lot of this stuff, you know. It's been like just to patch the hole and don't worry about it. Well, now we have the time and energy and the ability to focus on how to really fix it and make it better.

Lack of money does create family problems, but it is not the only stress related to jobs. Shift work, long hours, and physically painful work also act to overburden families. Terry's relationships with Kevin, as well as with Tanya, have suffered due to her night shift job, her added load of schoolwork in her attempt to get her college degree, and the resulting tiredness and grumpiness. Terry mourns the way her relationship with Kevin has changed:

> **Terry:** Yeah, it has changed. I'm trying to rechange it because when we first started, it was more of playing often. I think after moving here and starting the stress of everything else—

not just the stress of living, but the academy and working nights—and I got into a more . . . not really playing with him. It's just functional. And I want to change it back.

Terry and Tanya both wish for more time, together as a couple and with Kevin. Because of Terry's overburdened schedule, Tanya does much more of the parenting. This is stressful to Terry and makes her feel guilty. In her journal, Terry writes:

> A long work day for me. Tanya had sole responsibility for Kevin. I managed to come home to say good night but only really saw Kevin for a few minutes. Days like today I feel guilty for not being around to help out with parental duties.

Terry worries that Tanya never gets any time to herself, that the shift work isolates them from other couples and families, and that, when Tanya and Terry do have time together, they are in totally different spaces—Tanya is tired and winding down for bed while Terry is gearing up for work. In addition, couple time for Terry and Tanya is limited because there is no other parent that Kevin visits. The hope is that Terry will graduate from school and somehow time will be found to repair any damage in their relationships due to neglect.

Florence also has a lot of job stress which affects her relationships with the children. Her work demands long hours, due to overtime, and the long commute. In addition, the job is physically extremely difficult for Florence, leaving her not only tired, but in pain. Florence talks about the times when she has difficulty relating positively to the kids.

> **Florence:** Sometimes, too, I think, I am just . . . not I cannot be in control, you know. I'm just so wore out and in such pain that its all I can handle. It's all I can do to control that—not control it, because there is no controlling it.

So what does she do?

> **Florence:** Sometimes I just don't talk, withdraw—because if I do, I'll be snappy, you know.

Cady and Lori's jobs require a lot of responsibility and traveling away from home. However, this seems to create a positive, as well as a negative impact on their family relationships. Although the jobs are stressful and tiring and, particularly for Lori, take a toll on energy and mood, they also allow for time away from family responsibilities. These women have found a good deal of fulfillment and esteem from their work that helps keep family problems in perspective. The traveling also allows each of them to have one-on-one time with Molly.

Strategies that these women have used to cope with job stress include looking for another job, going back to school to improve one's status vis-à-vis the work world, attempting to limit one's involvement at work, and accepting either lower paying or less fulfilling jobs because of their better hours or insurance. Dory would like to find a more fulfilling job, or perhaps go back to school to enable her to get a better job, but she feels trapped due to her need for good medical insurance. Florence's job, as difficult as it is, pays well and has excellent benefits. She, too, feels trapped because she doesn't think she could get anywhere near the same pay at another job. Terry has gone back to school to get her degree. This will lead to a salary increase, but the added stress of school is damaging to her relationships with Kevin and Tanya. Both Florence and Becky talked about trying to keep down the amount of time they sign on for overtime. But this has to be balanced with an attempt to keep the supervisors happy at work, too.

The struggles that some of these families have with jobs illuminates the strength of the link between job and home. Time, energy, and money have great impact on the ability to build and sustain a healthy family.

CONCLUSION

This chapter has presented lesbian step families as similar in many ways to heterosexual step families. They are families who face challenges which confront all families—the challenges of creating cohesion while nourishing individuality, of monitoring and constantly adjusting parental guidance to fit the changing needs of children, of providing safety and security and love for all family members, and of nurturing the couple relationship as well as all family relationships.

This chapter addresses the erasure of lesbian step families in the research discourse on step families. It affirms for lesbian step family members and their helpers and allies that step families, lesbian as well as heterosexual, have certain challenges based on family structure and it illuminates how some lesbian step families have dealt with those challenges.

The need to claim "normality" is rooted in our struggle to be taken seriously as families and to be seen as legitimate. We wish to assert our commonality with all of humanity and to proclaim our families as having an equal potential as straight families to be healthy and affirming for adults and children.

On the other hand, we are not just like heterosexual couples or families. Because of our lesbianism, we are also unique and different. The next three chapters examine some of these differences.

Chapter 4

The Lesbian Couple
as Heads of Household:
Attempting Matriarchy
in the Shadow of Patriarchy

INTRODUCTION

Lesbian couples have two major differences from heterosexual couples: the partners are both women—with all of the socialization and gender expectations and prescriptions and discriminations that come along with the female role in this society, and they are both lesbians—with all the societal baggage and outsider status that accompanies that orientation. The second difference, that of being lesbians, will be discussed in Chapter 7. This chapter addresses the first difference. How does the fact that there are two women as heads of household affect family life?

This chapter examines the possible impact of gender on family life. In particular, it describes how the couples divide household tasks, the question of how parenting is accomplished in female couple households, and the model of coupling that the female partners offer their children. Blumstein and Schwartz (1983) write that, "The couple is a basic unit of society. It is the unit of reproduction, the wellspring of the family, and most often the precinct of love, romance, and sexuality" (p. 11). What, then, does the female couple offer, and what challenges does it incur, in its role as wellspring of the family?

FEMALE COUPLING

Johnson (1990) writes that lesbian couples have all the qualities of women doubled. There are both dangers and opportunities that arise from this female bonding. One of the dangers is the problem of overidentification, merging, or fusion. Lesbians have to be particularly careful not to lose the self in the couple. However, many feminist researchers feel that this has been overproblematized (Green, 1990; Slater, 1995). Women's growth depends on deepening relational ties, and, as Slater points out, lesbians, who come out to a hostile world, "can hardly be accused of lacking personal autonomy" (p. 66). The couples in this study seem to be capable of allowing their partners to express key parts of themselves, even when those parts are very diverse. However, they are also very aware of and proud of their emotional closeness as couples. They describe this closeness as originating in a mutual respect and nurturing. Cady discusses how she feels taken care of in this relationship, whereas when she was married, she felt *she* was the one responsible for taking care of others. In this relationship, the caretaking responsibility is equal and mutual. Tanya feels there is more equality—more equal sharing—it is "more of a partnership," than her former heterosexual relationship.

Florence says that their relationship involves a lot more discussion and planning since they are equal partners. There is a common joke among lesbians that we tend to process everything to death, but the good side of that processing is that it demands communication and connection. Everyone is going to at least express her needs and desires. Delia believes that lesbians, perhaps because they have had to (and continue to) go against mainstream society, often bring a kind of confidence into their relationships. It is not that lesbians don't rely on or depend on each other, but that:

> They are just confident. They appear strong; they appear sure of themselves. They just kind of go out there and—I don't know if we are trying to prove that we can do all this stuff. I don't know.

Certainly all lesbians aren't always more confident than heterosexual women—and there are many insecure lesbians. But perhaps the fact that one is different as a lesbian and that one accepts this difference creates or allows for a particular kind of confidence or defiance toward the mainstream thinking.

Whatever the source of the differences, whether it is the female upbringing or the lesbian stance or a combination of the two, these couples are unanimous in their beliefs that their particular couple provides a good role model of coupling for their children. It is a good model because the children don't see the same gender stereotyping that is prevalent in many heterosexual families. It is a good role model because the children are exposed to an intimate understanding of prejudice and discrimination and their effect on people. It is a good role model because of the extent of mutual caring and care taking that occurs. It is a good role model because it offers alternatives to the children.

> **Diana (20):** By having this out and loving relationship [they] have shown me there are other options out there and whatever I feel is right—that they would never tell me, "You can't be with this person," unless they were abusive.

The children living with these lesbian mothers see a relationship based on equal respect and caring and a relationship that is very highly valued. Lori testifies to the power and strength of their relationship and how that must impact on the children.

> And in any case, you know, one of the things we know we've done at least is, we've at least given them a model of two people who love each other, two people who fight, you know, and do everything else. But, you know, they know they can't play us off against each other—they can't divide and conquer in this relationship. And one way or another, they've at least, you know—what they didn't get out of their first family, unfortunately, and hopefully they'll get out of this—is the idea that you can have a relationship that will work—even if it's from massively different people and even if it's under all kinds of supposedly societal adverse conditions.

Because women in this society are taught to put relationships first, a female-to-female relationship will often mirror that strength.

HOUSEHOLD TASKS DEGENDERED

Blumstein and Schwartz (1983) discuss how the changing nature of male and female roles has created problems for all types of couples. They write:

> The question is not simply who cooks, who takes out the trash, and who repairs the leaky faucet. Such task arrangements are really only a small part of the division of chores in a partnership. The larger question is much more profound and less amenable to easy answers. The household provides symbolic occasions for the establishment of territory and authority. Couples are trying to grapple with how men and women, how men and men, how women and women, should relate to one another. (p. 45)

Equality between the partners is important for many couples—heterosexual, as well as gay and lesbian. Certainly the gender makeup of the couple does not dictate any particular type of partnership. However, heterosexual couples may have more difficulty maintaining equal roles in the home because their gender training makes it easy to fall into male/female gender roles. Hochschild's (1989) study of who did what regarding the home work and child care in heterosexual couples, found that even when couples claimed to share the work equally, the women were actually doing more. Half of her interviews were done in the mid-1970s and half were done in the mid-1980s. She wrote,

> How much had changed from 1976 to 1988? In practical terms, little: most women I interviewed in the late 1980s still do the lion's share of the work at home, do most of the daily chores and take responsibility for running the home. But something was different, too. More couples wanted to share and imagined that they did. (p. 20)

So, although changes are occurring in heterosexual couples, they are changing slowly. As Slater (1995) explains, "While many heterosexual couples are also working to redistribute power and responsibility within their relationships, lesbians are operating from much farther outside the traditional model" (p. 48). Lesbian couples often see equality as a key facet of their relationships (Johnson, 1990; Slater, 1995). According to Slater (1995),

> Lesbians cannot base their assignment of relational, sexual, economic, or parenting roles on gender differences between the partners. As two women, lesbian couples build from a clean slate, negotiating from scratch all aspects of the partners' roles. Individual abilities, interests, and tolerances form the basis for the complex construction of these couples' relational roles. (p. 47)

Even if lesbian couples do not share household tasks equally, the children still see women accomplishing the tasks and negotiating the power. If one partner is more powerful than the other, that person is still a female. That must have an impact on how children experience gender. Hite's (1994) study of the family found that boys typically learn to be boys by rejecting everything female ("Don't be like a girl!" p. 233) and that this training is likely to be particularly strong from fathers. An outcome of this masculinity training is that boys typically come to see their mothers as weak and ineffective. Hite found that boys who grew up with mothers only—either single parents or lesbian mothers—were much more likely to like and admire their mothers. She wrote:

> The data here shows that there are *beneficial* effects for the majority of children living in single parent families. It is more positive for children not to grow up in an atmosphere poisoned by gender inequality.
>
> This conclusion was foreshadowed in *The Hite Report on Men and Male Sexuality*. In that work, I was surprised to find that boys who grew up with their mother alone were much more likely to have good relationships with women in their adult lives. (pp. 372-373)

This does not suggest that sexism does not permeate the lives of lesbians. Lesbians may also fall into the gender trap of evaluating typically male roles as more important and/or requiring more skill (Slater, 1995). However, even if there is inequality of power between the partners, the children still see the powerful role being played out by a woman and this has to make an impact.

The couples in this study all valued relationship equality and attempted to make it happen in the homemaking arena. In terms of dividing household tasks, they attempted to do it equally, while making space for individual preferences and strengths. Delia describes how this works in their household.

> . . . it's funny the roles you take on. I have to take care of killing all the . . . well, I don't kill them . . . getting rid of all the spiders—everyone in this house is terribly afraid of anything that has more than two legs, except a cat. But as far as finances go, I probably couldn't tell you what the electric bill is because it's not my job. I look at it and I say, isn't this kind of high? Well, no, its not high, because of this. And I say, OK, fine, because she's always done that, because I am so bad in math.

The ways tasks are shared often took some time to negotiate as the couple came to know each other better.

> **Florence:** We eventually learned each other's specialty areas, who is better at this, who is better at that. Then we learned to give in to that, let them do that. It makes it much easier than saying, well, I want to do everything, and then screw it all up and have to redo it.

This process of learning how to share household tasks did not always occur without fighting. When I asked Becky and Dory how they divided household tasks, Dory responded:

> Flip a coin. Well, we didn't used to. I mean, it used to be really, really awful. We had fights continuously. It used to be, when we first got together, Becky was not working.

> **Becky:** I stayed home.

> **Dory:** So she took care of all that. We came out here and we both ended up with jobs and we fought for the first two years. Becky used to get home earlier, and I got home later—so it was all her responsibility. And we still fought. And then, this last year, in the last couple of months, we've sort of devised

the system and a lot of the stuff gets done on the weekends. But we started rotating the dishes and the dinner and that seemed to work out. Because for the first six months we kept going out to eat.

Becky: A lot!

Dory: And we kept looking at the checkbook and the checkbook just looked really horrendous. And so we finally started negotiating this split of the chores and it seems to be functioning, but there was a lot of chaos before that.

Sometimes household chores are divided not on an equality basis nor on skill or preference, but because one partner has strong feelings about the chore being done. Since Cady is more adversely affected by clutter in the household, she may do most of the picking up and cleaning, although they have worked as a couple to come to a compromise so that Lori doesn't make as much clutter as she used to.

Cady: But I would say that, generally—and I think you will agree—I do more of the yard and probably more of the housekeeping stuff.

Lori: Because you do freak out when things get out of order.

Cady: Yes, I'm very bothered by stuff out of order and by clutter.

However, the division of household tasks may change when one partner's job changes or has new demands. For example, when Cady was working on an advanced degree, Lori did more of the household work. Then, when Lori worked on her dissertation, Cady did more of the work.

Household tasks, then, are divided with consideration to factors of time, skill and preference, and who is more bothered by them not getting done. While the division of tasks is not always smooth, all of these couples made attempts to share the household work as equally as possible.

Several of these couples took pride in doing a majority of the work around their homes themselves, including car maintenance and remodeling work. Delia and Kathy specifically let me know that they tried to do traditional male tasks, such as working on the car or doing electrical repairs, as a model to their daughters that women could do these things. Terry and Tanya were in the process of scraping and painting their home when I visited them. Terry also spoke of working on the lights of the trailer they had borrowed. They took pride in the fact that they had removed some full-grown trees from their backyard so that they could have a garden. They built their own backyard fence and compost bins. Florence and Nisi are constantly working on remodeling projects in their home—including plumbing work, knocking out walls, plastering, and hanging doors. Florence enjoys working on and maintaining their cars and their camping trailer. This kind of "we-can-do-it-ourselves" attitude toward home work created a lot of pride for these couples.

These parents particularly treasured the equality and sharing of power in their relationships. They believe that their relationships impacted positively on their children because of the absence of a model of male privilege within the family structure. This structure encourages girl children to feel powerful and affirmed. It may also allow boy children to proudly claim their "feminine" (as pre-scripted by a society that separates human traits based on gender) traits. For example, Nisi and Florence tell the following story about Dale:

> **Nisi:** I love how sensitive Dale is. I mean, he loves to go get fireflies, but he won't keep them overnight, because he is afraid they'll die.

> **Florence:** He knows they are going to die.

> **Nisi:** I treasure that about him. . . . I hope . . . I don't know whether I told you this, maybe I did, when we go to the beach, there are all these toads and at dusk when there's just . . . I mean, you take a step, and there's like a parting of ways. These toads are jumping everywhere. And he said the only thing he doesn't like about going to the lake and standing on the beach is he's afraid he's going to step on a toad. And Florence and I are like . . .

Florence: There's plenty.

Nisi: Don't worry. There's so many toads.

Florence: There's nothing you can do—you can't miss them sometimes.

Nisi: But anyway, you know, then a little while later, he says—"Well, there's a lot of people, but if Frannie got killed, that would be horrible". . . . But I guess that's part of being who I am, you know, that I just really value a gentleness and a sensitivity toward life and that Dale has just taken a hold of that so much—I just really treasure that. . . . I think we are raising wonderful little boys and that they will be great men. They might not be the same as a lot of other men, but they will be wonderful. They will have a lot to add to the maleness of the world.

Of course, heterosexual couples can and do also raise wonderfully sensitive boys, but perhaps lesbian couples provide another window to see more clearly how this might be done. It is important to further explore how to raise children without male privilege, without the idea that women are passive with limited abilities, and with the clear understanding that being female is as wonderful and powerful as being male. This kind of family may provide an inoculation against the perpetuation of sexism. Since lesbians do not have differentiated gender roles to resort to when the going gets tough, combating sexism may be easier in lesbian families.

MOTHERING AND FATHERING DEGENDERED

One of my outsider collaborators, Sunshine Jones, suggested that I examine more carefully how both mothering and fathering are accomplished in lesbian families and how these activities may be less related to gender than to preference. There is currently much debate over whether fathering and mothering are necessarily gendered activities or not. Blankenhorn (1995) argues that fatherhood cannot be separated from manhood. He believes that fatherhood is necessary for males, first and foremost, to temper male aggression:

> Fatherhood, more than any other male activity, helps men to become good men: more likely to obey the law, to be good citizens, and to think about the needs of others. (p. 21)

In this sense, he sees fatherhood as an engendering activity—ties to and responsibilities for children create good men. Blankenhorn (1995) first assumes that male aggression is innate and biological. Second, he chooses to locate his socializing action designed to temper this aggression in fatherhood and the model it provides, rather than in challenging how boys are socialized into men. Both of these ideas are assumptions that have been questioned.

But, more pertinent to this study, are the activities that he attributes to fatherhood which, he says, privilege children. These are, primarily, to provide for them materially and also to protect them, to educate them, to represent his family's interests in the larger world, to provide day-to-day nurturance and care, and to provide "a father's distinctive capacity to contribute to the identity, character, and competence of his children" (p. 25).

With the possible exception of the last characteristic, female parents can certainly accomplish these so-called fathering tasks, just as many feminists believe that men can mother. Benjamin (1988) identifies "gender polarity" or the separation of human traits into male and female, as "the deep source of discontent in our society (p. 171)." Blankenhorn (1995) interprets feminist discourse as advocating that fatherhood is superfluous. However, I understand it as a degendering of mothering and fathering, rather than an argument that fatherhood is unnecessary. Both fathering and mothering are important for children. The question is, can they be accomplished in single-parent, female-coupled and male-coupled families?

For purposes of this discussion, I define the traditional fathering role as one in which the parent feels responsibility for and commitment to the children, but also spends more time interfacing with the community than the mother role. This may include volunteer activities, job responsibilities, and/or social activities. This parent spends less time doing the day-to-day maintenance, nurturing, and caring for the children. This slightly more distanced role from the child allows for a different perspective to develop and a freshness of energy in time spent with the child. The traditional mother role, on the other hand, includes the day-to-day care for and maintenance of the children. The mother role entails spending more time with the children and often results in an emotional attachment to the children which creates a closer, more intimate but sometimes myopic perspective on the children.

The participants in this study believe that they can provide for both the mothering and fathering of their children. There is agreement among these women that two parents, regardless of gender, made parenting easier. Some feel that two parents are generally better than one—others believe that a single parent can do a fine job on his or her own, but that it is harder. As Lori puts it, "So I'm more of a feeling that if we had more adults in children's lives, you know with their neighbors and their parents' friends, and everybody else actually treated them like they were important human beings— that's more important than anything. I guess we don't have enough general adult interest in kids." Delia believes that the issue is love, and not the gender of the parents. When I asked if she believed kids need a father, she responded:

> **Delia:** I'm going to say they don't because I know gay men that have daughters and they seem to be perfectly capable of raising that daughter with as much nurturing as any woman could possibly bring into that family. To me it's a matter of we all have that ability and this is just crap that men can't be. I will never buy it.

And Diana echoes her mother's sentiments,

> I don't need a father, and I really get very resentful when people tell me that I do, and [that] I'm not going to be as good as someone who has one. I need two loving parents who will love me and respect me as a person. And that's what I have.

Diana's (20) family has a running joke about who is being the "mom" today and who is being the "dad."

> **Kathy:** You know Diana's joke that Delia's the mom today and Kathy is the dad today, because Kathy is painting the house and Delia is making the dinner.

In Chapter 6, I describe how these couples divide the traditional mothering and fathering roles based on individual preferences and how that interacts with the added complexity of the step status. It is clear within this group of women that they have varying degrees of preference for tasks traditionally defined as fathering and mothering and that this is simply another adjustment that the couples make in parenting together.

WE CAN FATHER BUT WE CAN NEVER BE MALE

Blankenhorn (1995) argues that, beyond the obvious sexual differences, men have innately different personality traits from women. These participants agreed that males are important to children, whether it is because they are socialized differently or because of biological differences. Children need positive relationships with males and these parents made efforts to ensure their children had positive contact with men. Some of the children have fathers who are involved in their lives, although the women didn't always see those fathers as positive role models. Molly's father hasn't been a problem for Cady and Lori, but he also has not, in their estimation, provided a very nurturant and involved model of fathering. Diana and Talia's father has been very problematic for Kathy and Delia. They also see him as an extreme macho man whose values conflict with their feminist principles.

These couples have made varying efforts to provide their children with positive male models—some more proactively than others. The mothers of boys seem particularly aware of the fact that there are some things about being male that they simply don't understand. Terry talks about her attempts to help Kevin learn about erections.

> **Terry:** When it came to specifics, Kevin, I'm sorry I don't know what could help you as far as making it feel better and not be so uncomfortable. I told him some people rub them and its OK to experiment, go right ahead and do that. And he said, "I don't know what to do for experimentation." There are other people who experience what you are and, I said, it would be safe for him to talk to Konrad [a family friend]. I also

suggested [another friend], but he didn't want that—he's too goofy. He did say it was OK for me to mention it to Konrad, that he may come to him.

Both Kevin and Dale are the only males in their immediate families, which can lead to some difficult situations. Florence thinks that Dale must feel "so alienated, sometimes—being the only male and then dealing with all this other stuff [having lesbian moms]." Nisi feels that Dale is different than she is in a lot of ways—like being into sports, and Florence adds:

> Especially when he gets older and really starts developing his male sexuality and all that, it would be nice if he had a man to discuss it with. Because we don't know where he is coming from—we don't know how his body feels, you know.

And Dale (8) writes in his journal,

> It is Fathers Day and I don't have a father. I felt kind of sad. I think about what it would be like to have a father.

The mothers of girls also think that it is important for them to have a positive male influence:

> **Dory:** I think there are certain points in each child's life where a masculine figure may be of a benefit. We talked about this before and said, you know, there gets to be an age where compliments coming from a father can mean a lot, because there's that evaluation of this is—if you are a heterosexual child—who knows, but those compliments can be real important. There's one aspect that we really can't give—the mind-set of men, you know. So if you are preparing your daughter or your child to be in a relationship with an opposite sex individual, I think a father can help prepare some of that mind-set—I don't think that we have the ability. Now, whether it's a natural father or just a male figure in general—a grandfather, an uncle, a close family friend—I think it can be done by anyone who's close enough to the family. That would be something they would be able to do.

Lori tries to explain why she thinks children need solid contact with men who are close to them.

> There are certain ways because men in our society have certain roles, and because men just relate differently emotionally, and there are certain ways that they can give a child both a sense of protection and a sense of competence and relief from the emotional love that women will always go through.

She goes on to explain how important it has been to her as a boss to balance her workforce with men and women.

> So men have a certain lack of hysteria. I spend all my time calming my female staff down, over every God damn crisis, you know. On the other hand, there are other things that women add that men can't add, but, it takes all kinds to make the world. And I wouldn't want to live in a world where we only had women.

Because they believe that men have some unique perspectives to offer their children, these women make efforts to include men in their children's lives. Nisi's father and brothers are involved with her children, although she is hoping to get even more consistent contact with a male for Dale. Delia has good male friends at work that have some contact with the girls. Terry and Tanya's best family friends are a heterosexual couple with a male child who is about Kevin's age. The children also seek out and find males with whom to connect. Diana mentions in an interview that she has gotten to know a lot of her friends' fathers, who are "very good men." And Nisi talks about how Dale connects with a friend's father to talk about basketball. So it is important to recognize that children can and do act in their own behalf in seeking out male connections, if they are encouraged, or allowed, to do so.

Although these women recognize that men have a unique contribution to make to their children's' lives, they do not feel that their family structure is a handicap for their children. First, they believe that the children can get positive male modeling in other ways besides having a biological, involved father. Nisi, for example, realizes that her children are missing a biological piece of who they are by having an unknown donor father. Although she can tell them about some of his characteristics and she thought it was helpful for Frannie and Dale to go through the process with Florence and her for getting sperm for the new baby, she understands that it is a significant loss that they will not have a biological father involved in their lives. On the other hand, she points out that neither will they have to experience abandonment by a biological parent, as many children do. Cady says:

> I think what is most important is the stability and knowing that they are not going to be abandoned by somebody and that they are just that important. It would be nice if it happened to be their biological father or biological mother, but if it isn't, there certainly are other good alternatives, I think.

These participants do believe that men have an important role to play in children's lives, yet they also believe that children can be successfully raised by various parental structures. In other words, love, respect, guidance, and consistent involvement create the quality of a parental/child relationship—not gender. They were adamant about the fact that a female couple has unique strengths that they offer to their children. Just as heterosexual couples can offer certain perspectives to children and gay male couples have other strengths, there is a recognition that, because both partners are female and lesbian, they have some unique contributions to make to child rearing. Those contributions include an equality between the partners based on the shared female upbringing and that the children do not have male privilege modeled in the family home. These may be differences that have a positive effect on children and that also contribute to a societal change that allows men and women to be equally valued.

CONCLUSION

Lesbian couples, by definition, consist of two female partners. This chapter has examined how that configuration may affect the children and influence the transmission of sexism. These participants believe that they model couple relationships of respect and equality that encourage closeness, connection, and communication.

Because there are no adult males in these families, there is also an absence of male privilege. Adult tasks and responsibilities are accomplished by females, including traditional mothering and fathering. Tasks that are often divided on the basis of gender in heterosexual families are assigned based on preference, ability, or time. This may combat the sexism children experience outside the family; further studies of adult children of lesbians must be conducted to address this question.

These participant couples did not reject the importance of men in their children's lives. But they also did not believe that their families suffered by not including adult males. They believed children could benefit from close contact with men outside of the immediate family.

The lesbian family disrupts the societal prescription of male domination, refuting the splitting of human traits and tasks by gender. Within the family, children do not experience gender as being bound to a particular role. Although it is beyond the scope of this project to predict how this may affect the children as adults, it is clear that these adult couples are proud of their coupling models and agree that their children benefit from them.

Chapter 5

Outside/Insight:
Creating the Step Mother Role
and Redefining the Mother Role

INTRODUCTION

In heterosexual step families, the step mother does not generally love the biological mother. Certainly they rarely live together. As Minnich (1989) writes, "To get a Wicked Step Mother, one's mother must leave or die, one's father must remarry, and a new woman must move in" (p. 193). But this is not the case with lesbian step families. The mother is not lost—she is there, in the home, with the step mother. This usually means that the mother script must also be rewritten, in order to make room for the step mother in the family.

The step mother comes into a functioning (if not always functional) family, an outsider—at least in the beginning. How do these biological mothers and step mothers work together (and sometimes against one another) to create a new family? How do the children participate in this creation?

Feminist thinkers have long argued over the relative importance of the Mother to the children's well-being. While some describe Mother as a social construct with many harmful consequences (e.g., Firestone, 1972; Miller, 1989), others have rushed to the defense of Mother, as being critical and natural for the child's health (Friedan, 1981; Greer, 1984). Minnich (1989), a step mother herself, recognizes this nature versus nurture debate as the result of that simplistic, dualistic thinking that traps us so easily:

I have long said that those who argue for explanations by nature are really against change. What is by nature, they have told us, must simply be accepted. Whenever we have questioned our lot as shown, we have been told that it is "natural" in just that spirit. So what am I doing wondering if the primacy of the birth mother, enshrined within the insistence that there can be only one mother, is based on something "natural?" Perhaps I am trying to find a way to accept it more easily. And if it is by nurture? Then perhaps I could temper the hurt of the present with hope for change. (p. 198)

The biological role of Mother is so intensely tied to the social construct of the modern Western European family that it is extremely difficult to begin the process of untangling them. However, we can look outside of the modern (or post-modern) nuclear heterosexual Western European family for some illumination. Historically, we know that many biological mothers did not raise their children to adulthood—e.g., for reasons such as the mother's early death, or customs of sending children out of the home at a young age (Theurer, 1994). We also know that definitions of family, even father and mother, are culturally bound. Wade-Lewis (1989) in her study of African-American step mothers, writes of the acceptance of nonbiological, but parental status within the culture:

> Most of these six women recalled that in their childhoods a family was a family, parents introduced children as "my children," and most children, whatever the actual nature of the relationship, addressed parents using titles of respect such as Daddy and Mama. The forms of address may have hinted at step relationships—Daddy Sam, Mama Annie, Big Daddy, Daddy Two, Little Mama—but always they indicated respect for the station and role of parents. Parents were authority figures, not simply adults of the household. (p. 226)

She continues, "In the African-American family, there is the assumption that children belong to families, and that if a man or woman joins a family, it is a privilege, rather than a burden to assist in raising the children" (p. 227).

Certainly the primacy of Mother is not an immutable fact. Even if it is "natural," it can evolve. Mothering has been shared in the past and it is shared in the present—and this sharing can benefit not only the mother—by freeing her to live a productive (not only reproductive) life but also the children (Miller, 1989). What can the additional, nonbiological parent bring to the child? The child learns that she/he can depend on someone other than mother to meet some of her/his needs. A step mother, as Minnich (1989) writes:

> speeds up the painful but empowering process of separation. The children meet a stranger called "Elizabeth," or whatever, not "Mother." She is unfamiliar, in the true meaning of the word. Children are then forced to know that their mothering comes from an identifiable individual separate from them on whom they are nevertheless dependent. (p. 194)

In addition, because the step mother is an "outsider," integrating into a preexisting family unit, she may also offer the child and biological mother her outsider perspective on the child's needs and challenges (Crosbie-Burnett, Skyles, and Becker-Haven, 1988). If this perspective is offered with a "loving gaze" (Ruddick, 1989), it can contribute to the child's well-being and growth.

The outsider role, however, is often painful—for the step mother especially, but also for the biological mother who loves her partner. It creates an uncomfortable and, at times, excruciating vulnerability in the step mother. Minnich (1989) relates:

> I am vulnerable to the children, with whom nothing can be considered safe or established, and who not only have doubts that I will stay but who test to see if I can be made to leave. I am vulnerable, too, to the world of neighbors and schools and doctors and other parents that children connect us to whether we want to be connected or not. I must deal all the time with assumptions and expectations on their part over which I have no control. (p. 192)

Certainly the vulnerability of a step mother is intensified in a lesbian step family. In the first place, not only are the children there to question your authenticity as a parent, but the biological mother is right there with you, too—watching, feeling, approving or disapproving of your daily interactions with the child. Beyond that, the world we live in offers even less validation and support to lesbian step mothers. Heterosexual supremacy serves to make the lesbian step mother invisible to the outside world, which communicates that invisibility to the children, the biological mother, and the step mother. She is unnamed—and therefore erased. Surely the job of lesbian step mother is not for the faint of heart.

Lesbian step families, like the Chinese character for crisis, embody the essence of both dangers and opportunities. The dangers often present themselves like land mines, hidden and unexpected. But the opportunities are also there to create family tied together by love, familiarity, and steadfastness, rather than the blood and possessiveness which serve to bind some nuclear families. Maglin (1989), in her review of step family fiction, writes that "The harder tale to tell—bonding between women, the sharing of mothering, and the degendering of mothering—has yet to be written" (p. 271). These lesbian step families, and others like them, are living in uncharted territory.

This chapter examines some of the tasks these families faced in creating their families. These tasks include bringing the step mother into the family, as well as redefining the mother role. I then describe the unique roles these step mothers and their families built and a discussion of three distinct step mother stances found in these families.

Common themes emerged from the data from all of these families on how the step roles were created and are evolving. To integrate the step parent into the family, the family must negotiate these tasks. This negotiation is a long-term project, as heterosexual step family literature suggests (Kelley, 1995; Visher and Visher, 1990), taking up to six or seven years to complete. And, like all parenting, it is never totally finished because children grow and circumstances change. The necessary tasks include the biological mother making space for the step mother, however the family works out what that space will look like. In addition, the step mother must determine how to take the child or children into her life, and the children must do the same for the step mother. These tasks are ongoing and overlapping. They do not necessarily proceed at the same rate. They do not necessarily lead to the same definition. This unevenness can create pain and misunderstanding, but it may also force growth.

COMMITMENT OF STEP MOTHER TO CHILD

For all of these step mothers, getting involved with a woman who had a child or children was a big commitment. They realized from the beginning that they would be building relationships with the children as well as the mother, and that the children's needs would be an important part of the relationship. For some step parents, this meant taking more time to make the commitment.

> **Terry:** My problem was I didn't want to get involved in a relationship with a kid if I wasn't sure about it. I just couldn't do that to the kid. So I kept being wishy-washy in a sense. But then when I decided for sure that was what I wanted, then I felt more comfortable with someone with a kid.

Florence was concerned about whether her own upbringing, which was unstable and authoritarian, might cause her to be unable to parent appropriately. In discussing her own upbringing, she says:

> Yeah, you do what they, you don't ask questions, you don't say no. So, and because I knew through all of this stuff that it does carry over—you pass it on to kids. And I didn't want to do that. It took us a couple of years, maybe even three, before we really thought we wanted to do this.

For some step parents, the fact that they had always wanted children helped them and their partners to make the decision to commit.

> **Lori:** I wanted this relationship with Cady, and [kids] were part of the deal. And we had talked a lot about it, you know. She was really worried about anybody wanting kids in their lives. And I said to her, you know, I had had this idea that I was going to have ten kids when I was younger. And I always loved kids and baby-sat for kids and had been kind of a fairy Godmother to a lot of my friends' kids.

> **Kathy:** I always loved children. I still love children. I like to hang with kids.

As already noted, Becky stated that one of the best things about their family was that she got the kid she always wanted.

However, this wasn't so with all of the step mothers. Although Florence enjoyed children, she wasn't always sure that she wanted to be a parent. "Yeah, I never wanted kids at all—even when I was married. He wanted kids and I said, 'Nah.'" But, family life has changed Florence and now she and Nisi have a new baby to raise together.

The decision about commitment was also important to the bio-mothers, who were very concerned that they partner with someone who would also be a good parent. As Nisi describes it:

> I was very much in love with Florence and she was who I had fun with. She was my best friend. She was who I wanted to sleep with. So it was kind of silly. But I was really afraid of getting into another long-term relationship that wasn't going to work out and I really wanted us to have time in different situations together to really see if it would work.

And Tanya remarks:

> I thought there might be some kind of difficulties with Kevin and Terry and there were, probably the first six months. But I also thought that she would be a really good role model for him.

Dory was particularly concerned that her daughter not have adults "bouncing in and out of her life." She and Becky went to couple counseling when they first got together, in order to "set the ground rules" for the relationship—one of which was long-term commitment. In order to try to ensure some safety and stability for their children, bio-moms carefully scrutinized their potential partners. They wanted partners who enjoyed being around children and who could be generous with the children. Some bio-mothers seem to have consciously or unconsciously chosen a partner who could offer something to the child that the bio-mother couldn't. For example, Tanya, who is white with a biracial child, chose a mixed race partner. Dory, who has attention deficit disorder, chose a partner who is organized. Nisi wanted to be sure not to repeat the mistakes of her first long-term relationship—she wanted someone who liked to do things with the children.

The children, then, were an added factor to be carefully considered at the beginning of these relationships. Although some of these relationships developed quickly, and others took much more time to grow, all of these adults recognized the seriousness of the decision and tried to consider the children with honor and respect. However, even this careful consideration did not avoid the fact that one adult was coming into a preexisting family—an outsider. The enormity of that challenge often wasn't clear until after the commitment was made. Visions of what the new family would look like gave way to the everyday nitty-gritty work of creating family. Step parents soon discovered that they often felt like outsiders, leaving them hurt, angry, and vulnerable. All of these women describe the earlier years as harder. The existential question that had to be answered in those years seemed to be, if I am not Mother, then what am I?

THE NATURE VERSUS NURTURE DEBATE

This outsider status leads to a sense of insecurity that appeared to be persistent and pernicious. The themes of pain, hurt, and anger are prevalent in the voices of step mothers (Maglin and Schniedewind, 1989). The cultural myth of the wicked step mother haunts the actual step mothers, who question: Is it me that is creating this mess? Am I the bad guy?

As Terry relates:

> Partly because I had step parents, too, and I'm finding myself being a little on the harsher side with Kevin, and I think— gosh, I sound like my step father! And here I am the wicked step mother.

The step mother role is particularly painful for these women as they see how it contrasts with the biological mother's role. Lesbian step mothers live with the bio-mom and see this bio-mom/child interaction daily. The bio-moms have a security that is less easily shaken.

Cady: I mean, for me—I don't know if this has been your experience—but through all of this, I have never doubted my kids loved me. Never doubted it, even when they told me they hated me and I ruined their life. I don't believe that. And I don't think that for a step parent it's that easy.

Dory echoes this sense of security, in discussing Becky's anger about how Pauli's dad does very little for her and yet Pauli loves him unconditionally.

Dory: That's where Becky is at and she's just really, really angered by that. And I guess maybe that's part of this step parent thing. I mean, I know where my place is and I'm real secure with it.

This contrast may lead moms and step moms into questioning whether there is something unique and natural about the biological parent. This can be both comforting and disquieting.

Lori: I'm sure many lesbian step parents would say the same thing, that you're always coming into a preexisting family and forever you are not a member of that family. We may have another thing going here, but there's another family first. And that's a dynamic that the mother, the biological parent, contributes to, too. And I'm not saying that fault finding—that's just a reality. There's a relationship there and it is going to be there. And, for a long time, that made me crazy. And sometimes it still makes me feel totally alone. But I don't think that that. . . . I don't know . . . I don't know that that ever goes away!

This appears to be an ongoing internal and external debate among these mothers: Is the primacy of the biological mother bond inevitable, or can it be altered?

Becky: Well, sometimes I get hurt a lot because either Dory will, not so much say so, but the things she does and how she does it, says that I don't know what I am doing. You know, I don't necessarily think having birthed something makes you any better to parent. And I don't know that she consciously has that intent, but that's the way it feels. And I get told I'm hated on a regular basis by the little one.

Or perhaps, rather than challenging this primary bond, is it better for the child and the step parent to simply accept it?

Terry: I don't consider myself his Mom mom, in the sense I wasn't there from birth and I don't expect him to expect . . . I know that I am different. And maybe because I have step parents, too—I know I'm different. I will never be that mom to him that is a Mom.

There was a constant questioning in these adults about whether they were dealing with a step issue—or is this just pure and simple parenting? Kathy and Delia have struggled with this throughout their fourteen years of parenting together. Like the other biological mothers in this study, Delia is more likely to believe that it is just parenting.

Delia: So when I would tell [Kathy]—no, you're off the wall here. You are taking what they're doing personally and saying it's because they don't like me. And I'm saying no, it's because they're a brat and if I had been in the room at that time, I can guarantee you the reaction would have been the same. It doesn't matter that it was you or me. . . . the insecurity—like "it's because I don't have the authority or I don't have the respect you naturally get." And Jan, we had so many arguments about this "natural respect." Like I go, "This is a bunch of crap. Look at what you are saying. The other day what did they do to me? OK, and you had to step in and say don't talk to your mother like that. And I had to turn around now and say—you don't talk to this mother that way. We do it all the time. So what are you doing here? You are freaking." And sometimes I was more sensitive to that than others. Sometimes I'd just say—"Oh, I don't have time for this."

Step mothers are more likely to assume that when a child misbehaves, or gets mad, or says "I hate you" that it is because of the step relationship—not simply a child acting out. This creates an ongoing dialogue in these families. As Dory says, "[Becky's] perception has always been that Pauli doesn't listen to Becky on the important issues." Step mothers and biological mothers search for examples to disprove the theory that the children's misbehavior is a result of their distrust of, dislike of the step parent. Lori illustrates this search in a journal entry:

> We have had a number of days this month when Molly would gravitate to me and treat Cady like shit. Cady and I try to verbally raise this to collective consciousness and commit it to memory for hard days to come when I am Molly's target. It's these days of Cady "getting it" and that unusual openness of affection from Molly to me that convince us that this is adolescence and just not to be analyzed rationally as conscious behavior. So this is very helpful for some perspective.

These participants definitely disagree on how important and necessary they see the primacy of the biological mother. As will be discussed later in this chapter, there is a wide range of how the step role has come to be defined in this group. However, these struggles with the outsider status are found within all the families—regardless of how the step role is defined. All of these adults had to work hard at bringing the outsider in—a process of creating a new family.

STEP PARENTS DEVELOP UNIQUE RELATIONSHIPS WITH THE CHILDREN

These step parents developed several unique roles with their step children, which helped to create bonds. These roles were often based on the special strengths and characteristics of the step parent, the interests of the child, and/or the needs of the bio-parent. For example, one of the roles was that of adult playmate. Both Terry and Florence are people who really enjoy playing and that has helped them to make connections with the children. When I attended a school picnic with Terry and Tanya and Kevin, it was Terry who immediately ran off to play baseball with the kids, while Tanya and I set up the picnic blanket. Dale and Frannie's journals testify to the fact that one of their main activities with Florence is playing—Yahtzee games, running through the sprinkler, shooting baskets, etc. And Nisi recognizes that this is something special that Florence brings to the kids.

> **Nisi:** It's really neat to see her bring things to them that I don't have, or that I don't have energy for, or that kind of thing. Those kind of moments might be like when she'll just pick up the basketball and start really going at it with Dale, like playing basketball—or when her and Frannie get together and play Yahtzee together.

Another role some of these step parents took was that of protector. Sometimes the bio-parent may be less assertive and the step parent takes on the job of standing up for or advocating for the child.

> **Terry:** Kevin sees me as a person who will step in and confront.

Terry has dealt with teachers, principals, parents, and children in various ways to protect Kevin and to advocate for him in cases of racism, homophobia, unkindness, and unfairness. And Tanya says that one of the things she likes best about Terry's parenting is that she "stands up for Kevin—she's there for him."

Becky has found that she is more likely to confront the school on Pauli's behalf because Dory "doesn't have the gumption—she is timid." This kind of protector role builds trust and a sense of safety for the child. As Terry notes, now Kevin will sometimes ask her what she is going to do about something when he is feeling hurt.

One of the major roles that these step parents play with the children is that of Teacher—of certain skills, of responsibility, and of politics, values and/or ethics. Terry works with Kevin on the piano (although he may not appreciate it all the time). Florence bird watches with Dale. Becky and Pauli like to watch certain TV shows together. They find openings to teach what the biological parent may be less skilled at or unable to do. Florence describes her role as the following:

> **Florence:** I think guiding and teaching of the things that Nisi doesn't consider or think of, because she's more of an intellectual and I'm more of a doer, physical, mechanical type, I guess.

In their journals, Frannie and Dale discuss Florence as someone who will fix their toys, help them make costumes. They also spend a good deal of time working with Florence around the home—washing the car, being go-fers during home remodeling and maintenance projects, pushing Florence in her wheelchair when she had a broken leg. Florence has been an important force in teaching the kids responsibility—such as picking up after themselves, and respecting others' needs for privacy, or quiet, or less chaos.

Some of the step mothers enjoy the role of teacher of politics, values, or ethics. Becky, recognizing that Dory grew up in a racist, very conservative home, makes sure to take advantage of those teachable moments with Pauli to help her be accepting of difference. She also enjoys helping Pauli understand the effects of sexism and encouraging her to think about unfairness. Lori enjoys talking about politics with the children, commenting that Cady just doesn't have much interest in politics. "We have giant political talks—all of them driven by me."

Step mothers also found that they could sometimes be a friend to the children. A friend takes less of an authority figure role, concentrating instead on building a positive relationship and allowing the mother to do the disciplining. This might mean helping to negotiate an agreement between the bio-mom and the child. Cady describes in her journal a time when she and Molly were at a standstill in a fight that had been going on for days:

> Once again there was no way that Molly would understand my position and when she retreated to her room just a short time before the three of us were about to go out, Lori volunteered to try talking to her. It worked very well. Lori negotiated an agreement that Molly could live with and presented it to me on Molly's behalf. Her mediating brought us to an agreement. Lori seemed to offer an ally to Molly, and gave Molly a way of getting out of this mess with me . . . I was really happy with the way Lori was able to do this. . . . In some ways the step parent role may have been an advantage since Lori didn't use a parental approach, but one of a friend to Molly, offering to help find a solution.

Similarly, Becky finds that she sometimes advocates for Pauli with Dory, acting as a buffer to soften Dory's temper flashes.

The step parent, because of her slightly more removed stance from the child, may find that she can discuss issues with the child that are difficult for the bio-mom to address. For example, Terry finds it easier to talk with Kevin about sexuality.

The step parent may use her own personal experience to help the child. Terry uses personal examples to help Kevin cope with racism:

> **Terry:** It has been really helpful because we have been able to relate to him on an experience level. It's like, "Oh yeah, it was really hard for me too when I was growing up." So we have this great talk and he'll sit on my lap and talk about how we felt about it and how I felt about it and how he felt about it. And it doesn't necessarily answer his questions for him—why did they do it? I can't tell him why.

These friendship connections appear to provide a sense of security for the child. As Nisi describes:

> **Nisi:** Sometimes when [Florence] will just share who she is with them—her past, or how she was parented—that sort of thing. She also just brings a lot of love and security to them. They just—she is real important to them.

Step parents can also give the children love and show affection. Delia appreciates how nurturing Kathy is with the kids and says that that nurturance seems to come more naturally to Kathy. Cady appreciates that Lori can be open with her emotions.

> **Cady:** I think there is actually some value in showing that emotion and that's something I have a hard time with. It really, (the kids) have to push me pretty far to know how much pain I'm in and to know how much they are bugging me, and to know—and that isn't particularly healthy for them.

It is interesting that these unique roles which the step mothers have developed with the children parallel the roles Blankenhorn (1995) locates in fathering: protector, educator, day-to-day nurturer.

In addition, these step mothers, like some fathers, are material providers for the children, using their incomes to augment the children's standards of living. Step mothers, then, found special parenting niches to fill in the children's lives. Sometimes they adopted these roles by preference, acknowledging a particular comfort with a particular role. Other times they accepted the role because either the biological mother and/or the child(ren) were unable or unwilling to redefine the mother role in a way that allowed the step mother access to a greater share of traditional mothering tasks and status.

Biological mothers were able to relinquish, in part, some mothering power and control because they grew to appreciate the unique and special relationships that the step parents had with the children. As the step parents' relationships with the children grew and deepened, the biological mothers found it easier and easier to trust and to let go of some parenting. However, if the relationship between the child and the step parent became more distant, as in the case with Molly, who has distanced from Lori during adolescence, the biological mother appeared to step in and take up the slack. Lori's response to Molly's rebellion has been to withdraw somewhat—as a self-protective stance. In turn, Molly has interpreted this as a lack of interest in her. Molly turns to her mother more often and Cady responds. This has also happened somewhat with Terry, whose relationship with Kevin has become more distanced due to her lack of time. Tanya has increased her time and energy with Kevin in response. Relationships take time and energy to develop and to be maintained.

For the most part, as the step parents have deepened their relationships with the children, the biological mothers have trusted and made room for shared parenting. The biological mothers express a lot of appreciation and admiration for their partners, recognizing their unique contributions to the children. But they are also always protective of the children and sensitive to any perceived or real breach of trust. The step parent's relationship with the child, then, requires a delicate balance among the step parent's effort to build it, the child's willingness to accept and trust the step parent's effort, and the biological mother's trust and belief that the relationship is positive for the child. The next section looks at the different ways this balance has been established in these families.

DEFINING THE STEP PARENT ROLE:
THREE STANCES

But what creates a father—or a mother? McMahon (1995), in her study of Canadian mothers with small children, found that it was having the ultimate responsibility for a child that transformed women to mothers. Women in her study believed that mothering was different from parenting as a result of this responsibility and their special awareness or consciousness of their children and their needs. These mothers, even those who hadn't initially wanted to have children, found this responsibility for a child to be a morally transforming experience:

> It is the feelings of responsibility for children, therefore, that also endow motherhood with much of its sacred character. Thus we can understand how motherhood can be 'morally uplifting' to women even when it is not valued socially and even when it is not skillfully performed. (McMahon, 1995, p. 273)

Stack's (1974) study of urban, poor black families demonstrated that it was not simply biology, but rather responsibility that conferred the rights of parenthood. McMahon (1995) argues that this social and moral transformation experienced by the mothers in her study is the result of their connectedness, caring, and interdependence with children and that this relationship model can be extended beyond the mother-child relationship to "mothers and nonmothers, men and women" (p. 277).

The different step parent stances defined by these families result from a complex interplay of adult preferences for tasks traditionally defined as mothering or fathering or a combination of those roles, children's abilities and willingness to accept those preferences, and the division of responsibility for and power with the child(ren).

These five participant families have created three distinct step parent roles. I term these different stances as the co-parent, the step mother, and the co-mother.

The Co-Parent Stance

Three of the families define the step parent in a manner which I have named the co-parent—a helper and supporter of and consultant to the biological mother, an active parent of the children (although this is contested at times), and a dedicated and committed family member. In this family type, the power and responsibility for the children is weighted toward the biological mother.

The co-parent takes more of a traditional fathering role in these families—providing for, protecting, and playing with the children, and helping the mother with the daily routines and nurturing.

The co-parent spends less time with the children than the biological mother. This may be due to the requirements of jobs—such as with Terry's night shift work, plus school, or Florence's long hours and commute. However, there is also an element of choice involved. Tanya, for example, is underemployed—she has a master's degree and is employed in a paraprofessional job. Although she keeps her eyes open for other positions, she admits that her present job has advantages, especially the hours which allow her to be home with Kevin after school. Terry's higher paying job allows Tanya more freedom of job choice. So there is an element of agreement between the two partners.

Florence originally lived in another state and moved to Newville because Nisi did not want to move and disrupt the children. Although Florence was able to transfer to work in the same state as Nisi, she does still have a long commute. So, in some sense, her long hours away from home are the result of a compromise agreement made by the couple.

For two of the co-parents, Florence and Terry, this role appears to be based on preference. Terry, in my observations, makes decisions to engage in more activities outside of the home and enjoys that freedom to interface with the community.

Terry, in her journal, wonders if she would feel worse about the time she has to spend away from Kevin if she were the biological mother. "I wonder how I would feel if I was blood parent or with Kevin from conception. Would the guilt or expectations be worse or different? I don't know, but the thought crosses my mind." Terry, in an interview, tries to describe the difference in her parent status from that of Tanya.

Terry: Tanya is his mommy. If he was sick, it was mommy, mommy, mommy, and he would do that with Tanya. He would show Tanya more of his (chicken pox) bumps than he would show me. There was a different nurturing type thing with her, where I'm more of a provider type. And I don't know. I think that role was set maybe because I make more money—or, I don't know if it's my personality or that role was kind of set there.

She continues:

> But there is a different—there are times I need to step back because I feel there is a line, even though it is not a defined line . . . but there's time when I feel it's time for me to step back and Tanya to take over because she's the parent parent.

Florence also expresses the need for more time away from the children. This may be because parenting is difficult for her in her struggle to overcome her childhood abuse. For whatever reasons, the slightly more distanced, more connected to the outside community stance seems comfortable for her, although this may change with the addition of a new baby.

> **Nisi:** You know we haven't really played Florence as mom out in the world. She's been more parent than mom—my partner—than mom. So, you know, if we really play her as mom with the new baby, I think it might be different.

Nisi talks about how she thinks they will have more of a partnership with the new baby—partly because Florence has been there from the beginning:

> **Nisi:** To be a part of the planning and the decision, and the birth, and the early months, and having that attachment happen right away—I think there is a lot there. I think it will be more equal and I think she'll have more opinions about the decisions that are made. Whereas now, a lot of the decisions for Dale and Frannie—she'd just rather leave them up to me.

However, even with the new baby, Nisi plans to maintain a somewhat more powerful mother status. They have agreed that in the event of a breakup, although Florence would be equally financially responsible, Nisi would still be the primary caretaker of all of the children, with Florence having a significant time with them.

The third co-parent, Lori, has had a more difficult time with this role, mainly because the children have contested her role as parent. She talks about how she had hoped for a more formal kind of acknowledgment of her parenting role. Because Nell has refused to accept that parenting from Lori, and Molly, presently at least, has also rebelled against it, Lori feels hurt and tries to make some sense of it. Was it because Nell was already thirteen when the family formed? Was it because the children formerly lived in an alcoholic home? Is it possibly related to personality or relationship issues for Cady and Lori? These questions remain unanswered. However, both Lori and Cady agree that Lori was willing to and worked hard at taking responsibility for and building relationships with the children. Although the children have both, at times, rejected Lori's parental status, Cady and Lori both acknowledge it and operate under its assumption.

As a group these parents tend to believe that the biological mother has a unique bond with the child—whether it be by nature or because they have been with the child since birth. Lori does believe that the biological tie to Mother is unique and irreplaceable. Her own tie to her mother was so elemental and primary that when her mother died "my body was different, and it has been ever since. It's that simple, and this is—the body I came from is no longer on earth."

Cady doesn't know if the biological tie is that important, but she does feel that it becomes more and more difficult for a step parent to bond with a child as the child gets older.

Co-parents benefit from the fact that they have somewhat less responsibility for the children. It allows them more freedom and flexibility to spend time outside of the family. Lori believes that this has helped her to ease some of her pain:

> **Lori:** I think part of what has helped me a lot is I just have other interests and a lot of friends and I have a whole life. I think that's real important to my sanity . . .

Terry attends community meetings, umpires during the summer, and generally spends more time than Tanya "off doing my own little thing."

Florence uses her time away from the family as a coping mechanism, finding that it gives her some breathing space and allows her to return with a more positive perspective. When she is feeling depleted, with no energy for the kids, she will take time to visit with friends or family, go to a movie, play cards. This strategy is supported by Nisi. So this trade-off—the biological mom having more power with the children, but also more responsibility—seems to work when the parents agree and are equally committed to it. It is not always an easy balance to maintain, but it can permit a positive co-parenting situation, as long as everyone's needs for affiliation are being adequately met.

All of these co-parents maintained a consultant role with the biological mothers and those mothers found this to be immensely helpful. Cady gives an example of this in her journal:

> Lori and I exchanged information about Molly—a message left from school on our answering machine that Lori delivered; a discussion followed about what this meant about her attendance—consequences if there was a problem. I asked Lori to pick up a prescription I'd ordered that was for Molly. Molly thanked Lori for picking it up. (I did, too.)

Florence suggested that when they have to make decisions about the kids, Nisi consults her as a concerned friend. They each give their opinion and discuss their fears. And their different perspectives help Nisi to come to a better decision.

In addition to acting as a consultant, each of these co-parents participated in all parenting activities, although they may have done them less often than the biological mom. When I asked couples if there was anything that the biological mother did exclusively, I was consistently told no—the co-parent does everything the biological mom does with the children. Although Tanya has days when she is solely responsible for Kevin, she also depends on Terry to take over parenting tasks when she can—"because I know I can't be everything and do everything." Whenever I asked questions about parenting tasks, such as bedtime rituals, baths, attending sports events or school events, running errands, chauffeuring, cooking and feeding, and getting the kids through their daily routines, I was told that the co-parents had done it all at times. There are no limits. Perhaps one of the most poignant stories comes from an interview with Lori. She says that there is "almost nothing that I haven't done, that I can think of either." This included pulling Nell's head out of the toilet when she was throwing up and nursing her through a hellish drug trip.

> **Lori:** Because [Nell] was afraid to sleep alone, she was afraid to just sleep, and she would want to sleep if someone was next to her so that if she woke up and she saw you there, then she knew she was in the real world, because she had seen other stuff. And Cady had given me a wonderful soft bear and I was trying to think of what to do with this kid, to give her some other sense of reality. So I gave her that bear, ended up giving her the bear, and I told her that she should hold the bear and if she could feel the bear, she would know that she was OK. And she kept that bear, she slept with that bear for a couple of years after that. It was really kind of cute . . . So there's almost no parenting thing I haven't been willing to do that I can think of—and several that I didn't have in mind experiencing in my lifetime—neither did Cady.

And Cady concurs:

> **Cady:** Yeah, and she was always willing to do just about anything that they [the kids] would let her do. She was really eager to get involved. . . . and I think actually she gives too much sometimes, but that's her. She does that with everybody too—it's not just the kids—that's Lori. And she gets great pleasure from that. So I mean I think of those things as mothering, and fixing food for them, you know, doing, making sure they got the stuff they want on the grocery list, also looking out for them. Sometimes when they ask me for something and I would say no, she would sometimes pull me aside and say, "Wait a minute, Nell probably really deserves this. Maybe we can figure out some way to compromise a little bit."

The co-parent may not be an equal partner in power with and responsibility for the children, but she is recognized by the partner (if not always the children) as an extremely important parenting person—who has powerful impact on both the biological mother and on the child. The co-parent allows the biological mother to have a life outside of parenting and work, to get a break, to not always have to do it alone. As Nisi expresses it:

> **Nisi:** I think that it's easier to parent with two people. I think it's a lot easier. I certainly have my days where I'm just at the end and it's nice to be able to retreat and let Florence take over. It's really nice—like last night I went out to eat with a friend, and [Florence] took care of the kids, and I just got to go out as an adult. And that's just—it's wonderful to be able to do that. And it's wonderful having somebody who knows the day-to-day goings–on that I can talk to about parenting and I can talk to about what's going on and what the issues are and how to deal with them. And it's calming to me. I saw it a lot when Florence was just coming for the weekends and then going back [to the other state] for the work week. I was just calmer and just better able to deal with all of it with her here, than when she was gone.

The Step Mother Stance

One of these families, Becky and Dory and Pauli, illustrates a stance which I refer to as the step mother stance. It is different from the co-parent stance in that in this family the step mother actually does more of the traditional mothering kinds of tasks, although the power with the child remains weighted on the biological mother's side. It parallels, in this sense, the stance found in many heterosexual step mother families. In these families, the step mother enters the family with all of the societal expectations that she can and will naturally mother the children.

> We have learned that in a family a woman is nurturer, the emotional linchpin for family members, and has primary responsibility for meeting other's needs. Many women try to succeed in step families by attempting to live up to these norms. While some women have found this workable, others

have found it painful or self-defeating. (Maglin and Schniede-wind, 1989, p. 8)

The step mother role in heterosexual families is particularly difficult, then, since women are socially prescribed to be the main nurturers in the family, and yet fathers, by virtue of biology, legality, or simply time lived with the children, retain more power with them. This imbalance between responsibility for and power with the children creates tension.

Both Becky and Dory agree that Becky is simply more of a mothering-type personality. As Dory puts it, "Any of the mothering things would be like Becky's scope." Dory describes Becky as more nurturing, the constant one, the more consistent one. Because of the limitations of Dory's attention deficit disorder, Becky is the one who has to keep track of things. She tries to remember when Pauli's school assignments are due. She is the one that the doctors and the school personnel turn to when they need information on Pauli. Dory describes how she is becoming more responsible for that kind of task, because Becky's job keeps her away from the home more than Dory's job does at present:

> **Dory:** . . . and when Becky was handling all of it, everything was OK. But now, because of her job and my job, I have to get more involved in it, which means we are having more and more messy gaps of things that aren't being handled right. And I feel bad.

In the times that I spent with this family, it was quite obvious that Becky was very important to Pauli. She would often check in with Becky, seeking confirmation, saying such things as, "You buyed that for me, huh, Becky?" In her interview, Pauli notes that, "Becky does a lot of things for me—like she copied a book one day for me." She also respects Becky's opinions about things. She was telling me about the O.J. Simpson trial, which was going on at the time of her interview, and she said, "Like you know O.J. killed her." I asked her if that was what she thought and she replied, "I think so—that's what Becky thinks!"

In spite of her obvious dependence on Becky, Pauli has a contested relationship with her, too. In discussing her fighting with

Becky, Pauli observes that "I don't really fight with my mom as much." Becky and Dory have struggled to make sense of this combativeness that Pauli has with Becky. They wonder if it is just a personality difference:

> **Dory:** . . . but there has always been—I mean, [Becky's] more the nurturing, more patient. I think that sometimes Becky would like to be closer with Pauli, but there's a barrier on being able to interact. In other words, Becky's way of looking at things and Pauli's way of looking at things are not the same. And sometimes Pauli and I do look at things the same. So I can explain something to her and she'll get it. And Becky could be beating her head against the wall forever and she won't get it, you know. But I don't have the patience to do that on a continuing basis.

They feel that perhaps, since Dory and Pauli both have ADD that they understand each other better. The whole ADD issue is a major struggle for this family. Becky thinks that it gets used too often as an excuse for unacceptable behavior—Dory is more likely to believe that the misbehavior is unavoidable due to the fluctuations of the medication. On the other hand, Becky does emphasize with how hard it must be for Pauli.

> **Becky:** So when we are properly medicated things seem to go OK. It's when we are on that downer, that up again, that we are having the big difficulties. And I don't know—to me it would be awful to be like this all day long, all day long. Very stressful, I think.

Becky also worries that Pauli may be angry with her because she sees Becky as the one who took her away from her grandma. The transition from Grandma's care to Becky and Dory's care was abrupt, since Grandma had to go to the hospital. And since Dory was still in the military at that time, Becky became the major caretaker for Pauli.

Regardless of the causes, it is clear that all three of these family members see Becky and Pauli's relationship as the most problematic and contested. I did not observe this in my limited time with the family. I did see Pauli act out—refusing to put her gloves in her pockets so that they wouldn't get lost, cutting off the hair of her dolls, getting distracted and not accomplishing what needed to be done—but when I was there, Dory handled Pauli's misbehavior. And my observation was that Pauli did try to resist Dory's authority. However, apparently when Becky and Pauli are alone together, Pauli is particularly difficult for Becky to handle—often insisting that her mother wouldn't make her do that, or that her mother would change Becky's decision on discipline. And according to Becky, this continues to happen:

> **Becky:** This morning, we had Eggo waffles. Pauli knows she does not get any sugar on them—no syrup, no, no. "Can I have syrup?" No. "Can I have syrup?" No. Well, there is enough for a couple of waffles for me and I had a couple more and so I put strawberry jam on them. "Well, I want some strawberry jam." No. I'm not going to give you any sugar— I'm not doing it. "Yeah, I'm going to tell Mommy!" So, call her right now and tell her. "I don't know the number." Well, here, I'll dial it for you. "She'll make you change it!" I said, no she won't. "Yes she will!" No, she won't. "Yes, she will." Finally I said, I'll tell you what, when you are all done with these waffles, you tell me how much strawberry jelly you had. Well, she didn't get any. . . . But to this day, no matter what, no matter how much Dory has tried to start backing me, [she still thinks that Mommy will change it].

Neither Dory nor Becky believes that the biological mother necessarily has a unique tie to the child, but both of them agree that Dory may understand Pauli better at times, especially because of the ADD connection. In addition, they disagree about who has the power to make decisions regarding Pauli. Becky has a sense that she is less than equal—Dory disagrees. When I asked if they are pretty equal partners in decision making, they responded as follows:

> **Becky:** Sometimes, sometimes not. Because she's, "Well, I gave birth to her." She doesn't exactly say that . . .
>
> **Dory:** No, I've never said that. I have a tendency to be more, well, as we already discussed—I'll make a blanket statement

and Becky will take it for exactly what it means. This is how it's going to be. That, in my mind, is probably not what I intended, so there's decisions that get made without me realizing that that was "a decision." You know, I said something Becky took it to heart, and that's the way it goes. With the major or the larger decisions, where we actually have a discussion on it, I believe we are equal. Usually she's more equal, because she's got a memory, so she can remember what we discussed.

Like the co-parent families, both Dory and Becky participate in all the parenting tasks, from bedtime rituals to driving Pauli to appointments, to school conferences, etc. The difference is that in this family Becky takes on more of the nurturing tasks as well as the organizing and orchestrating of Pauli's parenting. They appear to be struggling with ways to cope with the impact of ADD in their lives, as well as how to address Pauli's resistance to Becky as a parent. They are making an effort to present a more united parenting front to Pauli as one strategy. Hopefully, they will have the time and energy now to work out some other effective strategies—this is one of their stated goals. As this happens, they may transition into one of the other parenting stances.

Clearly Dory is aware of and appreciative of the important parenting role that Becky plays in Pauli's life:

Dory: Becky makes sacrifices (for Pauli) continuously. And sometimes I'm not even aware. I mean, she just does things that, you know—she does them. I mean, there's times that I am probably more selfish as far as concerning myself with Pauli. But I think with Becky, Pauli always comes first.

This validation has been crucial to the health and developing stability of this family. But there is continuing tension with this step mother role since the responsibility and power are unbalanced between the adults. Whether this is a transition stance or one that persists remains to be seen.

The Co-Mother Stance

The third different stance I call the co-mother. One family—Delia, Kathy, Diana, and Talia—took this stance. The defining characteristic of this stance is that the two mothers have equal rights and responsibilities with the children. For Delia and Kathy, this was a conscious decision that they made at the beginning of their relationship.

> **Delia:** . . . from the very beginning I always said she was going to earn the status [of mother] and I kind of shoved it in everybody's face. And it wasn't like some of our friends would have relationships and they still seem to—the bio-mom still had more status. . . . Yeah, with a partner. The bio-mom was really kind of protective of this little nesting and kind of pushed, even the other mother may want to step in—the other partner may want to come in and be more involved. And she just told me that is not going to work. You got to let go and you've got to do this parenting thing on an equal turf. So that wasn't hard for me to say, in fact, I would sometimes say "I'm tired. I don't want to deal with this. You go be mom. You go tell them to wash their hands again—don't be coming to me and saying they're not listening to you. Figure it out. I ain't stepping in here now as the disciplinarian. You are going to have to weather it."

Even though they agreed to parent equally, it wasn't always easy—especially in the beginning. In discussing one of the most difficult times of the relationship, Kathy says:

> **Kathy:** I would have to go back to the early days, and I think the lowest point would be where, whether or not it was legitimate, I nevertheless felt . . . I really wasn't part of the family and I was somehow off to the side, despite all the talk.

Kathy reported that Delia was sometimes unsympathetic toward her insecurities, and Delia admits that was probably true. On the other hand, Delia was willing to share parenting—even pushing to share it—in spite of the fact that that was sometimes difficult for her, too. I asked Delia how she was able to let go so completely:

Delia: I guess I never saw the children as a possession. I saw them as little people that need to—they are in your care, you are their guardian. . . . And I don't think I ever thought it was easy to do it alone. . . . So sort of out of a selfish thing—I wasn't going to be the one that was the only . . . these are your kids if they are noisy. You deal with it—if they are crying at night, you get up. So selfishly I thought, no, this isn't the way I want it. I want some help here.

. . . I think I've mentioned before that I was a little jealous when Talia was really little because she would fall down and run to Kathy. And at times my nose got a little broken—I'm here, too—well, once in a while. But when you look at the situation, where I was the one working nights and not there—and who did wipe the nose and kiss the cut? It just made sense the child would run to that person. So I think with that I started to open up and see parenting as it really is. It has nothing to do with what you did physically—it's the kids focusing on who cares for them, who nurtures them, who listens. And even now, as they are older, I think the four of us have a preference for one or the other. And there are certain things that we can talk about easier. So we've picked up on our styles and different things, what's more comfortable, who listens better when I'm doing this, you know. And you go to that person for your needs and you can't always meet it all.

Personality wise, Delia feels that Kathy is a more nurturing person—"She's better at that than I am." She also sees Kathy as a softer touch than she is.

Delia: And I think I'm going to say she's the soft touch and I'm the one that, cause I pretty much . . . "Hey, this is it, you are grounded, end of story. Get out of my face. I don't want to hear any more whining." And I don't have a problem with that. Whereas, little miss mom over here, could rethink it, or say, Oh, I think two days is enough." Or she—to this day, and I have never done this—she brings them little treats.

At this point in the interview, Kathy jumps in to remind Delia that there have been issues that are important to her and she has been the stricter parent—such as practicing the piano, and following through on commitments. And Delia agrees.

Due to the flexibility of her job, Kathy probably spent more time with the kids, taking on more of the traditional mothering tasks. For example, Kathy did almost all of the connecting with the school. Delia reports, "I could never arrange it with my work schedule ever to go. So they just sort of started calling Kathy." And Talia agrees.

> **Talia (16):** . . . and my mom wasn't always able to do like—if I got sick, you know, Kathy was more likely to come and pick me up—not always, because my mom did it sometimes. But, I don't know, I always remember Kathy because, like right now in my school, she's like involved on like all these committees and stuff. She's always been really involved.

But Kathy still had to work twice as hard to earn equal parenting status, regardless of how willing Delia was to share the children. She says that a lot of work went into building the relationships with the kids—"I talked a lot. I just spent hours and hours talking to the kids." She also spent time with them and got involved in their lives. But she always had to bear the burden of the outside forces that denied her mother status. Certainly the girls' father tried to denigrate her status. But it was more than just him.

Kathy says that she didn't realize in the beginning of their relationship that she and Delia would have to work every day "at establishing my presence as parental." Even though the girls experienced Kathy as a mother within the home, it was constantly questioned outside of the home. As Kathy says, "So here we were asking them to reject what dominant society was telling them and accept what two people, at that point in their lives, were telling them. And I know it was difficult for them." Even now, Kathy feels insecure about how the kids' friends perceive her—as a parent or not. Society's insistence on heterosexual supremacy takes its toll on Kathy's security as mother.

But the children do see and experience Kathy as another mother. When I asked Talia how Kathy and Delia parented her, she said, "I don't know—they've always just been my parents." And Diana concurs:

Diana (20): Well, I don't like the term step family, because that's not what we are, because to me a step family is—you had your family and didn't, your parents didn't want to stay married. So they married someone else and that third parent is not as equal, you know. You can ask her for things and maybe she'll help raise you, but she's not as good as the two parents you had before. As far as I'm concerned, I had two parents— my mother and Kathy. And I had this weirdo thing on the other hand [her dad]. Because, I don't remember when my parents were married.

Within this family, Delia and Kathy are apparently equal parenting partners, both taking on traditional fathering as well as mothering roles. Outside of the family, however, Kathy's role is perceived in many different ways. That difference will be further examined in Chapter 7.

CONCLUSION

The participants reported that it has been difficult to create and maintain family, but they have been willing to work at it, to process and address the problems, and to reap some important benefits.

These families demonstrate the salience of preference, as opposed to gender, in determining how the tasks and roles of parenting are divided. They also illustrate how responsibility for children creates parenthood, regardless of biology and/or gender. This is not always a smooth process. Children's needs and fears may conflict with parents' needs and fears. Some parents, like Lori and Becky, may have to settle for lesser parental power with the children, even though they are willing to be responsible for them. But they have shown that they can persist, in spite of the difficulties, and that time may eventually secure a stronger parental role for them:

Lori: I think the bottom line for Nell may have been that she saw that even when she did her LSD trip and even when she went to live with her father and all of those things that we still had a relationship with her and wanted to have one, and I think maybe that surprised her.

and later,

> **Lori:** A family, these are relationships, that kind of thing. And that even if right now you don't . . . aren't . . . happy with somebody, they are still part of your life, and things like that. [The kids] don't always want to hear our reasons for this, but we try to give them to them anyway.

The co-parent stance appears to be a particularly good choice when the nonbiological parent prefers to take a more distanced parenting role and the biological parent enjoys the closer, more nurturing role. Children, especially if they are older, or are insecure about their relationship with their mother, or have lived with the mother in a single-parent home; may resist forming a parent-like relationship with another adult. Nonbiological parents may then have to adjust to less of a parental role with the children. However, they may still fill the role of co-parent in relation to the biological mother, who may rely on their advice and help with the children. It may also be that there are biological mothers who prefer not to share parenting, or prefer not to share certain aspects of parenting. The biological mothers in this study appeared to want to share parenting, although some clearly enjoyed taking the ultimate emotional responsibility for their children.

It is not completely clear whether biological parents in this stance chose partners who enjoyed the more distanced parenting role as a way of maintaining the ultimate power with and responsibility for the children, or if the nonbiological mothers simply accepted that role as available, or if it was a combination of preference and acceptance.

The step mother stance appears to be taken when the step mother, whether by preference or acceptance, takes the more nurturing parental role and the biological parent takes a more distanced parenting role. However, if the children or both parents don't fully embrace those roles, tension is created.

Pauli is presently rejecting this stance and Dory, at least in the past and perhaps even presently, has also resisted it. This makes me believe that this stance may be transitory in this family. If Pauli (and Dory? and Becky?) becomes more comfortable with Becky in the nurturing parent role, they could move toward a co-mom stance.

However, if the resistance continues, Dory may move toward fulfilling more of the nurturing parent role and Becky may move toward the more distanced role—taking on a co-parent stance. A third option, of course, is that they continue living with some tension regarding the roles. Persistence may eventually lead to more acceptance of and comfort with this stance.

In the co-mom family, Kathy, the nonbiological mother, may have initially taken on more of the nurturing tasks. Her job allowed her to spend more time with the children in the earlier stages of their family building. Perhaps this helped her to establish a strong mothering bond with the children. Delia was unique in this group of biological mothers in her desire and commitment to completely share mothering with Kathy from the beginning of their relationship. Diana and Talia, who were only four and one when the family got together, accepted Kathy as a mother rather quickly. So this stance was created with a biological mother who really desired a shared mothering partnership, a nonbiological mother who preferred an active mothering role, and children who grew to accept both women as mothers.

I have tried to illustrate that there are many circumstances which affect how the family determines what the step role will be. What seems important is not what kind of definition the family arrives at, but rather if that definition provides some measure of comfort and security for each family member. Any family, regardless of its structure, can have times of conflict and unrest. The real test of family health is whether they can continue to grow and and become strong. The data show that these families have struggled with challenges but have also learned from them.

Family is about connections—deep and enduring connections that keep us from unrelenting loneliness. As Kathy writes, "Our parenting activities included keeping track of Diana and Talia's whereabouts and feeding them." Keeping track of each other and feeding each other—that is family.

Chapter 6

Forging Families in a Heterosexual Supremacist Environment

INTRODUCTION

Bell hooks (1987) describes white supremacy as an all pervasive ideology and behavior in the United States' society—a value/belief system that is still embodied by whites, even when they do not embrace racism. Blacks, she says, can also be involved in the maintenance of white supremacy. For example, assimilation is a strategy that encourages the oppressed to become like the oppressors. This reinforces and helps to maintain white supremacy.

The term heterosexual supremacy is used here in a similar sense. A heterosexual supremacist society is one that idealizes the male-female love bond and male-female sexuality as superior—spiritually, morally, physically, emotionally, and intellectually. Based on this belief system, lesbian/gay/bisexual/transgender people should work toward affirming and demonstrating their similarities with, and try to be like, heterosexual people. This is assimilation. However, assimilation involves giving up what makes one unique and different, and works to perpetuate the system of domination. It is only in the acknowledgment that difference can be positive that the structure of domination is exposed and ultimately changed.

This chapter addresses how the participant families cope with the "mundane extreme" (McAdoo, 1986) environment of stress caused by heterosexual supremacy. The temptations to assimilate as a strategy for coping may be especially great for lesbian mothers for three reasons: (1) because we can often "pass" as straight; (2) because we were likely raised to be heterosexual and therefore have an intimate understanding of heterosexuality; and (3) because there is a constant underlying threat that we could lose our children (by being declared unfit mothers). It *is* important to illuminate our similarities with the heterosexual majority—similarities based on our common humanity. We can and do form loving partnerships. We can and do successfully nurture our children. But, in order to resist the trap of assimilation, lesbians must also celebrate and affirm our differences from the mainstream (Wright, 1994).

This chapter examines some of the impacts (both positive and negative) of heterosexual supremacy on children and their parents in lesbian step families, as well as the impacts on the family life itself. Using the model of minority family stress (McAdoo, 1986), I describe what the participants identify as stressors created by heterosexual supremacy and their strategies for coping with those stressors. First, the chapter addresses children's issues and strategies, then parents', and finally the impact of community on family life.

CHILDREN

Pollack (1987) identifies three erroneous assumptions commonly held by judges and mental health professionals who are called in to testify in child custody cases: That lesbians are sexually promiscuous, liable to sexually harm the children, and sexually maladjusted. Second, that the children of lesbian parents will grow up to be gay or will have confused sex-role identification. And last, that the children could be socially stigmatized and seriously harmed if the mother's lesbianism is widely known. Pollack discusses how the first and second assumptions have been clearly shown in several research studies to be untrue. However, she sidesteps the third assumption, claiming that it is, after all, an example of blaming the victim. What do the children of lesbians actually experience as a result of heterosexual supremacy?

These children tell us that they *are* sometimes teased about having lesbian moms, if and when people find out. For example, Kevin's moms recount a situation that was quite painful for him. Some kids had been talking about gays and lesbians on the school bus and Kevin told them that his mom was a lesbian. Then two of them started pointing at him, laughing and saying, "Kevin, gross! Kevin's mom is a lesbian! "And he didn't really understand why they would do that. He just thought that he was joining in the conversation and didn't really understand why they laughed at him. Pauli also reports that she has been teased about having two moms. She says that " a lot" of kids teased her about having two moms when she was in the first grade—calling her "mental" and "retarded," When I asked her why she thought that they teased her, she replied "They think it is funny that I have two moms." However, Pauli says that she has not been teased much in her second grade classroom.

Some of the older children have been suspected of or accused of being gay or lesbian themselves. Talia talks about her boyfriend's confusion. Once she made a comment about a girl looking very beautiful when she was dancing and her boyfriend wondered if being raised by lesbians might make Talia a lesbian too. Diana believed that her father was afraid that she might become lesbian because of her mother's influence in her life.

Children of lesbians (and all children) hear a lot of misinformation about gay and lesbian people. Talia "freaked out" when she was in the fifth grade and she read a pamphlet on AIDS that she got in school. She thought that it implied that if you were gay, you were likely to die from AIDS. She was so upset that she asked her mom if she had AIDS and had to talk it out with her. Certainly, children often hear derogatory statements about gay and lesbian people. Faggot is one of the more common put-downs in high schools. Cady tells about hearing a child call someone a "boy/girl" when she was chauffeuring her daughter to some event. Molly once made an offhand comment to Lori about the "weird things you and mom do"—an allusion to misinformation about lesbian sexuality.

Sometimes these children were misinformed or even rejected by extended family because of their mother's lesbianism. Delia, for example, thought that her father gave her children less attention and less affection than he gave his other grandchildren. And, as already reported, Delia's mother told Diana that Delia was "abnormal." So, while these children reported very little overt teasing of themselves personally, they still strongly get the message that lesbianism is not OK. They get this message through the absence of lesbians in their everyday existence outside of home. Heterosexuality permeates their lives at school, in books, on TV—everywhere except home. When they do hear something about lesbians or gay men, it is likely to be derogatory or frightening—conflicting with their experience and creating dissonance in their lives.

In fact, the children in this sample have experienced very little trauma from being teased by friends and classmates about their different family structures. Dale reports that no one really teases him about it. Frannie says that none of her best friends tease her at all, and writes in her journal: "Yosily nobody hurts my feelings about having lesbian moms." In some cases, children are not teased because they have successfully managed to hide the fact that their mother is lesbian. Molly simply hasn't told many people about it and she is not open about her family situation at school—so no one teases her. But even when the kids are open, they experience little teasing. In fact, they are probably more likely to be teased about other things.

Nisi reports that Frannie was teased by two girls at her gymnastics classes because they thought her haircut was too short and she looked like a boy. "I mean she was just shocked! She just couldn't believe that anybody could be that rude!" Dale told me that he hasn't been teased much about anything—except about how skinny he is. This is not to say that the children of lesbians don't get teased. There are documented cases and horror stories of the pain that some children experience (Rafkin, 1990). The somewhat astonishing lack of teasing experienced by these children may be due to the fact that most of them live in a fairly progressive and liberal community, or it may be due to the strategies that they and their parents employ to deflect or diminish such activity.

The striking revelation from this data was not that the children actually experienced a lot of trauma from the teasing, but rather how great their fears were about being teased. These children did have a lot of fears—even when they had not been the victims of any attacks. Talia (16) talks about the various stages she went through in dealing with her own fears:

> I was never teased. I just went through phases. Like when I was in fourth grade, you know, then I just thought it was neato. I would just go around like, "My mom's gay." I didn't know what it meant. I just knew it was different. But then, [in] sixth

grade, I was like, "Oh no," my mom's not gay. No—she just has a roommate. And then I lied about it for so many years, which was just stupid, because I had my big-mouthed sister, two grades ahead of me and she would tell everyone. It's like they all knew I was lying, but nobody really said anything. It was like, OK, sure. Then by ninth grade it was just, yeah, so what . . . . It's not like I ever got teased or anything. I think it was—I just thought that they would or something.

These children seem to carry around with them a certain uneasiness and anxiety, even when they haven't experienced any overt homophobia. When I asked Dale if he was sometimes afraid that people would find out about his mom's lesbianism, he replied, "Well, not bad—but it's just if they tease me."

Janet: But you said . . . has anybody ever teased you yet?

Dale: No, not really.

Pauli, who has experienced very little homophobia up to this point, tells me that she will definitely be straight when she grows up—because she doesn't want her children to be teased.

Pauli: I think that I don't want . . . I don't want to go through the hassle of my kids being teased by some other kids. So I'm going to get married. I'm going to get married with a man, because I don't want my kids to be teased. And I'm going to have four of them, so I don't want the four of them being teased. And I don't want to hear everything coming home saying that they got teased. I don't want to hear that. I want to hear a good report, like they didn't get teased today.

Janet: Do you think kids get teased about a lot of things though?

Pauli: Yeah, I do.

Janet: I mean, you said that you get teased about your name.

Pauli: Lots of kids get beat up in that school. Lots of kids get pushed. Lots of kids get their teeth ripped out—well, not the teeth. But, you know, it's an angry world out there.

Janet: So, even if you get married, your kids may get teased about something else, huh?

Pauli: You know, like maybe because they . . . boys go to ballet, you know. But I hope that my kids don't do it, because it's awful hard to grow up being teased. And I don't like being teased so I certainly know that if I do grow up having four kids, I don't want to hear them being teased because it's awful for me. Because, you know, if it's hard, it certainly will be hard for them. So I don't want that happening, though. But, I do want . . . would like to pass on what my mother did—you know, get married with a gay . . . but I think that my kids would get teased a lot. I don't want that to happen. But I would like to pass it on, you know. I would like to pass it on if kids would be more nicer.

Pauli, at age seven, is so afraid of teasing that she has already determined that she will not be lesbian and will not put her own children in this position. Even children who experienced little or no teasing during their grade school years may become particularly secretive and protective when they reach middle school. Although Talia experiences her big sister as a loudmouth who kept coming out for her, Kathy and Delia can remember a time when it was Talia, at the time in grade school, who was more open. She wanted to bring in an article about her lesbian mothers that was in the newspaper for show-and-tell at school. Diana, who was in fifth or sixth grade at the time, was adamant that Talia could not bring that to school. Cady and Lori report that Molly became more secretive and afraid when she was in fifth or sixth grade and "she didn't want to be different."

Lori: Yeah, in her opinion, they had nobody there [in her school] who was divorced or any other kind of thing. So it was an issue that year, but it was also an issue that year because she was having a big tug of war with me about her mother's attention. Her mom had attention for me—she had less.

Although children have complex emotions, they do seem to become more afraid of being different in any way during the middle school years. If they have been relatively open until that time, they will likely return to an accepting state when they mature. The key point here is the extent to which all of these children had fears about being in lesbian families—regardless of whether or not they had any personal experience with homophobia. Nisi describes it as a "free-floating anxiety" and tells this chilling story:

> **Nisi:** I think it was a year and a half ago—we went to a winter solstice—you were there. As part of the ceremony, the celebration was letting go, you know, what do you want to let go of as a family. What do you want to leave behind as a family. And we went like into a blanket amongst this group of trees and then talked about it ourselves. And what Frannie said at that time was what she wanted [to let go of] was [her fear] that somebody would kill us because we were a lesbian family.

> **Janet:** Wow, that gives me the chills.

> **Nisi:** And that was what she wanted to let go of—that feeling. And so it really is a big issue for them. So I think life would just be less anxious [if there were no homophobia]. They'd feel like they wouldn't have to be on guard; they'd feel safer; they'd feel like it was easier to be themselves with their friends and let everybody know who they were and what their core identity was. Introductions would be easier—I mean, everything would be easier.

For the most part, in these families, it is the fears that stress the children more than actual occurrences of homophobia. What causes such strong fears in the children of lesbians? I believe it may have more to do with the covert messages of heterosexual supremacy than with the overt teasing that children experience.

The place where children spend most of their time, outside of home, is in the schools. What impact, then, might the schools have on creating and maintaining these children's fears? I am reminded of a story I heard once in an attempt to illustrate what it is like growing up in an alcoholic home. Even though there is an elephant in the room (the alcoholism), no one talks about it and everyone acts as if it is not there. It is this secrecy which gives birth to a host of fears and insecurities. Children of lesbians don't usually experience the elephant in the room at home, where lesbianism is accepted as normal. But I believe that they may experience something similar to that at school, and in society in general, where their most basic and important experience—their safest haven—is simply erased. It either doesn't exist—or it is defined as bad in those few instances when it is addressed.

The children in this study did have a few overtly negative experiences with the schools. Talia, when she was in second grade, wanted to make two Mother's Day cards at school and her teacher said that she could only make one. When Diana was a senior in high school, her moms sent one of her baby pictures in to the yearbook with the caption "From your two moms" and the picture was mysteriously lost and not printed.

Sometimes the teacher's attempt to be inclusive may be interpreted negatively by the child. For example, Pauli feels like her teacher is outing her:

> **Pauli:** But sometimes she tells all the kids. You know, like, when she's telling me something what to do, like maybe I did it wrong—maybe I did something wrong or something like that—she yells out sometimes. She says that I have two moms and like nobody cares. But I have this boyfriend in my class who really doesn't like me and I think he doesn't want to like me because I have two moms.

> **Janet:** So sometimes your teacher says to the other kids that you have two moms and that embarrasses you?

> **Pauli:** You know, like when you get in trouble or something like that and you get mad and they might accidentally say something about your parents—and she says out all the time, she says moms.

The teacher's intentions are not totally clear in this case. It is difficult to say if this is an attempt to be inclusive or a subtle put-down. But it does appear that Pauli experiences it as a put-down.

On the other hand, most of these participants had positive things to say about particular schools or teachers. The two adolescents who attend alternative schools felt that their schools were generally very accepting of differences, although Molly is not out at her school. Diana feels that the private grade school that she attended for awhile had a very accepting atmosphere. It seems that in schools where there is a lot of diversity based on race and/or family structure the children are more likely to encounter a sense of acceptance. These participants expressed that daycare centers, alternative schools, and private schools that they attended were likely to be less oppressive than public schools. Perhaps this is because daycare centers and private schools can be selected based on whatever issues parents and kids see as important, and alternative schools are often dedicated to working with children who haven't fit in well to the traditional school setting.

But the participant families who are out to the school personnel (all of the families except Lori, Cady, and Molly) have generally had positive or at least neutral reactions. Kevin has, so far, been very open about having two moms in his open classroom school setting. As Terry says, "And he does it [says that he has two moms] in an environment where we are open with his teachers and we expect his teachers to protect him and they do." When I asked Nisi how her beginning of the year school conferences went, she said that she was really impressed with Frannie's teacher, who really seemed to hear and respond to Frannie. She liked Dale's teacher, too. She came out to their teachers at the school conferences because she wanted the teachers to know so that the kids would feel comfortable and safe with it. The children whose teachers know about their mothers' lesbianism all felt that their teachers were OK about it. So, just as with the issue of teasing, there seems to be few overt, personal negative experiences that these children had as a result of homophobia in the schools.

Instead, once again, what seems to affect the children most is the absence of any positive or even neutral feedback or information on lesbian families. There are at least three factors that may work to increase and maintain children's fears. The first is their accurate understandings of the very real threat of violence against lesbians and gay men. In a national survey of antigay/lesbian violence, the

National Gay and Lesbian Task Force (1984) found that 19 percent of the sample reported having been punched, hit, kicked, or beaten at least once in their lives because of sexual orientation, 44 percent had been threatened with physical violence, 94 percent had experienced some kind of victimization. As the AIDS epidemic and the controversies over gays and lesbians in the military and other issues have increasingly pushed gay men and lesbians into mainstream media attention, the attacks against us are also more visible in society's discourse. Young people may be especially subjected to antilesbian/gay violence, even if they are not gay or lesbian, but are for some reason perceived to be. In a survey of 2,823 junior and senior high school students, for example, the New York State Governor's Task Force on Bias-Related Violence found respondents to be not only negatively biased toward gay persons but "sometimes viciously and with threats of violence" (DeStefano, 1988, p. 7). Children in lesbian homes cannot help but be aware of this devastating violence. As Berrill (1992) points out:

> Although more research is needed to better understand the scope and nature of anti-gay violence and victimization, there is ample evidence to show that the problem is severe. Indeed, the quantitative and qualitative data gathered thus far are a frightening testament to the human cost of anti-gay bigotry. What no measurement of the problem can adequately convey, however, is the fear and anguish experienced not only by the survivors, but also by the communities of which they are a part. (p. 40)

I would add that the toll on our families and children is equally high. This is the context in which our children live. In addition to expecting their own fearful reactions to the culture of antilesbian/gay violence, children also vicariously experience their parents' anxieties. When parents are protective toward children, children may experience fear as a result. I will discuss this protective stance taken by parents further in the next section.

Finally, the scarcity of positive images and feedback these children get about their families from society, creates a sense of fear and secrecy. The societal message is that they are not supposed to be proud of their families.

What are the children's strategies for coping with the heterosexual supremacy that permeates their lives? One of the most difficult issues facing gay men and lesbians is the problem of authenticity. When do I come out and when do I not? What helps me make that decision? If I don't come out, am I lying? Although all of the adults in this study saw honesty as an important value, they also recognized that it wasn't always necessary or smart to come out. Sometimes it just isn't appropriate—it isn't the level on which we are dealing. Other times it is too nerve-wracking, or a lost cause, or even dangerous. The children of lesbians struggle with this issue, too.

Molly (15) simply doesn't talk about it with her friends or anyone else. She says, "I never really told anyone." She knows that some of her friends are aware of her mother's lesbianism, but she doesn't talk with them about it. When I asked Cady and Lori how the kids have explained their family to their friends, Cady replied, "As far as I know, Molly doesn't explain it, although she knows that friends know about it." And Lori adds, "She calls me your friend, or her aunt, and stuff like that." Cady continues:

> I think now she just introduces you as Lori and doesn't explain it much. Most of her friends are pretty stable—she's had a group of friends for about three years and we've had discussions at times about how they feel about this and how she feels about how they feel. And those close friends all—I've said to her that they seem very, very accepting. And she [replies], "Well, of course they would be. That's the way they are. But not everyone is that way."

Cady later mentions in her journal that when she went to a school meeting she didn't consider inviting Lori. "Molly would have a fit." She goes on to say that she and Lori feel OK about it—that "these people don't have to know the details of my relationship or household situation." So Molly's strategy of not telling seems to fit fairly comfortably with her parents' stances toward coming out.

A strategy of not telling may not work so well for children whose parents are more out in the community. In that case, a child who longs not to be different, particularly a young adolescent, may decide to lie. In Talia's case, she even lied to a friend who knew the truth and the friend never confronted her about it. "She knows [my mom] is a lesbian but she's never mentioned the fact that, 'Oh yeah, so you were just lying about it all those years, huh?'"

Younger children may especially struggle with this issue because they know it is not OK to lie, but don't yet understand situational ethics. When I asked Dale if there were times when he has been afraid to tell people, he answered yes. When asked what he does then, he responded, "I don't tell . . . . I don't lie, because they don't ask me." It would help younger children particularly if their parents would do some strategizing with them on this issue of honesty versus not telling so that children feel less confused about making this decision—a decision which some of us find very difficult even as adults! Frannie (8) suggests that a compromise on this issue may be the best policy at times. She says that she will often wait until other children get to know her as a friend before she tells them about her moms:

> But then after the kids start to get to know me and I tell that I have three moms, you know that they don't really mind because after they start to know that I'm not different or I'm not mean or I'm not different just because I have lesbian moms, they start to realize that it's OK to have a friend.

> **Janet:** That's smart. Good thinking. I think you are right. That happens with me, too. I'm a teacher. At the beginning of every semester, I tell the students that I'm a lesbian because I want them to know somebody who is—so they can see that I'm not really that weird.

> **Frannie:** Yeah, and sometimes I hesitate. I'm worried that someone will tease me at the beginning of the school year. So sometimes after I get to know them better then I tell them and they can't say, well, you are weird, because they've been playing with me.

Children do use several other strategies to cope with homophobia, potential homophobia, and ignorance. Once people do know about it and if they begin to tease or make derogatory comments, younger children often use the strategy of ignoring them. Pauli says that when kids tease her and try to hurt her feelings, "It doesn't do anything to me because I ignore it." Although it is clear from Pauli's interview that teasing does indeed "do something" to her, the strategy of ignoring the perpetrator does often work to stop the abuse. Kevin (8), Dale (8), and Frannie (8) all use the strategy of ignoring mean comments and find that it does sometimes stop the attack. Teasing is meant to get a response.

Both younger and older children also use the strategy of simply coming out. Coming out can actually have a protective function because it puts others on notice that you are not ashamed. Diana used this strategy with a friend who has a gay father when they were both new ninth graders at the high school. Delia explains:

> **Delia:** Well, when Diana and [her friend] Tilly got to high school, I think, in order to jump the gun on the other kids, realizing that everybody by now knew their situations—Tilly has a gay father. And so they would kind of skip down the hall and say things like, "Oh, so how's your gay dad doing?" And "Oh, fine, and how's your lezzie mom?"

Both Diana and Talia found that joking about it was a way of disarming their friends and potential attackers. Diana says, "I would just joke about it so that people would feel comfortable talking about it." And Talia says, "Now I just . . . nowadays I just basically come out and say it, kind of like in a joking manner—like, just warning you, my mom is gay."

Younger children also use the strategy of coming out as the following story about Frannie illustrates. Florence and Nisi went to Frannie's Brownie troop dinner. When the daughters were introducing their parents, Frannie whispered to Nisi, asking her what she should do. Both Nisi and Florence encouraged her to do what felt comfortable for her. But when her turn came, she introduced Nisi as her mother and Florence as her mother's partner.

The strategy of coming out works as a way to separate our friends from our enemies, or a way of identifying peoples' levels of acceptance and/or comfort. It is easier to come out when one can accept the idea that everyone doesn't have to be a friend or to like oneself. As Delia and Kathy comment, Talia (16) was able to stop lying about her moms when she matured enough to realize that "if they are so stupid [to react negatively], I don't need to have them as friends and I don't care." This attitude change occurred as Talia went from middle school to high school. It may also be easier to come out when we are in touch with our righteous anger. Anger can be an empowering emotion when it names oppression. As Dale (8) wrote in his journal, "It makes me mad when I think about Lesbian parents not giving as much rights." And Frannie (8) says in her interview, when asked why she thinks some people don't like lesbians:

> Well, they might think that someone is different and they don't like that. They might think that we are mean, just because we have a partner. But I don't think it's any different—they just love a woman instead of a man. I mean, there's no law about not liking a man or something, liking a woman instead. And . . . I mean, it wasn't very—I don't think it's very, not really good thinking that someone is different makes them mean.

Children, then, are empowered as they understand that lesbianism is not the problem—homophobia is. Even Molly (15), who is probably the child in this study who is least out, says clearly when asked if she has a problem with the fact that her mom is a lesbian, "I don't really have too much of a problem with the lesbian issue." Once children identify the problem as being *outside* of the family, they may also see the negative impact on their parents. Children may take a protective stance with their parents by not telling them about instances when their feelings are hurt by others. Delia and Kathy found out about some of these hurtful times only after their daughters were older. This is not necessarily negative, if the children are able to feel successful in how they handled the problem by themselves. On the other hand, children need to know that they can come to their parents and they can get help if they need it. It is that fine line that parents must walk between adequate and overprotection of children.

In fact, children may find strength in being a member of a lesbian family. Sometimes it is good to be different. As Dale (8) writes in his journal, "Being in a Lesbian family [makes] me more unekie." Children may enjoy the shock value of telling people about their mothers. Younger children often find odd moments to come out, as

Pauli did when she told the woman who was giving her a hair perm that her mothers slept in the same bed. Older children who are out about their families may even grow weary of their status as such a fascinating specimen that everyone wants to discuss. As Talia (16) says, "I'm really sick of writing about, oh, my mom is a lesbian—end of story. Mom said I should just write a story and photocopy it and just give it to all my teachers every time the assignment comes up, because it's all they want to hear about." Over and over again I heard these children say that their families were just "normal"—a term that surprised me, at first. They tend to be amazed at all the fuss that is made about their families.

How do children get to a place of feeling acceptance of and even pride in being members of a lesbian family? These children talked about two crucial factors in their lives that made a difference: positive books and other media about lesbians, and contact with other children of lesbians and/or gay men. Several children talked about the influence of positive media on their ability to accept their situations. When I asked Pauli (7) why she thought that some people don't like that she has two moms, she gave a response that illustrates the power and importance of books. Children need to see their families reflected in books:

> **Pauli:** They think it is weird, you know. Like in the book, it says that some grown-ups don't like other grown-ups that are gay. And one of the signs this person is holding [says], "Please go away." So you know some kids like people that, kids that have gay (parents).

Media may have an even more powerful impact on Pauli because she is one of the more isolated children. She does not know other children with lesbian or gay parents. Books, movies, and TV shows that depict lesbians and gay men in a positive light are very powerful for children because they address that aspect of invisibility in their lives. They also convey the message that there are lots of people out there somewhere, powerful people, who accept lesbians and gay men. They are not alone. Diana (20) talks of watching movies about lesbians as a way of increasing her understanding of the issues. It also may help children to name their anger at homophobia and to label it as righteous and justified.

The second factor that these children mentioned as an important influence in their lives is knowing other children of gay and lesbian parents. One of the crucial aspects of knowing other children from similar family structures is that children are reassured that they are not alone. As Talia (16) puts it, "So I always knew that there were other kids like me. I always knew that I was not alone." And Dale (8) writes in his journal:

> I was talking with Nicky. He is in a lesbian family too. I said to him I have three moms! Nicky has two moms and a dad.

Although Dale mentions here that he talked about his family structure with his friend, mostly the children do not talk about it. Talking and processing about their lesbian families seems less important to them than simply hanging out and playing. Further on in his journal, Dale reports, "I went over to Nicky's and I like playing with people that [have] Lesbian parents." And when I asked Diana (20) if she and her sister ever talked with their friends who had lesbian parents about their family structure, she replied:

> Really, I don't think that when we were with Kelly and Tara or any other kids when we were really young, we never—we took it for granted that they [our families] were, we knew that they were different. And we knew that they were different in a way that other people would find unacceptable and we knew why. But we never—it wasn't a strange thing for us. It wasn't —until recently that even like now that I'll sit down and go, wow, my mom is a lesbian, and I'll think about what that is and then think about the images we see in the media, and stuff, and I'll go—that's not my mom, you know. She's just mom and Kathy and they've been there all my life. But I'll sit down with Sara and I'll go—Sara, our moms are lesbians. And she goes, I know. And like, wow. But no, I never personally saw it as anything weird [when I was little].

The need to talk about having a lesbian mom with friends may come later in life, then, but it seems most important for younger children to simply have play connections with children from lesbian families. Some of the parents talked about the efforts they made to connect their children with others like them. For several years, Delia and Kathy attended monthly potluck dinners with other lesbian families.

> **Delia:** I don't know if your kids do, but our kids still remember those potlucks we used to have. I mean, it really did mean something to them. They, I think, enjoyed the safe space of being with kids and not having to worry about [anything].

Nisi also talks about how important it is to children to experience this safe space. When I asked her if she thought it had been important for her kids to know other kids from lesbian families, she answered:

> **Nisi:** Oh, absolutely, very important. I mean they identify with them early on—that they had two moms versus other kids have moms and dads. And part of them feeling comfortable and good about us as a family unit had to do with them knowing other kids who had lesbian moms. I think it would have been really hard if they didn't. It seems less important, I think maybe, as they get older, because they have that, kind of that, core belief, that they are not alone, that there's others. And then now, they just make friends with whoever they make friends with, whoever shares their interests, and their personality, and they get along with, but. . . . They still want to go to Lesbian Families Group.

Both media about and connections with other lesbian families seem to be extremely effective ways to combat the pervasive sense of invisibility which can haunt the children of lesbians. I did specifically ask children about whether or not they knew other children who had lesbian moms, however, the issue of the importance of the media came up entirely spontaneously as a children's concern. Although their parents have other strategies they use to help their children combat heterosexual supremacy, these were the factors that the children themselves were aware of and mentioned.

When I asked the children if they had any advice to give to other lesbian step family members, they addressed several issues that were important to them. Molly (15) suggests that it is just something that you have to accept, "you can't control other people, you know." And that, if you are lucky, you will get someone decent who joins your family. But even if it is a struggle at times, it can still be OK. Dale (8) says, "It's not different. It's OK. It's not bad at all. . . . Well, it is different—it's not something worse, though." And his sister Frannie (8) echoes his advice of acceptance.

> **Frannie:** If they were scared that people would tease them, I could say to them, "Nobody will tease you if they get to know you. It's really not that big of a deal, you know."

And Kevin (8) agrees, saying that "It's fun having two moms."

Diana (20) and Talia's (16) advice was to moms and kids—don't hide. Talia explains that it was harder when she tried to hide it.

> **Talia:** If anything was hard it was me making it hard, like me trying to hide it, you know.

And Diana tells this story to illustrate how important it is for parents to be proudly out:

> I think it helped that my parents were out. Because then it was me who was doing the hiding and it wasn't them. If they were telling me that this is right and this is OK, our relationship, but then they weren't out in the public, then that would have given me a real clear signal, and I probably would have had a lot more hard time. Because I know a girl . . . I just met a girl that just recently went to college—she was a friend of my friend who lived in the dorm—whose father is gay. But he's not out. So she was writing him letters, like, "Dad, I'm going to the [college gay and lesbian] dances. And I've met this girl and her parents are lesbians, and we're hanging out and it's really cool." But he's not out, so she doesn't, she only told me this, and she didn't even know me, so she was really looking for someone to say I feel bad—she feels bad for her dad that he can't be out.

> **Janet:** That he can't be more proud.

> **Diana:** Right, so she's got the mixed feeling that yes, I know this is not wrong, and this is something he should be proud of,

but I also understand that this society says it is. And it hurts her that he has to be so secretive.

These children, then, would tell other lesbian step families to accept it, that it's really not so bad, that it can even be good, and that it is easier and healthier to try not to hide. The next section addresses how the parents understand, experience, cope with, and attempt to help their children deal with heterosexual supremacy.

PARENTING IN THE MOUTH OF A DRAGON

Parenting is a difficult task for anyone and is perhaps more difficult when the parent is a member of a minority group that is disliked or even despised by much of society. As Lorde (1984) wrote, "Raising Black children—female and male—in the—mouth of a racist, sexist, suicidal dragon is perilous and chancy" (p. 74). However, it is also an opportunity. "Living in a lesbian family can be an empowering experience for children, teaching them to stand up for their personal choices and convictions," according to Joanna Rohrbaugh, a psychology instructor at Harvard Medical School (Freiberg, 1990, p. 33). She lists other possible positives for the children of lesbians, such as learning to tolerate and even value diversity. However, these positive outcomes for children are not guaranteed. Lesbian families live in a perilous environment, which creates enormous stress on both parents and children. This section examines what those stressors are for these participant parents and how they have worked to meet and overcome them.

Lesbian parents, like their children, have many fears. The most often expressed fear is that the children will be hurt or shunned because of their mothers. Dory expresses this dilemma very well when she says, "I want Pauli to grow up knowing that this is an OK life, you know, and reaffirm that, but at the same time, I don't want to put her out there as a target." And later, she adds, "There's always this fear of well, how are they going to treat Pauli, what is going to happen." Tanya expresses the fear that it is our lesbianism that may cause pain or rejection for our children:

> I think about whether or not a kid will befriend Kevin and if he does start a friendship with someone, will that friendship con-

tinue or not continue because of us. And just in dealing with other parents of his friends, just whether or not to open up to them about my being a lesbian and when to do that and how they find out and what their reaction is going to be.

This fear creates a constant anxiety in the parents, which Terry describes as very similar to the anxiety created by racism. Here she talks about her feelings when a new friend invited Kevin over to his house to play:

> Well, I think I was most concerned for Kevin that these kids know that Kevin has two moms at home, but in reality they don't have to deal with it all the time, so my concern was that this was a kid who is a third grader that Kevin looks up to him and really wanted this kid to like him and I'm afraid for Kevin. If homophobia wasn't there I wouldn't be so worried. I'm protective in a certain way. If racism wasn't there would I be worried. No. But it's there so I'm worried about racism. It's the same with homophobia.

These fears extend to feelings about how we are with our children's friends. These adults found themselves being particularly cautious around their children's friends, especially if they thought that the friend's parents might disapprove of their lesbianism. Delia talks about how she acted differently when children with straight parents spent the night:

> I think when the straight kids . . . the kids with straight parents were here I acted differently than when Sara or some of the lesbian moms' kids [were here]. I wasn't quite as—what's the word—cautious? I felt more at ease, because I knew these kids wouldn't go home and miss a trick of what went on. Whereas I didn't want that to happen. I didn't want something that a child innocently said, and then the parents were saying, "Well, you know, I did trust them to be decent; maybe they shouldn't go over there." I didn't want that to happen. So I must admit that I was cautious—you can't be completely at ease. There is something that makes people uncomfortable.

This unease is a result of not wanting to play into any of the stereotypes that some people may have about lesbians—as if we are somehow more likely to exhibit sexual indecency around children. This anxiety can be so great that it leads us to isolate ourselves to avoid dealing with it.

> **Cady:** When Nell was a little grade school kid, I was the scout leader for several years and when Molly was starting softball, as a fifth or sixth grader, I volunteered to do the coaching. By then I was living in a relationship [with a woman]—I hadn't been when I was a Girl Scout leader.
>
> And I thought about what are these parents going to think? And, isn't this the stereotypical thing—coaching softball. I didn't feel quite—again it was on my mind. And I wish I could be like some of the women I know, who just really are so self-accepting that they don't give a damn about that.

This constant monitoring of the environment is somewhat like the way a partner of an alcoholic might monitor the alcoholic's behavior. It pulls the lesbian mother outside of herself. As with other minority groups, lesbians can experience a kind of victim paranoia—always wondering what someone meant by what they said or what they did, always wondering if homophobia played a role in a rejection, a slight, a snub, and never being really sure. Did Diana's high school yearbook group actually lose the baby picture that her moms sent in with the inscription, "Love, from your two moms"? Or was it another case of homophobia? Delia writes about this struggle in her journal. Their family is nervously anticipating a camping trip family reunion with Kathy's family of origin.

> I suppose this isn't just unique to our family situation but we do all worry that our [difference] makes people uncomfortable—we can never just relax and do whatever is happening. Sometimes I know our assumptions are unfounded. We also have heard enough stories from other families to know that dealing with the in-laws is not easy.

It helps to have heterosexual friends with whom we can test our assumptions. Lori is surprised at how often her friends at work reassure her that a child's misbehavior or reaction has nothing to do with her having lesbian parents. "I often talk to my colleagues at work and say 'This must be because I'm a lesbian,' and they [say] 'No, my daughter does this, and unless I'm wrong, I'm not a lesbian.' And so it surprises me; a lot of it is just kids feeling out two adults who are power figures in their lives."

This anxiety and sometimes paranoia may even lead to questioning our own children—wondering if they dislike us or like us less simply because we are lesbian. We are not sure if our children are angry or acting out because they are behaving like normal children, or because they have grown up in a heterosexual supremacist environment and have bought the homophobic message. Talia (16) writes in her journal that she feels as if Kathy is "convinced that I don't like them because they are lesbians." And later in the same journal, she writes, "I hope she [mom] doesn't think I don't have people over because they [my moms] are gay. I'm just shy in general. I think she knows that still."

While this constant vigilance and anxiety is probably not very helpful for ourselves or our children, it is certainly understandable since lesbians are victims of and survivors of homophobia on a daily basis.

Legal discrimination may have the largest impact on lesbian families because of its immense weight—society condones discrimination against lesbians. Two of these families continue to suffer because of the fear that society could take away their children, based solely on the fact that they are lesbians. This is emphasized by Delia's acceptance of joint custody with her ex-husband, and in Dory's fears that her ex mother-in-law will initiate a custody battle. This fear also limits Pauli's access to her father. These custody fears are not paranoia—lesbian mothers do lose custody of their children and they lose custody solely because of their lesbianism (Polikoff, 1987).

But custody is not the only form of legal discrimination these families face. When I asked Dory and Becky what they would wish for if they could have three wishes, their overriding wish would be to "allow us to get legally married." This would give Becky some rights and status with Pauli, but would also allow them the benefits that go with legal marriage, especially the benefit of health insurance. Becky explains:

Well if we can't legally get married, at least it would be nice if we could work something out with my getting them on my insurance or something, so that we get . . . It's frustrating to know that there's people out there that they go out willy-nilly, have kids, and they don't consider anything and they get all these benefits from the IRS and everything. We certainly weren't willy-nilly about what we did, and we are trying to make a go of it and everything. If I could at least make an inroad so I can get them on my insurance and make things financially better for us. Because it's the only way I can do it. I don't get any tax exemptions or anything.

Florence feels this same frustration, saying that "there's nothing that would carry over to Nisi or the kids" in her benefit package at work. Lori recently discovered that Cady couldn't even get her retirement monies if Lori were to die before she retired. Only a legal spouse can get the full contribution. This new awareness has led to the conclusion that, if she doesn't die before retirement, she will need to take all her retirement monies immediately, and then perhaps reinvest them elsewhere. Sometimes lesbians aren't even aware of the extent of the legal discriminations against us. Lesbians must take extra precautions to take care of their investments and benefits in a manner that includes their lesbian family members, and sometimes that is impossible even with the special precautions.

The lack of legal family status adds to the unique outsider status of the lesbian step parent. It requires extra energy and time to insist on the inclusion of the lesbian step parent in the children's lives in the outside world. As Delia says, "But some of the recognition like, just with the schools, and health care providers, you have to go in and you have to actually say, look, this is how we want it." Cady feels that the discrimination and homophobia acts to "support that sense of Lori feeling left out." That, for instance, when she was the one doing the homework with Molly, "Molly's dad went to the conferences and I went to the conferences. Lori knew more about where Molly was academically than either of us, probably." This leads to a "lack of recognition for her contribution."

Discrimination also means that lesbian couples are not always recognized or accepted as couples. Nisi writes about this in her journal:

> Today I was frustrated and angry with my [perceived] lack of recognition as Florence's partner. Florence had an orthopedic doctor's appointment. I dropped her off to get her X ray, made a quick stop at the library, and then meant to join her in time for her consult with the doctor. When I got there with the kids, she was already with the Dr. The receptionist would not let me join her, saying, "There is not enough space in the cast room." I was angry, feeling that if my title were "spouse" rather than "friend" I would have been permitted in.

The families who are generally out in the community have experience with discrimination and homophobia. Sometimes, as we have seen, it comes from our families of origin, who cannot quite accept us when we are out as lesbians. Kathy's born-again Christian brother sent her an e-mail message as part of a long e-mail discussion about a difficult family reunion. He says, "I can separate you from your situation. We are who we are, not what we do. You are my sister and I'll always love and accept you. That doesn't mean I can accept your situation. Are you OK with this?" Certainly this is a double-bind message. Many families have adopted Clinton's military policy, "Don't ask, don't tell," as a method for not having to deal with their daughter's or sister's lesbianism—a clear message of shame. You are not OK as you are.

But these lesbians and their families also experience homophobia from strangers and/or acquaintances, as when Delia was the only one on an elevator and a group of people didn't get on with her when they noticed her gay rights T-shirt. Or when the bank refused to let her deposit Kathy's paycheck, leading Delia to respond with righteous anger:

> I got back to work and I got on the phone and called the bank, and I said "I just had an incident with this bank and I've got to talk to somebody higher up." So I said to them, "I don't care what you gotta do. You put a pink triangle on the card when you call up on the computer, you do whatever you got to

do—these are the dykes of the bank—but the next time I come in there and I want to cash her check, I want to cash her check, otherwise the money in the bank and CDs whatever, we will find a way to transfer them. Because I'm not taking this." . . . So now what you get is, they look at you and they smile and they have to bring like three or four other people from the bank to come and look at the lady in the car. I'm going, I don't believe this! They have yet to not do my transactions, but it's almost like, OK, I'm the freak in the circus now.

Tanya tells of a time when some neighborhood children were over at their house and Kevin told them that his family was going to San Francisco for a vacation.

> Kevin was playing with these guys [who] are older. They came in the house and were sitting on the back porch and Kevin said something to the boy: "You haven't been around for awhile." And he said, "Yeah, we were just in San Francisco." And Kevin said, "Oh, we are going to be there in a couple of weeks." And he said, "Well, you better watch out." "What?" "Yeah, they are going to be after him."

> **Janet:** They said that to you?

> **Tanya:** To me! I couldn't believe this kid was saying this to me in my house!

Tanya and Terry also had an incident with some neighborhood boys who wrote "Homo" in the snow on the side of their car. The next morning, Tanya and Terry watched to see if the boys would do anything else and, sure enough, they stood outside in the yard posturing and throwing snowballs.

> **Terry:** After I see these kids I'm mad and I'm gonna go and confront them—they are not going to do that to us. So I threw some sweats on and I come running down the stairs and the hair's totally a mess, so I grab one of my baseball hats and I had a jacket and sorrel boots, basically I looked like the dyke from hell. And I go storming out of the house and the dog

came running out with me and we jumped in the car and took off. So I go racing up and catch the kids just as they are trying to turn the corner to go into [a private Catholic school] and I stop in front of them and say, "You come here right away and I will get someone from the school." And one of them said, "Can I help?" and I said "I want to talk to somebody who is in charge" . . . . [And I told her] they were harassing me and my family. And the woman was like, "Well, we're ever so sorry; what happened?" And I explained that the other day they put Homo on the car and this morning they were making faces and [throwing] snowballs at our house and dancing around like fools in front of our house, making gestures like they didn't like us and harassing us. I looked at the kids and said, "How would you like it if my kid came by your house and started making faces at you and your family and threw snowballs at you for no reason at all that you know of?" And they started crying.

Sometimes these women chose to ignore the homophobic remarks or actions, and other times they confronted it. This choice seems to be based on the personality of the person assaulted, as well as her mood at the time and the type of homophobic behavior. But these lesbian parents were not only confronted with acts of overt homophobia, but also with heterosexist assumptions. Early in their relationship, Delia and Kathy's pediatrician made the assumption that Kathy was Delia's ex-husband's new partner, even though Kathy and Delia often took the girls to the pediatrician together! Step mothers may be assumed to be biological mothers, as with Becky when the receptionist at her former workplace asked how long she was in labor. Becky and Dory, since they have the same last name, are sometimes wrongly identified as sisters, as I observed when I attended church with them.

Tanya told me about how someone from Kevin's soccer team called one day because they were collecting money for a present for the coach. The woman asked, "Do you or your husband come to the games?" Tanya said she was taken aback because she thought everyone on the soccer team knew. She responded, I don't have a husband; I have a partner, and we do come to the games." Heterosexism is a pervasive challenge to lesbian parents to come out, even when sexuality and affectional preference really aren't a salient part of the discourse at hand. Lesbian families are often reminded about how they don't fit in and are sometimes met with a lack of acceptance.

This lack of acceptance is isolating. Cady hasn't found a church where she feels comfortable and accepted, so she doesn't often attend church. Florence feels self-conscious at Nisi's Lamaze class with all the other heterosexual couples and this mars her experience. Tanya at times avoids talking with the other parents at tae kwon do classes and soccer games. Dory wishes that society would be more accepting. "I mean I really have some major concerns for her (Pauli) when she hits high school and she has to try to have a 'normal life.' And we go to her graduation or she wants to go to these events and we're there. I mean, I want her to blend in, or to be everything that everybody else is."

The constant stress of managing one's identity to the outside world can be exhausting. We manage by restricting the information we give, but then wonder about the toll it takes. Cady writes in her journal about how she doesn't kiss Lori good-bye when she leaves on a plane for a business trip. "I don't think much about how nice it would be to never have to think about people around us being offended or disgusted." Sometimes we end up disclosing more than we wanted to, leaving us feeling vulnerable and exposed, as Florence describes in this story about approaching her foreman to request days off:

> And you wouldn't have to think about, well, did I just slip? Because I did. When I first got in this area, I asked my foreman—I called him over—and I said, did I get my vacation days approved? And he said, "Well, summertime isn't the best time to be requesting days off." And I said, "Well, my partner, that's the only time that she's off." And I thought about that. Did I really say she?

Or, someone else ends up exposing you, as when Dory and Becky's minister preached a sermon on acceptance of difference, including sexual orientation, on the day that they stood up to become members of the church. Even when the reactions of those around seem to be mainly positive, it is stressful because we cannot predict what might happen and therefore, we must always be on guard. The unknown is frightening. Tanya and Terry each describe what it is like for them as they attend an entertainment evening at Kevin's summer camp. Terry writes about feeling like they "stick out" as a lesbian family in a room full of straight families.

> It's awkward in an environment of large groups like this and the majority of people are strangers and assumed straight. I try to act normal and confident so Kevin does not see that inside I feel worry that he will be judged and discriminated because of his parents.

And Tanya describes her feelings at the same event:

> It is a bit awkward being with 100 other families who are 99 percent straight. Kevin unabashedly introduces us to other campers and their families as his two moms. We get mostly quizzical looks from the kids and friendly gestures from the parents' family. Kevin also introduces us to the camp counselors as his two moms. The counselors are mostly teenagers and are friendly enough. Mostly I see their interactions with Kevin as very positive and I think he endears himself to most of the staff. He seems to be popular with the other campers. I see this as acceptance of Kevin, regardless of the fact that he has two moms.

Simply put, being different is stressful because the difference of lesbianism is often considered unacceptable and shameful. As Delia explains it:

> Because, even through the years of kind of being callous, to, OK, fine, I can take the snickers. I can take your condescending, "oh, that's cool." It just adds a stress I know that doesn't need to be there. Something. There is enough you have to deal with just being a family, and when other people have issues, like race, or whatever, that adds to it and I think it's really sad, because it is a divisive element.

Clearly, these parents do experience homophobia and heterosexual supremacy as a mundane, extreme stress in their lives. What resources do they draw on to combat it? What are their parenting strategies for dealing with heterosexual supremacy? And how do they interpret it in a manner that is affirming and strengthening?

Family stress theory (McCubbin and Figley, 1983) postulates that there are two types of mediating factors that help families cope with stress: the way in which the crisis is interpreted by the family members and the resources they have to combat it. The most common interpretation used by these parents was that of pride in being lesbian and the way that they modeled this for their children was generally by being out whenever they felt they could. Being out is preceded necessarily by a sense of pride in, or at least acceptance of self. This was easier for some of these women than for others. Dory has struggled with this issue. When she met Becky at the twelve-step lesbian retreat, it was actually her very first step in coming out. Becky was already out and Dory has found this difficult throughout their relationship:

> **Dory:** When I got together with Becky, a lot of my life was evolving and changing. Going to a Metropolitan Community Church was a big, drastic change for me. Being out for me meant that there were people that were gay in the military that knew who I was and going to the bar—that was about being out, not necessarily getting drunk, but that was out! But for her [Becky] it's like there's this whole society. I go to this meeting and it's a gay meeting. I go here, and it's a gay church. I mean, her whole life was out and mine wasn't.

For Dory, being out is often "a really uncomfortable, unsettling situation for me." As Dory becomes more comfortable with her own lesbianism, though, she may find that it will help to reduce Pauli's fears. It is pride that allows us to deflect the negative images of others. Delia writes about her own evolving thinking on this in her journal:

> I used to think that I wanted to be treated like every other "normal "person or family member, however, as I grow older and experience more, I now believe that I want to be identified as "normal" and as a lesbian.

It is particularly difficult to manage the tangle of lies when we are not out, as Dory reports:

> **Dory:** What gets complicated is when I start having interactions with and we try to talk about, well, what happened over the weekend. And I have to screen everything that I say, "Well, my spouse and I, we did this." Or I just come up with "We did this or we did that." And, you know, when I get quizzed, that's when it gets tough and I find it real hard.

These parents agreed that having children, particularly when the children are young, has the effect of pulling the parents out of the closet, sometimes beyond their own comfort levels. Nisi explains how this happens:

> **Nisi:** When they were really young, I felt like I was pushed out, very often, much more than I would have chosen on my own, just because they would identify two moms very readily in any environment . . . And then, at work, I feel like it's always a choice whether I come out or not. It depends on who the person is and how well I know them, and whether I'm comfortable with it or feel safe. It's always my choice whether I come out or not. But, like when they [the kids] would start having sitters, or a day care center, I felt very obligated to be very clear with what my family form was. It didn't feel like it was a choice for me anymore.

> **Janet:** Why did you feel that obligation? What's the purpose?

> **Nisi:** Well, I felt like they needed to be validated on who their family was and without [it] that would be detrimental to them.

> **Florence:** And also just to let the staff know that this other person has the right to come and pick this child up, or be, if it gets injured, you know, make decisions.

> **Nisi:** Make contacts.

> **Florence:** You know, that's very important.

Janet: Yeah.

Nisi: So I felt like I was really outed, and I foresee that as they get older, it might be the opposite. Whereas Florence and I might like to hold hands in certain situations or may be out, they might feel less safe about it, if it's more their environment.

Janet: That's a good point.

Nisi: And so they might want us not to have books out when their friends are over and that kind of thing. I don't know that [it] is going to happen. I mean, it certainly hasn't in any way, shape, or form so far, but it could.

The families with adolescents did try to respect their children's need for increased secrecy which manifested itself especially during early adolescence. Kathy and Delia encouraged their children to do what was comfortable for them, but they tried to discourage any outright lying at the same time: "We hate lying!" Molly has been very closeted about her family situation and, although this has been hard at times for Lori and Cady, they have accepted it. For Diana and Talia, this period of hiding their family structure has turned out to be a stage, as they are both open about their lesbian moms now. It remains to be seen how Molly will handle this as she gets older.

It appears that the more open the parents and children are when the children are young, the more quickly the children go through the hiding stage as adolescents. However, each parent has to make decisions about being out based on her own contextual situation. Some communities, some workplaces, and some schools are safer and more open than others. Women who are teachers, or who are in the military, for example, have less choice about being open and must figure out how to manage their identities. These choices can be communicated to children, however, in a manner that allows them to maintain pride in their families. Instead of trying to get children to talk about the children's decisions and problems, it may be more helpful to them if the parents talk openly about the issues that are confronting them.

Dory says that she has tried to get Pauli to talk about her experiences at school and that "she has not confided in us." As we tell our children about our own experiences with coming out, our challenges, how we feel, they become empowered to make better choices for themselves.

Although all of these parents agreed that having young children makes the parents come out of the closet more, it may also make it easier in some sense to do so. Having children imparts a kind of normalcy to a woman. As Cady puts it, "Do you know what else, there is something about it [having children] that helps you feel normal, too." And Lori adds, "I do think it helps you feel like you are [normal], because family life—let's face it—family life is a big part of the American culture." Having children, then, allows us to say, look I am different in that I am a lesbian—but see how normal I am in terms of being a mother. Lesbian mothers then, who feel they have to come out more, do so in the context of motherhood. This may put lesbian mothers in the somewhat unique position as bridges for heterosexual people to begin to understand lesbian (and gay) lives in a less threatening context.

The negative aspect about being out is that prejudiced people can then target you for their abusive behaviors. The positive aspect on the other hand, can be a protective stance, as we have seen in the discussion about children. Being out puts people on notice that we are not ashamed. It may also help us avoid uncomfortable homophobic situations—such as jokes told about gay and lesbian people. Second, being out may allow us to get more support from people who are not homophobic. As Lori says, "I am out at work because it's important to me to have people know this." And Kathy writes in her journal about coming out to a new person at work, "It felt good letting Kerry know about my family." Being out helps us differentiate between those who dislike us and those who support us, and allows us to develop those supportive relationships and avoid the others.

It helps us to maintain a positive definition of our families and allows us to garner support when we have contact with other lesbian mothers. Three of these families have significant contact with other lesbian mothers, two do not. Dory and Becky do not know any other lesbian mothers and Cady and Lori have minimal contact with the few lesbian mothers of teenagers that they know. The other three families have all belonged to some kind of group for lesbian families. Even though this group may not have their very best friends in it, it does provide a context of safety and understanding for the mothers. As Delia says, "They understand—you don't have to explain." And Kathy talks about the importance of hearing from other lesbian mothers:

> **Kathy:** I really appreciated it because, as I said, we thought we were one of four families in the world trying to do this. So the more women we met and their kids, the better we felt about ourselves. It was important for me to hear about the experience of the mothers and the co-mothers. So that I could understand what Delia was dealing with and hearing it from some other mothers. . . it was good to hear other mothers having the same experiences—we found parallels there. . . . so that was so important.

Contact with other lesbian families, then, is not only an important resource for the children, but also for the parents. It establishes not only that we are not alone, but gives us other ideas and experiences to understand and perhaps to emulate or avoid. Becky and Dory, and Cady and Lori all expressed a wish for more connections with lesbian parents—especially parents with children who are at a similar age as one's own.

These parents provide their children with models in terms of being out and how they cope with the challenges incurred by being out. They also model how to get support from others in similar situations. However, they go beyond simply modeling behavior for their children. They are active teachers of their children in the struggle against heterosexual supremacy—teaching children strategies to combat homophobia, to increase pride in lesbian culture, and acceptance and celebration of diversity in general.

There were several strategies that the participants taught their children to help them cope with homophobia. They tried to prepare the children for the possibility that it might happen to them. Nisi talks about her children's lack of experience with homophobia:

> You know, my kids haven't really come into contact with a lot of it. A lot of what they know about homophobia is my trying to prepare them for the world. And letting them be exposed to

a small extent to what might happen in the news and what
issues are going on. So that they are aware . . . I mean otherwise they wouldn't know. They wouldn't have a clue. . . . And,
but they really haven't had, yet, to deal with much, as far as
somebody really harassing them about their family. I don't
want to put the expectation on them that they have to defend
us, because that might not be what's comfortable or safe, when
that happens. So, I hope that they realize that they can go to
adults for help if the situation is uncomfortable.

While preparation is helpful in giving children a context for
understanding why someone might be mean to them, parents are
also concerned that they not unduly frighten their children. Terry
says:

There are certain things you can prepare people for and
certain things you can't. You don't want to take away somebody's childhood, and so we don't tell him, you are going to
experience racism or you are going to experience homophobia
because your parents are lesbians. We do tell him there are
going to be things you are not necessarily comfortable being
around because of different people's perspectives in life.

Rather than dwell specifically on the issue of homophobia, then,
the emphasis is on teaching children skills to help them handle any
kind of adversity. These skills include ignoring people who are
mean. Delia writes in her journal that, when Diana talked of having
to confront a homophobic co-worker, they supported her and recommended that "with totally confused and biased folks, it's probably best to state your case and then move on to other topics."
If ignoring it doesn't work, then children will need to rely on
good conflict resolution skills. Terry and Tanya have taught Kevin
to tell people to stop and to let them know how they are affecting
him—what he is feeling. Nisi says that she hopes she has taught her
children to stand up for themselves and to deal with it through
communication and compromise. She helps her children practice
these skills with each other at home where they have established
certain guidelines. If that doesn't work, then the next line of defense
is to get help, which Nisi hopes they see as a last resort—but use it

if they need it. When children do ask for support, it is important that they get it, whether it is helping them to process it, or having the adult confront the abuser. Kevin experiences a sense of safety because he knows that Terry will stand up for him. Parents also teach their children about how to make decisions about coming out, by giving choices within certain parameters. Kathy and Delia discuss how they handled this issue with their daughters:

> **Delia:** But I think we even sometimes said to them, "Are you sure that's what you want to do right now? Are you sure that coming out to your friends or being that open—let's think about this. What are the risks?" So not always expecting—I don't think we ever wanted them to lie intentionally, to hide their family. We didn't accept that. But I think we all knew there were times when it made sense and maybe times when it didn't. And you don't always have to be out there with this issue and so open and whatever. Let's think about what will happen to you. Don't you think?

> **Kathy:** Yeah. But I think there were—I think we also sat down and [determined] strategies for dealing with jerks: We did tell them that we wanted to know if they were having problems. That would be the first thing they should do, is to tell us of any problems. I think the other basically was to just avoid such people, ignore and avoid them, but let us know.

The main message from these parents is that lesbian parents need to be especially focused on teaching their children good generic skills for conflict resolution. These skills will then be in place for use in homophobic incidents. In addition, children need to learn to understand what goes into decisions on coming out and to realize what choices are acceptable to their parents on this issue.

Besides teaching conflict resolution skills and strategies for addressing homophobia, parents are also actively involved in teaching their children about lesbian and gay cultures, encouraging a sense of pride and belonging. Children do not learn about this anywhere else, so it is up to the parents to introduce them to the positives of lesbian culture. This also, as we have seen, may sustain them against the erasure they feel from the outside. This is done by presenting children with books about lesbians and gays, and other appropriate and positive media when it is available. It occurs when we identify public figures who are out as gay. For example, Nisi says that her children were delighted to learn that Melissa Etheridge is lesbian. They were also happy when she told them about the cruises for lesbians organized by the Olivia record company. Diana and Talia enjoy reading the gay/lesbian newspapers and magazines that their moms have in the house. Parents can foster pride in their children by identifying and discussing openly the positive aspects and people in gay/lesbian culture. This pride can carry them through times of adversity.

These parents also work hard at teaching their children to accept and enjoy human differences in general. There seems to be a strong consensus among these participating parents that children be taught a whole paradigm of inclusiveness. This has a protective function for the children of lesbians because they come to understand that all differences, including their own, have value and something to offer to the world. But it goes beyond protection. These parents felt it was an important value to teach their children, regardless of whether it served to help them personally.

Like many progressive parents, these women found themselves talking with their children often about the unfairness of various kinds of prejudices and discrimination. Nisi says that these topics come up frequently in their family discussions, as well as in shorter comments on various issues—such as something in the news. Parents gave many examples of how they used teachable moments to address these issues with their children. For example, the issue of handicaps and mental and physical challenges are common in children's lives. Becky and Dory tell the story of how Paul asked a handicapped child who she knew from riding the bus to not say hi to her in front of the other children because it embarrassed her and her friends laughed at her. "So we had a big go-round about how that is not appropriate." Kevin rides the bus with a boy who is autistic and his parents spent time to help him understand this handicap.

Tanya: The kids just have a hard time with this particular boy and so we talk to Kevin about how Kelly is different and why he is different and we relate that to—it would be as if you should treat Kelly nicely or with respect or whatever, even though he is different. It would be just as if people were picking on you because you are brown or you had two moms or something—trying to make him put himself in that situation.

Race and religion are topics that the participants discuss with their children, too.

> **Lori:** I think we've gone out of our way, because [our town] is such a lilywhite little place. It's not as homogenous as we think, but it sure is racially homogenous. And we have gone out of our way to try to say that being bigoted racially, or about Jewish people, which are the only two things [the kids] ever brought up, [was not OK]. I mean, once Nell said, do you think there are any Jewish people in [our town]? And I said, of course there are. How do you expect to find them? With a star on their head? So we've talked a lot about that, and probably lots of different times—talked about how it isn't OK to be bigoted. We understand how people can feel about things being threatening, but that people who make this sexual choice are not inferior and that we don't know if it is a choice or a biological given. We just know that the issue is: Are we in a healthy relationship?

Tanya and Terry are particularly aware of issues of race and racism, probably because of personal experience. This awareness permeates their lives. One of the first questions Tanya asked me about my study was whether I would address racism. At Kevin's class picnic, Tanya commented on how there were more people of color there this year than last. Race is an ongoing, open discourse in this family, keeping the awareness high and allowing for plenty of learning opportunities for Kevin, as well as for Tanya and Terry.

Sexism was another common topic in these families. Although half of these women don't identify themselves as feminists, all these parents want to be sure that their children understand that women and men are worthy of equal respect. Becky talks about how she always tries to use inclusive terminology, such as police officer, instead of policeman (which is used at school). "So I always try to use the more politically correct [term] and say that it's not a man's job because you could do it if you wanted to." Delia and Kathy have spent much of their spare time working for women's rights, so these issues were part of the ongoing discussions and actions as the girls were growing up.

While some parents were less sure of whether they made a point of discussing gay and lesbian issues, such as Cady who mentioned that she wasn't sure if they did much of this in their household; others, such as Florence and Nisi and Kathy and Delia, talked often about it. In her journal, Delia writes about a typical family discussion that occurred as a result of an article in a gay and lesbian parenting newsletters:

> Diana couldn't understand why some of the daughters were upset when their mothers came out. We tried to explain that not everyone—even children of gays—is comfortable with the issue. We were all struck by the article about second generation gays and lesbians. None of us could figure out why homosexual parents would be upset with their children if they turned out to be gay. We ended our discussion sad that homophobia is so strong in our society and how tragic its effects are.

It is interesting how it seemed to be easier for some parents to discuss other prejudices rather than homophobia. Perhaps this is related to the internalized homophobia that Delia alludes to above. Lesbians, for example, have always been among the leaders of the feminist movement, but, for years, were not allowed or safe enough to include lesbian rights in the platform.

Parents also spent time talking with their children about acceptance of diversity in general. Kathy mentions teaching Diana about the concept of "hypothesized forces—society just says something is true [even though it may not be so] and it has to be this way and they do terrible things to cultures." There is an effort, then, to encourage children to challenge what some folks might say is true—to search for one's own truth and to follow one's own path.

Dory, who was raised in a very bigoted household, still has to struggle with the "rhetoric in my head." As a result of that, she tried very hard to live life as her parents taught her, but it turned out to be a self-destructive path for her. Now she tries to teach her daughter acceptance, by words and actions:

> **Dory:** If I'm going to teach Pauli anything it's that everybody is entitled to live their life the best and the fullest that they can, whatever it is. And that God loves you just the way you are. So acceptance is, I think—and if I live my life any other way, then I'm not teaching her that and she'll learn just the opposite.

Beyond talking with children about diversity, there is an effort among these parents to expose their children to it. Some do this by where they choose to live, or choose not to live. Terry says that they could never live in the country, even though they would like to, because it would be too homogenous racially and Kevin would be isolated. They encourage their children to have diverse friends. They choose books and toys and movies that reflect and celebrate diversity. Tanya says that they have always made a major effort to find multicultural books and toys. "Toys, at this point, well, maybe *Star Trek* can be considered not really nonsexist or nonviolent, but anyway, multicultural. I think that was a really conscious effort to focus on *Star Trek*." And because they have also involved themselves in learning about and enjoying *Star Trek*, this provides an opportunity for easy and fun family connection and learning about multiculturalism concurrently.

The children in this study do appear to have an awareness and understanding of diversity. Becky proudly tells this story about Pauli:

> I remember watching the Thanksgiving parade yesterday and Pauli thought that those outfits, you know, the real high cut legs, were gross. And she's on and on about this. And I said, "Well, you know, men really like that kind of stuff. They think that's real great. I personally don't think that they need to be stereotyping women like that." And she goes, "Well, the band looks beautiful without them." And I was so happy.

Molly told me that she thought racism was "stupid" and based on "ignorance." Diana refused to buy a camera case with the insignia "Stars and Stripes" because "that was the name of that awful boat that beat the women's boat in the America's Cup race." Talia speaks with distaste of a kind of minority quota system they have in her school—they want to show they have 25 percent minority students so they want her to identify herself as Hispanic.

In fact, the children in this study also taught their parents about acceptance of diversity. Delia tends to use terms for people that can be heard as derogatory—"I have this thing about not being able to control this terrible mouth." For example, when she said something about the skinheads downtown, one of her daughters replied, "Well, you don't want to say skinheads around my house because some of those skinheads are my friends." And she goes on to tell this hilarious story:

> The funniest time was when Talia brought over this boy, and, Jan, he had tattoos. He had a mohawk that was, I think, that fluorescent kind of blue. He had more pierces than . . . at that time . . . this was a few years back—that I'd ever [seen] . . . This was when piercing just started and I'd heard about it but I hadn't really seen anybody with these things in their noses, a guy with a safety pin in his eyebrows, and oh, I don't know how you can do this. And I'm sitting here, trying not to stare, but this is amazing. A very nice young man. You know, you go through the whole thing, he's a very nice young man; some of my best friends are pierced, you know. But, just that, again, that acceptance [that the kids have]!

Because the children of lesbians have personal experience with prejudice and see how it affects their mothers intimately, they may integrate it more easily and have a deeper understanding than children who have not had this personal experience. Diana talks about how her friends and even acquaintances will approach her with problems and fears about their own sexual choices and says, "I can sympathize with them and I know what it means, what it feels like to be prejudiced, I mean, to be discriminated against because of something you cannot control." It is interesting to note how the parents, when talking about other prejudices, encourage their children to relate by pointing out their own differences, as we can see in the earlier quotes. Identification and personalization leads to increased understanding.

> **Nisi:** I think that just because they are in a lesbian family they see that there are differences among people and that those differences are OK. And I think that's part of it. The other part is that they realize they are an oppressed minority and they feel that fear and that oppression and when you are in that situation, I don't think you can help but identify with other minorities, other people that are oppressed. And I mean, you've walked in their shoes; in a way, you can identify what it's like.

Parenting in the mouth of the dragon, then, seems, in spite of the obvious hardships, to offer an opportunity for children as well as parents. That opportunity is to look around and notice who is in that mouth with you and to correctly identify the dragon as the problem—not them and not yourself. The next section will examine some of the community factors which can support or isolate lesbian families.

IT TAKES A WHOLE VILLAGE

Communities have the potential to offer resources that support and nourish families. In examining this aspect of the data, I found information that conforms with findings from other studies on lesbian families, namely that place does make a difference (Levy, 1989; Pollack and Vaughn, 1987; Rafkin, 1990). The participants living in Newville, which is generally known as a progressive Midwestern city, acknowledge that they live in a sheltered environment as lesbians. Lesbian parents make choices to move to or stay in the city of Newville because they believe it will be easier for their children to grow up there. There is a city ordinance that allows domestic partners to register as such and city employees reap some benefits. But, beyond the benefits, such an ordinance makes a statement of tolerance that impacts positively on all lesbian families in the city. Dory and Becky, who live in a less progressive city, do not experience this same level of openness or tolerance.

A substantial lesbian/gay population exists for the size of the city and it is a visible community. Out lesbians/gays are employed in the police department, university, fire department, city, county, and state government, and other city departments and private businesses. The school administration at least will listen to the concerns of gay and lesbian peoples. This allows for a sense of community and a less isolated status.

The lesbian community in Newville has a Lesbian Family Group which meets monthly and has a mailing list of 150 families, although substantially fewer families attend the meetings. Lesbian mothers provide an important source of support for each other, as we have seen in the section on parenting. However, child-free lesbians can also have an impact on the well-being of lesbian families. Several participants mentioned their important connections with lesbian friends who do not have their own children. They found it particularly helpful when their child-free friends included their children in activities, thus establishing an extended family feeling or fictive kin. Terry gratefully tells about some of their lesbian friends, saying, "And they're really great. Well, they are not really great with kids, but when they invite us over there, they are really conscientious of Kevin's [presence] and they try to have stuff for him."

It is particularly important for Dory and Becky to get this support from their lesbian friends, since they do not know any other lesbian mothers. Becky mentions that some of their friends "always make sure Pauli gets something (for her birthday)—kind of like a surrogate niece or something, you know." Lesbians who are not mothers can offer tremendous assistance and support to lesbian mothers. However, they can also increase the sense of isolation for lesbian mothers. Traditionally, some lesbians who are not mothers have had free and independent social lives, often centered on going out to bars or other lesbian establishments or ball games, etc., after work. Lesbian mothers may find themselves feeling isolated at work or in social situations since they do not have the same kind of freedom of time. Although this also sometimes happens with heterosexual couples after they have children, they may have an easier time finding and connecting with new friends who share similar interests.

Lesbian mothers have fewer choices. Terry works at a place where there are other lesbians, but most of them are child-free. Terry finds this very isolating. She finds it ironic that in a department where it is OK to be an out lesbian, she feels more alone than when she had to be closeted. Because lesbians rely on each other so heavily to maintain self-esteem in a hostile world, rejection by or even lack of attention from other lesbians can be very difficult. As Terry says, "I think the isolation I feel—I mean now anyway—is definitely that I'm not fitting in with the rest of the dykes." It is crucial for lesbian mothers to find supportive lesbian nonmothers, especially when the number of lesbian mothers in one's community is limited.

Although the previously mentioned issues have been discussed in other research on lesbian mothers, there were two additional factors from this data, related to support from community, that took me by surprise. The first factor was the striking lack of connection with what would seem to be an obvious potential community ally—gay men. In fact, it was so completely absent that I wouldn't have noticed it myself if Terry hadn't mentioned it briefly in passing:

Terry: I didn't realize how different—I mean, my dad—I always wanted to be like my dad. My dad had kids and how different it is, even the cultural stuff, even from when he came out in the fifties, and living through the sixties and seventies and how different it is to be gay now than it was back then, and, but . . .

Janet: Because a lot of people in that time had their families as heterosexuals, like I did, so they had that experience of family life and they kind of carried that over?

Terry: Well, I'm even thinking of when I grew up. To me, being gay or to be lesbian or a gay person is—everybody is just—well, I see a lot more separatism now, I guess is what I'm getting at. Because my dad . . . there was always men and women over at the house, always. And when I go to Carl's [her father's partner] house for his parties, there's always men and women and a couple of token straights, like my family, my sisters and my mom's there, usually with her husband and stuff.

Janet: So you're saying that segregation between gay men and lesbians is much bigger here in Newville, or . . .

Terry: Yeah, well, not just here in Newville, but with our age. When you're older or with the older gay men and lesbians, it's more a family—its men and women. And now, family are women friends, or men friends; it's very separate. And ever since coming out it's been that way for me and I'm like totally confused, because it's different from what I was raised with; it's different from my dad.

Janet: I wonder if part of it is, there might be two things. One might be just in the fifties and before, you had to band together. There was just so much awful stuff. But also, the feminist movement kind of split women off.

Terry: . . . Well, that's how my dad explained it to me. It makes sense, but the to me, my image of fulfilled life is to have the combined thing. He was my role model, so . . .

The feminist movement and the increasing visibility of gays and lesbians seems to have created a split in the lesbian and gay communities. Gay men are still socialized as men in a misogynist society. Many gay men have not confronted the issue of male privilege in their lives. Some lesbians find this impossible to ignore. Although gay men and lesbians will often coalesce regarding political and advocacy issues, there appears to be less combined socializing, particularly in extended familylike groupings. This separation of gay men and lesbians may occur at the expense of our children, who have less opportunity to experience men and women as loving, comfortable with each other, and completely nonsexual friends. Gay men also model for children that it is OK for men to touch each other in nurturing ways—a crucial understanding for boys who are confronting the prescribed and enforced rules for maleness. This may also be a loss for both the gay men, who have fewer opportunities for real connection to children in their community, and gay fathers and lesbian mothers, who have limited connection with each other and therefore less exposure to what each has to offer the other.

The second factor caught me by surprise not because of the lack of information but rather because of the strength of its appearance in the data—that is, the crucial connection with heterosexual allies for both parents and children. These women expressed relief and gratefulness when their contacts with heterosexuals were positive. This was important with strangers and mere acquaintances, as well as with good friends and co-workers. It is helpful when neighbors show acceptance, because then the family doesn't feel left out. Terry and Tanya have presented themselves in their neighborhood as a family, signing up for the neighborhood association as a family unit. Although they have experienced some homophobia in the neighborhood, they have also experienced acceptance.

> **Terry:** I think some of the closest neighbors, the neighbors you can see just looking outside of our house, have all been wonderful as far as accepting. There is the older guy who lives across the street—I think he was the person who really made me feel more comfortable as far as just saying this is a great neighborhood. 'Cause he was one of the first residents in the neighborhood; they built that house. I think what he did one of the first years we were here, [at] Christmas, he called up and asked if we wanted family tickets to go to the pancake feed that [the Shriners] had with Santa. And he wanted to send our family to go to this. I think we accepted, but I couldn't go. And then the next time he had family tickets to the circus. He said, "I want your family to go."

Acceptance from neighbors creates an atmosphere of safety around the home and allows the family to feel comfortable participating in neighborhood activities. It also helps when families are accepted by the professionals with whom they must interact—doctors, teachers, insurance agents, etc. Nisi writes in her journal of how wonderful it felt that their Lamaze instructor always used the word "partner" when referring to the nonpregnant spouse—even though everyone else in the group was part of a heterosexual couple. Acquaintances can impact on the family's comfort level by showing acceptance. When I went to Dale and Frannie's baseball game, several of the other parents chatted amicably with Nisi and Florence about their recent family trip to the Badlands. And, after Frannie introduced Florence as her mother's partner at the Brownie event, Florence was relieved when several of the parents later went out of their way to talk with Florence and "really made an effort to help us be comfortable." These small gestures of acceptance have a big impact on lesbian family members.

These parents are also very appreciative of the acceptance and friendship they receive from their heterosexual family members and friends and co-workers—the heterosexual people who are closest to them. We have already seen the huge impact that families of origin have on their lesbian family members and their children. Acceptance from family is a treasure and lesbians put high value on even small signs of acceptance. It is also a wonderful relief to have people at work who know you are lesbian and accept it. Becky talks about coming out to some of her co-workers:

> I said, "Well, you know, I'm gay," and I said, "I'm bringing my partner [to the office Christmas party]." And he says, "Well, hell, I'm ready for you to come. . ." So from that point on, we already had kind of a little bit of a bond because of both of us being recovering alcoholics.

Janet: That's really nice. I bet that felt great.

Becky: Yeah, and then when I found out we were planning on moving and I mentioned it to him, he said, "Well, hell, I'll come down and help you out," and he came down and helped us move.

Janet: Oh, that's sweet.

Becky: And then one of the other fellows that had just started [asked who was with me at the Christmas party]. "Was that your sister?" I said, "No, that's my spouse." "Oh," he said, you know, my cousin is gay and has a lover. "Boy, we don't think anything less of her, you know.'"

Janet: That's great.

Becky: And then he, of course, offered to come down and help us move, too, you know.

As this illustrates, lesbian families can only get this support for their families when they take the risk to come out. Sometimes we are surprised by the acceptance we find. Terry and Tanya's closest family friends are a heterosexual family that they met through Kevin's day care. This relationship is affirming for them and for Kevin. Since the other family has an adopted child, they have talked about different kinds of families together. But, more than the talking, the experience if not just acceptance but joy in difference is powerful. Delia and Kathy have some heterosexual family friends who live in the neighborhood. Delia also works with the father of the family. She writes in her journal about walking over to their house with Kathy to see their son off on a trip:

> He [the son] also told Kathy that he liked her piece in the parenting book. We ended our visit happy and hopeful about changes regarding how people view gay people. We have a certain "parent-like " relationship with this young man and he respects us and appreciates this relationship.

Delia was so impressed by a letter from one of her co-workers that she included it with her journal. He wrote to congratulate Kathy on the article she had published in a book on lesbian parenting. Then he went on to reminisce about how Delia came out to him after he had simply assumed for a long time that she was married. When he once casually asked her what her husband did, she replied, "You mean you don't know?"

"Don't know what?" I answer.

Now I'm thinking, "You idiot, he's dead or paralyzed or in prison for some horrible crime. It was probably in the paper and on TV and you're so stupid you missed the whole thing! She'll probably have three years of therapy just because you brought the subject up!"

"You really don't know, do you?" "No, what is it?" "My partner is a woman," and as she looks straight into my eyes, "DOES THAT MAKE A DIFFERENCE?"

Complete relief. "Absolutely not!" I answer.

I tell this little story to illustrate how in all our discussions about family and kids and parenting, never did I consider that

Delia was in a lesbian relationship. I assumed, and rightly so, that she was in a loving, open, lasting, and, above all, normal relationship. And that is exactly what you all have.

Positive relationships with heterosexual people affirm our relationships and our families. They are immensely important to these families in their struggles to overcome the societal message of heterosexual supremacy and also in their efforts to positively define and interpret their families.

CONCLUSION

Family stress theory (McCubbin and Figley, 1983) identifies two mediating factors that serve to reduce stress and encourage creative coping—resources and interpretation. In confronting the mundane extreme environmental stress of heterosexual supremacy, these families rely heavily on both of these factors.

Positive resources include a tolerant community, a significantly open lesbian/gay population, other lesbian families to socialize with, any legal status for lesbian/gay families and people, and a connection with supportive heterosexual friends, family, and acquaintances. These participants have relatively few close connections with gay men, who would seem to be another possible ally group. This division between the gay and lesbian communities would be an interesting future study.

The most widely used presentation these families employ to interpret themselves to the community is that of being a "normal" family. They change written forms to accommodate their families, the adults present themselves as the children's parents, they attend activities as a family. As Kathy puts it, "I think our presentation is believing we are a normal family; just present it that way. Why set it up differently?" As we have seen, the children think of their families as normal and try to present them that way, often being surprised that anyone sees it differently. Talia (16) speaks to this in an interview:

> I mean, look at our house, it is extremely normal. Just the other day in school, the teacher told us to write something different about our family. I'm sorry, my family is just too normal. He

just looked at me and said, well, they're really not. Come on, aside from the one little, tiny detail, we are so incredibly normal.

This presentation works to lessen distance and create acceptance based on similarity. It is important as a first step toward overcoming prejudice to proclaim one's similarities with the majority. But it is also important to celebrate one's strengths and uniqueness (Wright, 1994). This celebration of difference leads from toleration and acceptance toward true appreciation of unique strengths and offerings. We are, as Lorde (1984) wrote, "outriders for a queendom not yet assured" (p. 73). This pride in uniqueness is an important part of liberation struggles (Friere, 1989). As we become accepted as "normal," we begin to push for recognition as both "normal" and "special." It is this dual presentation of our families that serves to strengthen and affirm them—allowing us to be whole and healthy families. We do this when we perceive our families as offering unique opportunities to its members. These families were at various stages of embracing this uniqueness, but all of them recognized the possibility. Delia writes eloquently about this issue in her journal:

> Being a lesbian is part of my identity and I no longer want this ignored. I am part of a larger community of gay and lesbian and bisexual families, and I now believe we are different from the heterosexual community and should be acknowledged and respected in our own right.

Parents try to instill a sense of pride in their children by teaching them about gay/lesbian culture, illuminating historical and popular positive lesbian and gay role models and contextualizing homophobia as one of many types of unjust forms of domination and oppression. Coming out is often interpreted as a brave and proud stance.

In spite of the use of these stress-mediating factors, parents and children live with significant fears. They use several strategies to address potential and real homophobic incidences. These include preparation, secrecy, and hiding or just not telling, ignoring and not caring, using good conflict resolution skills, joking, coming out, reframing difference as good, and seeking help. When homophobia is clearly named as the problem, fears may be somewhat transformed into righteous anger. Taking action may help to lessen fears. Lorde (1984) writes:

> My anger has meant pain to me but it has also meant survival, and before I give it up I'm going to be sure that there is something at least as powerful to replace it on the road to clarity. (p. 132)

As lesbian families struggle to raise responsible and loving children, we are very aware of the dragon of heterosexual supremacy which constantly threatens that quest.

Chapter 7

Free to Be You and Me

INTRODUCTION

This in-depth exploration of five lesbian step families illuminates some of the challenges and opportunities faced by families that are defined as "different" (and therefore generally seen as inferior) by much of mainstream society and its institutions. A particular family structure has been championed and supported by the dominant groups and their institutions throughout most of U.S. history—the male-female dyad with the dominant male as economic supporter and the subordinate female as homemaker and their children as their private possessions. Religions, capitalism and economics, education, child care, legal, media and information, social service, and government systems are intricately and inexorably conjoined with a vision of family as heterosexual, nuclear, white, Christian Protestant, middle- to upper-class, and male dominant.

The fact that this family type is no longer, if it ever was, the majority family form in the United States has resulted in very few substantial institutional changes. This lack of goodness of fit between society's vision of the family and its actuality creates upheaval and unrest. Society's institutions support a family structure that is no longer tenable for the majority of families. There is a considerable movement to turn back—to attempt to enforce the (actually fairly recent) "traditional" family form as the bedrock of society. However, although it is important to look back and to understand the lessons of the past, attempts to return to the past are sure to fail. The world has changed and families are part of that world. As Einstein (quoted in Covey, 1990) wisely advised, "The significant problems we face cannot be solved at the same level of thinking we were at when we created them" (p. 42). To find creative solutions to family problems, then, we must look outside of our traditional paradigm. One way of pursuing this quest is through the exploration of various diverse family forms, such as lesbian step families.

Lesbian step families, living immersed in the dominant paradigm of family, experience an ongoing tension between presenting and seeing themselves as "normal" families versus presenting and seeing themselves as different and unique. The stories told here are replete with life tasks that face all families—how to nurture, guide, nourish, promote growth, and maintain security for all their members—physically, emotionally, spiritually, and intellectually.

While these families' stories clearly tell the tale of attempts, successes, and ongoing challenges to fulfill the tasks of nurturance, economic survival, and growth, they also address the struggles to be unique in a society that enforces conformity. Conformity, after all, is more efficient and less complex. The stories that need to be clearly heard in today's climate are those that reject stereotypes and embrace complexity.

In addition to telling the tale of "normalcy," then, this research project addressed three major differences found in this particular family structure: (1) a biological mother sharing parenting with a nonbiological female parent, (2) the couple dyad consists of two females, and (3) these families exist in an environment of heterosexual supremacy. Each of these differences created challenges for the families, which were addressed with various tactics and with varying degrees of success. Each of the differences also created opportunities for their family members. Differences in family structure and context provide windows to view family and family tasks from fresh perspectives. This allows other kinds of families to adjust to provide additional positive experiences in their own families or to avoid pitfalls made more visible. Our diverse experiences will guide and enrich our progress in life.

MODELING GENDER FLEXIBILITY

One of the strongest opportunities embedded in lesbian families is that of challenging inflexible gender prescriptions. This challenge is not only actively pursued, but also passively exists in the family structure. As Hite's (1994) research pointed out, simply not having a male father figure actively involved in the family changed children's attitudes about gender and women. This is not an argument to end men's involvement in the family. These women and children felt strongly that men's involvement in their lives was important. Instead, this argument examines the magnitude of harm done (to men and women) by gender dominance and male privilege. Hite (1994) explains:

> most boys get a particularly negative indoctrination into "masculinity" from their father; the majority complain that their father did not explain in any clear or positive way how to "be a man" [an adult], but only criticized them for doing the wrong things, e.g., "Stop acting like a girl." (p. 235)

Male dominance and privilege teaches boys to discount, fear, even hate what is defined as female. It teaches girls to acquiesce, to give up, to accept a lesser role in the world. Lesbian families, not through any particular virtue or superiority, avoid reinforcing male privilege simply because they are two female *heads* of household. Half of the women in this study did not even identify themselves as feminists. I am not discussing active pursuit of feminist principles here, but rather the ubiquitous nature of male dominance that permeates this society. Just as lesbian families must struggle constantly against the destructive forces of heterosexual supremacy, the family with male parent(s) that hopes to discourage the assumed inheritance of male privilege will need to work diligently against such a message. Simply put, the struggle against recreating the acceptance of a male-dominant system is less difficult in female-headed households.

In addition to this passive, structural challenge to gender dominance, these couples also actively fought against sexism and encouraged their daughters and their sons to pursue their interests and develop their personalities based on an acceptance of human traits, rather than gender-specific traits. Taking the step toward claiming one's right to be a lesbian may provide some impetus to do this, but certainly heterosexual (feminist or antisexist) men and women can do this with their children as well.

Mothering and fathering tasks, which have traditionally been aligned with gender, were divided in these families on the basis of preferences of the mothers and the children. Some of these women exhibited clear preferences for traditional fathering tasks over mothering tasks, or vice versa. Some step mothers, certainly Becky, but also Kathy and Lori to some extent, were more comfortable in mothering roles. Some biological mothers preferred fathering. These families, then, illustrate that traditional mother and father roles are dictated neither by gender nor biological parenthood.

Female couples, because of the female upbringing that emphasizes the importance of relationships and the skills of negotiating them, may also provide children with a different model of coupling. These couples believe that they provide good role models of coupling—because of the mutual caring and respect they feel and show for each other, the sense of equality between them, the emotional closeness they feel with each other, the high value they place on the relationship, and the fact that they have chosen to be authentic, in spite of the societal pressure to hide who they are. We know from research that female couples do emphasize certain traits and exhibit certain unique characteristics (Slater, 1995; Johnson, 1990). These couples are proud of the models of coupling that they provide for their children, believing them to be positive, respectful, equal, and loving.

SHARED PARENTING

All of these couples shared parenting to a certain degree. This included not only all parenting tasks, such as feeding, protecting, and guiding, but also a strong emotional connection—caring for the children, a willingness to consider the children's needs as equally important in the family, a desire to be someone special to the children, to be family. Biological mothers realized that this shared parenting gave them more freedom to pursue their own interests as well as allowing them to share decision making and problem solving concerns the children's issues. All of these biological mothers felt that having this adult partner helped them be better parents. Step mothers, co-parents, and co-mothers brought additional perspective, energy, money, and skills into the family enriching family life.

What determined the type of shared parenting stance was the balance of power with and responsibility for the children. In the co-parenting families, the biological mother retains more responsibility for the children and more power with the children. This is a common stance with heterosexual step families, too (Kelley, 1995). It appears to work well when the family members agree and are comfortable with this stance.

Older children tend to be less willing to accept a step parent as a parental figure so these families may have to adjust to a stance where the step parent that involves less directly in overt parenting (Kelley, 1995). This happened in Lori and Cady's family, which came together when Nell was thirteen. This more distant stance has been difficult for Lori, who would have liked to be more active and clearly identified as a parent. Cady, on the other hand, feels as if she may have given up too much of her own parenting style in her effort to bring Lori into the family. Even so, Lori has taken on mothering duties, allowing Cady to actively pursue her advanced degree and profession. So the cooperative co-parenting has happened, perhaps in spite of the significant resistance from Nell, and now, to a lesser extent, from Molly.

In the other two co-parenting families, the children were much younger when the families formed and they have clearly accepted their step parents as family. Although time and energy spent on the children is not equal in these co-parenting relationships, an agreed-upon balance exists between the partners that seems to serve the needs of the family members well. This stance has worked to allow some relief from mothering responsibilities for the biological mother while encouraging significant bonding between the children and the step parents.

I chose the label, "step mother stance" to describe the relationship among Dory, Pauli, and Becky because it is similar to some heterosexual step mother families in terms of balance of power with and responsibility for the children. In heterosexual step families, step mothers report more role strain than step fathers. Whitsett and Land (1992) found that women are still expected to fill the primary nurturer and caretaker roles, and that even when these expectations are not overtly stated, societal forces and the woman's own expectations prescribe that role. McGoldrick and Carter (1988) claim that traditional family gender roles have "no chance at all in a system where the children are strangers to the wife and where the finances include sources of income and expenditures that are not in the husband's power to generate or control" (p. 400). The role strain is created with the step mother's responsibilities for the children are greater than her power with them.

This role strain may be caused by the gender expectations in step mother heterosexual families, which lead to an unbalanced sharing of responsibility for and power with the children. There is also an unbalanced sharing, or has been in the recent past, between Dory and Becky. The step mother stance is unbalanced in this lesbian step family because of a complex interplay of the limitations incurred as a result of Dory's ADD, Pauli's verbal (but not, in my observations, emotional) conflict with and sometimes rejection of Becky, and Becky's perhaps more nuturant personality. As Dory discovers more ways to compensate for her ADD and as these parents take a more proactive stance with guiding Pauli, this family may find a more balanced stance as either co-parents or co-moms.

One family takes the co-mother stance, which involves an equal sharing of power with and responsibility for the children. This stance works well for this family, yet it is continuously contested by the outside world. Although issues of gender may make it more difficult for the heterosexual step family to assume this stance, the pervasiveness of heterosexual supremacy creates problems for the lesbian family to assume this stance. There is nothing legal to buttress the co-mother role and the heterosexist and homophobic attitudes in the outside world act to erode this stance. Lesbian families in which the mothers have chosen to have a child together, biologically or by adoption, may also suffer from this lack of acceptance. The nonbiological or nonlegal mother may have to constantly battle for mother status in the eyes of society.

All kinds of step families provide us with an opportunity to examine how parenting can be and is shared. Men can and do provide all kinds of mothering, and as these families exhibit, women can accomplish fathering, as well. These are differences between heterosexual and lesbian couples in what appear to be the limiting factors in sharing parenting, however. For heterosexual step families, one of the major limiting factors is the gender expectations and prescriptions that divide and separate male and female tasks, roles, and even acceptable "traits." In lesbian step families, the major limiting factor seems to be the ever-present heterosexual supremacy which delegitimizes us to our children, our families, our workplaces and social support systems, and ourselves.

THE IMPACT OF HETEROSEXUAL SUPREMACY

Clearly, the pervasive presence of heterosexual supremacy is a source of mundane extreme stress for these families. Although the children did experience some teasing and the adults also had negative experiences to report, these participants have not been actively harassed or abused to any great extent. This does not negate the fact, however, that the homophobic world we live in *is* dangerous. The statistics on hate crimes against gay men and lesbians are frightening (see Herek and Berrill, 1992). These children of lesbians are very aware of this reality and express a startling ongoing fear of the possibilities for experiencing direct homophobia. Although there needs to be further research on this issue, I found two factors beyond the knowledge of antilesbian/gay violence, which may contribute to this "free-floating anxiety" in children. The first was the invisibility of their kinds of families and of lesbian people in general in the institutions outside of the family. This invisibility creates a sense of unreality—as if one is seeing something that others cannot see. When the comments that children do hear outside of the home about lesbian and gay people are negative, this creates the stone of fear in the child's heart. As one of my sons put it, "*I* know it isn't bad, but other people don't."

A second factor which may act to increase the child's anxiety is the fear of the mother. When a parent takes a protective stance toward a child, the child recognizes that there is something to be protected from. Once, when we were discussing how we learned about racism in one of my college classes, a student recounted that whenever his family drove into the big city from their small town home, his mother would tell the children to lock the car doors as they approached the city. This seemingly simple message planted the seeds of fear of people of color in this white child's heart. Of course, all parents feel protective of their children. But by being aware of the child's reaction to this protectiveness, we may be able to manage that protectiveness in a way that creates less anxiety for the child.

One set of strategies that seemed to be particularly helpful for children were those that worked to reduce the invisibility—to stop the erasure of lesbian people and their families. These strategies include seeking out and inundating the child with positive images of lesbians and gay men—books, TV, movies, newspaper articles, her-stories, pictures, and identified lesbians and gay men who are famous. It also means finding and spending time with other lesbian and gay families, lesbian and gay people in general, and heterosexual people who are accepting and affirming. The importance of affirming heterosexual allies in our lives was strongly supported in this data. Our children are bombarded with invisibility and unacceptance. We strengthen them by presenting a broad and diverse community that stands with them.

The second set of strategies parents used to combat these fears in their children was teaching them conflict resolution and problem-solving skills. When skills such as ignoring, walking away, telling how you feel, talking it out, and seeking help are taught in a generic way (not just emphasizing homophobic situations), children are empowered to take care of themselves in all kinds of situations. If parents have confidence that their children can handle common childhood confrontations, they may communicate more confidence and less fear to their children.

Another strategy used effectively by some of these parents was that of reframing or interpreting homophobia as the problem, rather than their own lesbianism. People are empowered when their fears and self-doubts are transformed into righteous anger—not the anger of hatred, but the anger of action. Education, connection with a larger community, the acquisition of skills, and taking action are empowering tools for children and adults.

Finally, the parents in this study used the opportunity of being in a lesbian family to help their children make connections to other oppressed individuals. It was very important to these parents to teach their children that differences were not bad and that being authentically who one is can be a good and positive experience. The fact that these children have personal experience with oppression may help them connect and be more empathic with other oppressed persons.

THEORETICAL IMPLICATIONS

This project examined three theoretical questions: (1) Can mothering be shared, allowing mothers to be adults outside of family and allowing unmothers to be parents? (2) Does female-only motherhood perpetuate sexism? and (3) How does the particular oppression of heterosexual supremacy affect the lesbian family?

These participants demonstrate that parenting can be shared by two women who divide parenting tasks by preference, without regard to gender or biological parenthood. All of the women participated in both traditional mothering and fathering tasks with the children, including day-to-day nurturing as well as providing for them materially. However, some women showed a preference for the daily nurturance and routine care of the children, traditionally defined as mothering, while other women preferred to spend more time interacting with the world outside of the family, traditionally defined as fathering. These preferences were not based on biological parenthood but rather, apparently, on self-identity.

It appears from this study that responsibility for children and power with them creates parenthood. Familiarity, endurance, time, and full participation in all parenting tasks create a sense of shared parenthood in the adults. Some children, particularly younger children, also appear to confer parental status based on these factors. However, it is not completely determined in this study whether or not all children eventually will embrace the nonbiological parent as a parent. It *is* clear that the adults accept each other and relate to each other as co-parents of the children, albeit not necessarily equal parents in terms of responsibility or power. The biological mothers agreed that shared parenting gave them increased time and energy to be adults outside of parenthood status. They also believed that their partners helped them to be better parents because of their additional perspectives, time, and energy.

Step families, both heterosexual and lesbian/gay, have the potential to transform motherhood and family. As Maglin and Schniedewind (1989) write:

By relinquishing some of the power of motherhood (which we have only one step removed, if at all), we can relate more fully as women. By challenging the myth of biological motherhood we can help create diverse forms of family in which parenting is shared. By replacing the "good mother" with mature adult women, we can create the space for women concurrently to be autonomous and connected in loving relationships with others. By sharing our stories we can see our connectedness and catalyze change in the broader social fabric shaping our lives. With such revisioning and concomitant social action, families can then have the hope of becoming collectives of individuals, living democratically and cooperatively together, sharing responsibility, power, and love. (p. 13)

These lesbian step families are examples of how shared parenting can work. Because they operate outside of gender restrictions within the couple system, parenting tasks are distributed based on family members' preferences and acceptance.

The second theoretical question addressed in the project was how sexism is perpetuated within the family structure. This study design did not allow any conclusive results in terms of how the lesbian couple family affects the children's attitudes and values as adults. Further studies of adult children of lesbians are needed to understand the impact of lesbian couples on the transmission of sexism. However, this study did illuminate the lesbian parents' strong positive feelings about the models of coupling and the models of strong and effective females that they presented to their children. These female couples experienced their coupling as unique—strong, respectful, nurturing, and equal were the terms most often used to describe their unions. They believed that they modeled relationships free from domination and subordination and that this would have a powerful and positive effect on their children. Children in lesbian families do not experience male privilege within the family structure which may influence their adult attitudes toward female persons.

Finally, family stress theory provided a helpful paradigm for understanding the impact of heterosexual supremacy on lesbian family members. Two crucial resources appear to be visibility of gay/lesbian people and families and supportive communities. An interpretation of pride in one's lesbian family was important for both parents as well as children. Perhaps one of the most interesting findings is the strength of erasure as a source of stress within the construct of mundane extreme environmental stress. This erasure and invisibility appears to resemble the act of shunning that takes place as a method of discipline and control in some Amish sects and Native American tribes. It creates an ongoing anxiety and realistic paranoia that can only be combated by building a supportive alternative community that celebrates this difference.

This study illustrates how family stress theory and liberation theories (such as Freire, 1989) may complement and inform each other. Family stress theory emphasizes the important mediating factors of resources and interpretation in coping with stress. (McCubbin and Figley, 1983) It also defines oppression, as a mundane extreme environment of stress. Liberation theorists (Friere, 1989; hooks, 1984; Lorde, 1984) assert that domination is the root of human distress and that it is challenged in two major ways: through a *reinterpretation* of power that replaces "power over" (domination) with "power with" (familiarity, effectiveness, dialogue); and a *reinterpretation* of difference as a strength and a *resource*. Liberation work, therefore, consists of building positive interpretations and resources with the oppressed. This study illustrates how lesbian step families are involved in liberation work as they cope with the daily stress of heterosexual supremacy and its impact on their families.

IMPLICATIONS FOR RESEARCH AND POLICY

This exploratory research certainly raises as many or more questions than it answers and indicates a continuing need for further research. As more children of openly identified lesbians grow into adulthood several themes may be explored with them. What kinds of adult intimate partnerships are they forming? What choices are they making in their lives—not necessarily on sexual orientation, but on any difference? What are their attitudes toward other oppressed peoples? Are there significant differences between women and men who were raised by lesbians? How do they understand and practice gender distinctions? What strategies did they find most helpful for coping with prejudice? Studies of adult children will help shed light on the various outcomes of growing up in a lesbian family and will give us better information for our parenting. They may also more clearly define some of the strengths and challenges of lesbian families.

More studies are needed of various kinds of lesbian step families. This study examined a basically healthy step family population, most of whom lived in a relatively progressive area of the country. What are the major clinical problems presented by lesbian step families? What interventions work to help them? What about complex lesbian step families, into which both mothers bring children—what are their unique challenges and strengths? We need more information on lesbian step families who got together when the children were older—what works for them in creating healthy families? How must strategies change when the family lives in a more overtly homophobic atmosphere?

Comparative studies may help us understand the transmission of sexism and gender dominance more thoroughly. What values and meanings are transmitted through families with gay men as heads of household, heterosexual families with profeminist fathers and mothers, single parent (male and female) families? More information is needed on lesbian families of color and biracial and multiracial families. What are their special needs, challenges, and opportunities? Information is sparse on all kinds of lesbian families, such as those with disabled children or adults, adoptive families (including transracial and/or transcultural adoptions), combined gay father/lesbian mother families. Information creates understanding and understanding can lead to appropriate action. The need for lesbian and gay studies is crucial to the struggle for justice.

In addition to implications for research, this study clearly reinforces the need for two major policy changes. One is the importance of same-sex marriage or a legal equivalent to legitimize the co-parents in the eyes of the children, society, and ourselves. Some of us may reject all marriage as the creation of a patriarchal paradigm, but as long as we exist within that paradigm we must demand legitimate status from it. Even if this step is seen as a transitional goal along the way to some new system of family formation, it is one worth pursuing because of the crucial impact it would have on acceptance.

The second policy change projected in this data is that of increasing inclusiveness in the school curriculum and atmosphere. Since our children must spend much of their lives within the schools, it is crucial that they see themselves reflected there. Inclusion in all institutions—religious, medical, therapeutic, etc., is important in our fight against erasure, but the schools remain a dominant force in the lives of children.

Implications for Lesbian Step Family Members and Their Allies and Helpers

Guidelines that can be extrapolated from this study to inform lesbian parents and their allies and helpers include:

1. *Redefine "normal."* Difference is not synonymous with abnormal. Difference does not mean deficit. Much of the good information on building healthy relationships, parenting, and step families can be applied to lesbian step family situations—however, we must be aware of when difference may mean that adjustments should be made. I highly recommend *Step Families Stepping Ahead* (1989), published by the Step Family Association of America. They outline eight steps to creating a healthy step family that I find generally applicable to lesbian families.

2. *Step families need to define a role for the nonbiological, nonlegal parent that creates a balanced stance in responsibility for and power with the children.* All family members, including children, are active agents in creating this definition. Children who are older when the new family forms, or those who have lived for a while with their mother as a single parent may require a looser bond with the step mother. Any balanced stance, which allows the parents to balance power with and responsibility for the children in a manner that is acceptable to the children, can be healthy. Parents can consciously determine how they will share the parenting tasks. Counselors and therapists can work with lesbian parenting couples to help them find a balance that meets their needs as individuals, couples, and families.

In addition, it may be helpful to acknowledge the parenting function of the step parent through some kind of affectionate and/or familial name. This may be a name which delineates family, such as Mama Kathy, or Nana, or it could simply be an affectionate nickname which declares familiarity. Naming can be a powerful tool of affiliation and inclusion.

3. *Lesbian step families, because they get little validation for their family form in society, may need to devote special attention to family building activities.* Ceremonies and rituals can be important stabilizing forces in families. According to Butler (1990), "Rituals have come to be understood as essential modes of revitalizing, sanctifying, and empowering, representing both celebration and transformation" (p. 41). In spite of this fact, none of these families has participated in any special ceremony to acknowledge the creation of a new family. Becky and Dory are the only couple who actually had a public ceremony to recognize their coupling—although some others had private ceremonies. Heterosexual step families generally gather in a ceremony to celebrate the couple's marriage, which allows the children to experience the parents' promises to each other. But the children of lesbian step families rarely have this experience. Such ceremonies might help the children understand more fully the love that binds their parents. Kwambe Omdahda discusses the impact of her union ceremony on herself, her partner Patricia, and their daughter Kashiko:

> For me, in my heart, the ceremony didn't really make any difference in how I feel about Patricia or Kashiko; I'm committed with or without symbols. But I think our holy union made a big difference in Kashiko's life; she stands grounded in what our relationship is now. I wanted to give her that foundation and let her carry it on from there. (Omdahda and Omdahda, 1990, p. 275)

It is difficult to determine how important such a ceremony might be in helping the children accept and adjust to the new family. But it is interesting that Dale and Frannie have created their own anniversary of their family coming together.

> **Nisi:** But [the kids] were ready—they really wanted her to move by the time [Florence] came, too. They were really happy and it was a whole family celebration that she could move. In fact, the kids still talk about that as our anniversary.

Even without a formal ceremony, it might be useful to lesbian step families to seize a moment, like the act of moving in together, to celebrate as a "family anniversary."

Rituals and celebrations sustain us as families. And these families have created a myriad of rituals—from going to church together as a family on a weekly basis, to familiar and beloved celebrations of Christmases and birthdays to dinners together. One method of family unification that I found striking was the use of pictures and videos. Pictures evoke memories and they can be incredibly powerful for children.

Ceremonies and rituals that celebrate the family may help to validate its existence and reinforce its concrete reality. It is important to consciously create and nurture traditions. Structure, including rules and chores, delineate boundaries and help secure a sense of safety in the home. Regular family meetings provide a forum for open discussion of issues, as well as time for connection.

We can also claim family status through any legal means available to us, such as power of attorney, wills, and domestic partnership agreements. These strengthen our ties and diminish our fears.

4. *Building family pride is an important inoculation against heterosexual supremacy.* One of the ways this is done is by emphasizing that difference and uniqueness is good. Everyone is different and that is their gift to the world. Exposing children to books, movies, newsletters, journals, and various groups of people that celebrate and affirm their uniqueness—lesbian-affirming, as well as any minority or oppressed or unique group—gives them an affirming and strengthening worldview. Children also need to know that not everyone has to like them, that they can steadfastly affirm themselves even in the face of those who try to put them down. We can talk with them about this and we can, perhaps more effectively, model it. When we adults feel fear, when we read in the paper of a gay-bashing incident, or when we are harassed by an anonymous phone caller, we need to be aware of how we convey this to the children. These are horrible and fearful events, but we cannot only talk about them with our children, but also let them know what we and/or others are doing about it.

Righteous anger is more empowering than fear. We can get ourselves and our children involved in direct action—gay pride marches, writing letters to the editor, calling local, state, and federal representatives, attending Martin Luther King Jr. celebrations, pow wows, etc. We can teach history about oppressions that have been fought against and the successes of those peoples. Children (and adults) can put fear in perspective and cope better when they feel some sense of control, when they can *do* something about it. It is hopelessness that creates chaos and feeds on itself. Hope is an action word.

5. *We can teach children (and ourselves) good generic conflict resolution and problem-solving skills.* My partner and I have found it helpful to follow the guidance of a good parenting book in this endeavor—we use Jane Nelson's (1987) *Positive Discipline,* but there are many that might be useful. Children need to talk about the issue of teasing, for example, and brainstorm various solutions.

Our children need to hear about and understand what goes into our decisions concerning when to come out and when not to, and our values regarding those decisions. We need to talk with our children about the positive results we get sometimes when we come out, so that they see how it can build protection and support, as well as clearly identify those who will not accept us.

Although talking with children is crucial, an even stronger teaching tool is to employ these conflict resolution skills and problem-solving skills in our own families. This modeling creates the foundation which makes it possible for them to apply it elsewhere.

6. *Humor and having fun together revive us and help us to survive the hard times, reminding us what we like about each other.* It is important to make time for fun, and to maximize the potential for its occurrence by choosing activities that everyone can enjoy together. The double meaning of recreation—as recreating as well as having fun—has an important meaning for family cohesiveness. Bonding is created and cemented by having fun together. These families found that playing together was healing, as well as enjoyable. Family trips are often extremely successful, if not 100 percent enjoyable, because all the family members are away from the pressures of daily life. It is particularly worthwhile in step families to create situations in which the step parent and the child can have fun together. This is not only wonderful for them, but warms the heart of the biological mother, too.

Families can discuss and structure into their lives the restorative and relationship-building activities that are *fun.*

7. *We need to continually build and strengthen a support system for our families that radiates positive feedback.* This means finding other lesbian families—child-free (but child-affirming lesbians), gay men who honor women and children, and heterosexual men, women, and families who affirm and support us in our families. It also means searching for service providers who are accepting—doctors, dentists, teachers, religious leaders, counselors and therapists. Or, if we cannot find those accepting people, it means committing ourselves to the sometimes tedious task of educating those who are willing to listen. As families with children, we may be especially effective as bridge people—the ones who may make it possible for others to open their minds about lesbianism at deeper and clearer levels.

Finally, for some families, this need to create a strong support system may even lead to a geographic change—to move closer to a more supportive neighborhood or community. For others, it may mean making a commitment to even more time spent driving or traveling to connect with those support systems.

These are some of the strategies that the women and children in this study found helpful in creating strong and healthy families. It is hard work to build family, perhaps even more challenging to build loving and connected step families. But I think these families clearly show how meaningful and fulfilling that work can be.

CONCLUSION

"The Family," as constrictively and prescriptively defined in modern America, is dead—long live *families.* Postmodern definitions of family have made room for diversity and exploration. As Stacey (1990) writes:

> An ideological concept that imposes mythical homogeneity on the diverse means by which people organize their intimate relationships, "the family" distorts and devalues this rich variety of kinship stories. And, along with the class, racial, and heterosexual prejudices it promulgates, this sentimental fictional plot authorizes gender hierarchy. Because the post-modern family crisis ruptures this seamless modern family script, it pro-

vides a democratic opportunity. Efforts to expand and redefine the definition of family by feminists and gay liberation activists and by many minority rights organizations are responses to this opportunity, seeking to extend social legitimacy and institutional support to the diverse patterns of intimacy that Americans have already forged. (pp. 269-270)

If, then, family can connote a variety of forms and situations, what is left to give distinct meaning to this particular human configuration? Hite (1994) suggests that there are two characteristics that define family: "Wherever there is lasting love, there is family" (p. 372). Family, then, is not only a group of people who love one another, but also people whose love endures over time. As Pogrebin (1983) writes:

Love and time are all we have. Time use *is* family history. What we do together counts. It adds up to years. It makes memories. (p. 230)

Enduring love is patient. It is unyielding in its consistency. It bears pain and struggle. It forgives. It continues, steadfastly.

The lesbian step families in this study are part of a revolutionary expansion of the definition of family—the partners are lesbians, they are both women, and the children are not legally related to both parents. These differences offer new possibilities for family life. They also allow us to understand more clearly some of the challenges and stumbling blocks that may impede our expanded re-creation of family.

However, these families are not only, or even predominantly, about revolution. They repeat the age-old wisdom of healthy families of all kinds—they love each other deeply and lastingly. That makes them family.

References

Allen, J. (1986). *Lesbian Philosophy: Explorations.* Palo Alto, CA: Institute of Lesbian Studies.

Allen, K. R. and Walker, A. J. (1992). A Feminist Analysis of Interviews with Elderly Mothers and Their Daughters. In Gilgun, J., Daley, K., and Handel, G. (Eds.), *Qualitative Methods in Family Research.* Newbury Park, CA: Sage Publications, pp. 198-214.

Alpert, H. (Ed.) (1988). *We Are Everywhere.* Freedom, CA: The Crossing Press.

Arnup, K. (Ed.) (1995). *Lesbian Parenting: Living with Pride and Prejudice.* Charlottetown, P.E.I., Canada: Gynergy Books.

Baptiste, D. (1987). The Gay and Lesbian Stepfamily. In Bozett, F. (Ed.), *Gay and Lesbian Parents.* New York: Praeger, pp. 112-137.

Benjamin, J. (1988). *The Bonds of Love: Psychoanalysis, Feminism, and the Problem of Domination.* New York: Pantheon Books.

Berrill, K. T. (1992). Anti-Gay Violence and Victimization in the United States: An Overview. In Herek, G. and Berrill, K. (Eds.), *Hate Crimes: Confronting Violence Against Lesbians and Gay Men.* Newbury Park, CA: Sage Publications, Inc, pp. 19-45.

Berzon, B. (1988). *Permanent Partners.* New York: E. P. Dutton.

Blankenhorn, D. (1995). *Fatherless America.* New York: Basic Books.

Blumstein, P. and Schwartz, P. (1983). *American Couples.* New York: William Morrow and Company, Inc.

Briggs, C. L. (1986). *Learning How to Ask.* Cambridge, England: Cambridge University Press.

Brown, L. S. (1989). New Voices, New Visions: Toward a Lesbian/Gay Paradigm for Psychology. *Psychology of Women Quarterly,* 13 (4), pp. 445-458.

Burke, P. (1993). *Family Values.* New York: Random House.

Butler, B. (Ed.) (1990). *Ceremonies of the Heart.* Seattle, WA: Seal Press.

Chodorow, N. (1978). *The Reproduction of Mothering.* Berkeley: University of California Press.

Chodorow, N. and Contratto, S. (1982). The Fantasy of the Perfect Mother. In Thorne, B. and Yalom, M. (Eds.). *Rethinking the Family.* New York and London: Longman, pp. 54-75.

Clunis, D. M. and Green, G. D. (1988). *Lesbian Couples.* Seattle, WA: Seal Press.

Copper, B. (1987). The Radical Potential in Lesbian Mothering of Daughters. In Pollack, S. and Vaughn, J. (Eds.), *Politics of the Heart.* Ithaca, NY: Firebrand Books, pp. 233-240.

Covey, S. R. (1990). *The Seven Habits of Highly Effective People.* New York: Fireside Book, Simon and Schuster.

Crosbie-Burnett, M. (1984). The Centrality of the Step Relationship: Challenge to Family Theory and Practice. *Family Relations*, 33 (3), pp. 459-464.

Crosbie-Burnett, M., Skyles, A., and Becker-Haven, J. (1988). Exploring Stepfamilies from a Feminist Perspective. In Dorrbusch, S. and Strober, M. (Eds.), *Feminism, Children, and the New Families*. New York: Guilford Press, pp. 297-326.

Daly, M. (1973). *Beyond God the Father: Toward a Philosophy of Women's Liberation*. Boston: Beacon Press.

Davis, L. (1986). A Feminist Approach to Social Work Research. *Affilia: Journal of Women and Social Work*, 1 (1), pp. 32-47 Spring. ©1986 by Sage Publications. Reprinted by permission of Sage Publications, Inc.

DeStefano, A. M. (1988, May 10). NY Teens Antigay, Poll Finds. *Newsday*, pp. 7, 21.

DeVault, M. L. (1990). Talking and Listening from Women's Standpoint: Feminist Strategies for Interviewing and Analysis. *Social Problems*, 37 (1), pp. 96-116. ©1978 by The Society for the Study of Social Problems. Reprinted from *Social Problems*, 37 (1), pp. 96-116, by permission.

Dinnerstein, D. (1976). *The Mermaid and the Minotaur*. New York: Harper and Row.

DuBois, B. (1983). Passionate Scholarship: Notes on Values, Knowing and Method in Feminist Social Science. In Bowles, G. and Klein, R. (Eds.), *Theories of Women's Studies*. London and New York: Routledge and Kegan Paul, pp. 105-116

Elshtain, J. B. (1981). *Public Men, Private Women*. Princeton, NJ: Princeton University Press.

Emerson, R., Fretz, R., and Shaw, L. (1995). *Writing Ethnographic Fieldnotes*. Chicago, IL: University of Chicago Press.

Erikson, F. (1990). Qualitative Methods. In Linn, R. and Erikson, F. *Quantitative Methods/Qualitative Methods*. New York: Macmillan Publishing Company, pp. 77-193.

Ettorre, E. M. (1980) *Lesbians, Women & Society*. London: Routledge and Kegan Paul.

Ferguson, A. (1989). *Blood at the Root*. London: Pandora Press.

Firestone, S. (1972). *The Dialectic of Sex*. London: Paladin.

Fraiberg, S. (1977). *Every Child's Birthright*. New York: Basic Books.

Freiberg, P. (1990). Lesbian Moms Can Give Kids Empowering Models. *American Psychology Association Monitor*, December issue, p. 33.

Freire, P. (1989). *Pedagogy of the Oppressed*. New York: Continuum Publishing Co.

Friedan, B. (1981). *The Second Stage*. New York: Summit Books.

Gilligan. (1982). *In a Different Voice*. Cambridge, MA: Harvard University Press.

Green, G. D. (1990). Is Separation Really So Great? *Women and Therapy*, 9 (1/2), pp. 87-104.

Greer, G. (1984). *Sex and Destiny: The Politics of Human Fertility*. New York: Harper & Row.

Hammersley, M. and Atkinson, P. (1983). *Ethnography: Principles in Practice.* London and New York: Routledge.

Hanscombe, G. and Forster, J. (1981). *Rocking the Cradle: Lesbian Mothers: A Challenge in Family Living.* Boston, MA: Alyson Publications, Inc.

Harding, S. (1986) The Instability of the Analytic Categories of Feminist Theory. *Signs: Journal of Women in Culture and Society,* 11 (4), pp. 645-664.

Hartsock, N. (1981). Political Change: Two Perspectives on Power. In *The Quest Book Committee,* (Ed.). *Building Feminist Theory: Essays from Quest.* New York: Longman.

Herek, G. M. and Berrill, K. T. (Eds.) (1992). *Hate Crimes: Confronting Violence Against Lesbians and Gay Men.* Newbury Park, CA: Sage Publications, Inc.

Herman, E. (1988). The Romance of Lesbian Motherhood. *Sojourner: The Women's Forum,* March, pp. 12-13.

Hill, R. (1949). *Families Under Stress.* New York: Harper and Row.

Hite, S. (1994). *The Hite Report on the Family: Growing Up Under Patriarchy.* New York: Grove Press.

Hochschild, A. with Maching, A. (1989). *The Second Shift.* New York: Avon Books.

hooks, bell. (1984). *Feminist Theory: From Margin to Center.* Boston, MA: South End Press.

hooks, bell. (1987). *Talking Back.* Boston, MA: South End Press.

Ingersoll, B. (1988). *Your Hyperactive Child.* New York: Doubleday.

Johnson, M. (1988). *Strong Mothers, Weak Wives.* Berkeley: University of California Press.

Johnson, S. E. (1990). *Staying Power: Long-Term Lesbian Couples.* Tallahassee, FL: The Naiad Press, Inc.

Joseph, G. (1981). Black Mothers and Daughters: Their Roles and Functions in American Society. In Joseph, G. and Lewis, J. (Eds.), *Common Differences: Conflicts in Black and White Feminist Perspectives,* Garden City, NY: Anchor Press/Doubleday, pp. 75-126.

Kelley, P. (1995). *Developing Healthy Stepfamilies.* Binghamton, NY: The Haworth Press.

Kitzinger, C. (1987). *The Social Construction of Lesbianism.* Beverly Hills, CA: Sage Publications.

Lather, P. (1986). Issues of Validity in Openly Ideological Research: Between a Rock and a Hard Place. *Interchange,* 17 (4) (Winter), pp. 63-84.

Lazarus, R. and Folkman, S. (1984). *Stress, Appraisal, and Coping.* New York: Springer Publishing Co.

Levy, E. (1989). Lesbian Motherhood: Identity and Social Support. *Affilia,* 4 (4), pp. 40-53.

Lewis, K. (1980). Children of Lesbians: Their Point of View. *Social Work,* 25 (3), pp. 198-203.

Lightburn, A. (1992). Participant Observation in Special Needs Adoptive Families: The Mediation of Chronic Illness and Handicap. In Gilgun, J. Daly, K., and Handel, G. (Eds.), *Qualitative Methods in Family Research*. Newbury Park: Sage Publications, pp. 217-235.

Lofland, J. and Lofland, L. (1984). *Analyzing Social Settings*. Belmont, CA: Wadsworth Publishing Co.

Longres, J. (1990). *Human Behavior in the Social Environment*. Itasca, IL: F. E. Peacock Press.

Lorde, A. (1984). *Sister/Outsider*. Freedom, CA: The Crossing Press.

Maglin, N. B. (1989). Reading Stepfamily Fiction. In Maglin, N.B. and Schniedewind, N (Eds.). *Women and Stepfamilies*. Philadelphia: Temple University Press, pp. 254-278.

Maglin, N. B. and Schniedewind, N. (1989). *Women and Stepfamilies*. Philadelphia, PA: Temple University Press, pp. 254-278.

Martin, A. (1993). *The Lesbian and Gay Parenting Handbook: Creating and Raising Our Families*. New York: Harper Collins.

Martin, B. and Mohanty, C. T. (1988). Feminist Politics: What's Home Got to Do with It? In deLauretis, T. (Eds.), *Feminist Studies/Critical Studies*. Bloomington: Indiana University Press, pp. 191-212.

Martin, E. P. and Martin, J. M. (1978). *The Black Extended Family*. Chicago and London: The University of Chicago Press.

McAdoo, H. (1983). Societal Stress and the Black Family. In McCubbin, H. and Figley, C. R. (Eds.), *Stress and the Family, Vol. I: Coping with Normative Transitions*. New York: Brunner/Mazel, pp. 178-187.

McAdoo, H. (1986). Societal Stress: The Black Family. In Cole, J. (Ed.), *All American Women: Lives That Divide, Ties That Bind*. New York: Free Press.

McCracken. (1988). *The Long Interview*. Newbury Park: Sage Publications.

McCubbin, H. and Figley, C. R. (1983). (Eds.) *Stress and the Family, Vol. I: Coping with Normative Transitions*. New York: Brunner/Mazel.

McCubbin, H. and Patterson, J. M. (1983). Family Transitions: Adaptations to Stress. In McCubbin, H. and Figley, C. R. (Eds.), *Stress and the Family, Vol. I: Coping with Normative Transitions*. New York: Brunner/Mazel, pp. 5-25.

McGoldrick, M. and Carter, B. (1988). Forming a Remarried Family. In Carter B., and McGoldgrick, M. (Eds.), *The Changing Family Life Cycle: A Framework for Family Therapy*. New York: Gardner Press, pp. 399-429.

McMahon, M. (1995). *Engendering Motherhood*. New York: The Guilford Press.

Mies, M. (1983). Towards a Methodology for Feminist Research. In Bowles, G. and Klein, R. P. (Eds.), *Theories of Women's Studies*. London and New York: Routledge and Kegan Paul, pp. 117-119.

Miller, A. (1983). *For Your Own Good*. Toronto: Collins Publishers.

Miller, C. (1989). Lesbian Stepfamilies and the Myth of Biological Motherhood. In Maglin, N. B., and Schniedewind, H. (Eds.), *Women and Stepfamilies*. Philadelphia, PA: Temple University Press, pp. 281-287.

Minnich, E. K. (1989). Choosing Consciousness. In Maglin, N. B., and Schniedewind, H. (Eds.), *Women and Stepfamilies*. Philadelphia, PA: Temple University Press, pp. 191-201.

National Gay and Lesbian Task Force. (1984). *Antigay/Lesbian Victimization: A Study by the National Gay Task Force in Cooperation with Gay and Lesbian Organizations in Eight U.S. Cities.* Washington, DC: Author.

Nelson, J. (1987). *Positive Discipline.* New York: Ballantine Books.

Omdahda, K. and Omdahda, P. (1990). Building a Family: Together We Soar. In Butler, B. (Ed.), *Ceremonies of the Heart.* Seattle, WA: Seal Press, pp. 267–276.

Pasley, K. (1988). Contributing to a Field of Investigation. *Journal of Family Psychology,* 1 (4), June, pp. 452-458.

Pogrebin, L. C. (1983). *Family Politics.* New York: McGraw-Hill Book Company.

Polikoff, N. D. (1987). Lesbian Mothers, Lesbian Families: Legal Obstacles, Legal Challenges. In Pollack, S. and Vaughn, J. (Eds.), *Politics of the Heart.* Ithaca, NY: Firebrand Books, pp. 325-332.

Pollack, S. (1987). Lesbian Mothers: A Lesbian-Feminist Perspective on Research. In Pollack, S. and Vaughn, J. (Eds.), *Politics of the Heart.* Ithaca, NY: Firebrand Books, pp. 316-324.

Pollack, S. and Vaughn, J. (Eds.) (1987). *Politics of the Heart.* Ithaca, NY: Firebrand Books.

Rafkin, L. (Ed.). (1990). *Different Mothers.* Pittsburgh and San Francisco: Cleis Press.

Random House Dictionary (Second Edition) (1987). New York: Random House.

Rich, A. (1980). Compulsory Heterosexuality and Lesbian Existence. *Signs,* 5 (4) pp. 631-660.

Riddle, D and Arguelles, M. (1981). Children of Gay Parents: Homophobia's Victims. In Stuart, I. and Abt, L. (Eds.), *Children of Separation and Divorce.* New York: Van Nostrand Reinhold, pp. 174-197.

Ruddick, S. (1989). *Maternal Thinking.* New York: Ballantine Books.

Sager, C. J., Brown, H., Crohn, H., Engel, T., Rodstein, E., and Walker, E. (1983). *Treating the Remarried Family.* New York: Brunner/Mazel.

Schaffer, R. (1977). *Mothering.* Cambridge, MA: Harvard University Press.

Schulenburg, J. (1985). *Gay Parenting.* Garden City, NY: Anchor Books.

Simmel, G. (1950). (translated by Wolff, K.). *The Sociology of Georg Simmel.* New York: The Free Press.

Slater, S. (1995). *The Lesbian Life Cycle.* New York: The Free Press.

Stacey, J. (1990). *Brave New Families.* New York: Basic Books.

Stack, C. B. (1974). *All Our Kin.* New York: Harper and Row Publishers.

Stake, R. E. (1995). *The Art of Case Study Research.* Thousand Oaks, CA: Sage Publications, Inc.

Stepfamily Association of America, Inc. (1989). *Stepfamilies Stepping Ahead.* Lincoln, NE: Stepfamilies Press.

Theurer, S. L. (1994). *The Myths of Motherhood.* New York: Penguin Books.

Visher, E. B. and Visher, J. S. (1983). Stepparenting: Blending Families. In McCubbin, H. and Figley, C. R. (Eds.), *Stress and the Family, Vol. I: Coping with Normative Transitions.* New York: Brunner/Mazel, pp. 133-148.

Visher, E. B. and Visher, J. S. (1990). Dynamics of Successful Stepfamilies. *Journal of Divorce and Remarriage,* 14 (1), pp. 3-12.

Wade-Lewis, M. (1989). The Strengths of African-American Stepfamilies. In Maglin, N. B. and Schniedewind, N. (Eds.), *Women and Stepfamilies.* Philadelphia: Temple University Press, pp. 225-233.

Walker, A. and Thompson, L. (1984). Feminism and Family Studies. *Journal of Family Issues,* 5 (4) December, pp. 545-570.

Whitsett, D. and Land, H. (1992). Role Strain, Coping, and Marital Satisfaction of Steppparents. *Families in Society,* 73 (2), pp. 79-92.

Witt, S. H. (1980). Pressure Points in Growing up Indian. *Perspectives,* Spring issue 12, pp. 24-31.

Wright, J. (1994). Overcoming Heterosexual Supremacy. In Sears, J. T. (Ed.). *Bound by Diversity.* Columbia, SC: Sebastian Press, pp. 153-157.

Appendix A

Informed Consent Forms

Dear Participant in the Research Project on Lesbian Step Families:

My name is Janet Wright. I am a lesbian mother with five children who range in age from twenty-one to five. I am also a PhD student in social welfare at UW–Madison doing a dissertation on lesbian step families. I define step families as families into which one or both mothers brought children from a former relationship (i.e., marriage or former lesbian partnership).

This study is for my PhD dissertation. At some point, I also hope to be able to publish this study in book and/or article form.

I am conducting an ethnographic study of six lesbian step families. This is an in-depth look at these families which will require several interviews including at least an interview with the couple, and an interview with each individual family member. Interviews may range in length from less than one hour (with children) to two to three hours (with couples). In addition, I will spend a significant amount of time (about ten hours or more) simply being with your family, observing how you interact. These periods of observation will always be arranged with you ahead of time and you can cancel and rearrange these at any point. Family members will also be asked to keep a structured journal for one week. These journals will be copied, replacing names with pseudonyms, and returned to the authors. This period of concentrated contact (interviewing, observations, and journals) with each family will take place over a two- to three-month period, although the entire study may not be completed for two or three years.

The interviews (but not the observations) will be audiotaped. They will be transcribed or I will take extensive notes from them. The transcriptions and/or notes will use pseudonyms instead of real names. The tapes from all interviews will be kept by the researcher in a locked box and will not be available to anyone else (except possibly a paid transcriber who will adhere to confidentiality guidelines). All written materials (including my dissertation and any publications) will use pseudonyms and other identifying characteristics will be changed to disguise your identity. Also the names of communities will be changed. However, I cannot guarantee that persons reading a publication won't guess or surmise your identity, so please consider all possible risks to you and your children before signing the consent form. In particular, if you have concerns regarding the custody or safety of your children, your participation in this project may not be appropriate.

The University does not provide reimbursement for medical or psychological care or other compensation.

You have the right to withdraw from this project at any point or refuse to answer any individual questions without penalty.

You are free to participate or not with no prejudice toward you.

If you at any time have any questions or problems concerning this research, you may contact me, Janet Wright. If you have complaints about me or my conduct, you may contact my major advisor and supervisor.

If you are willing to participate in this research study, please sign the statement(s) below.

I have read the above explanation of the research with lesbian step families being conducted by Janet M. Wright and I have the phone numbers for questions and grievances. I agree to participate in this study.

———————   ————————————————

Date   Name

For Legal Mothers

I also understand that my child(ren) will be interviewed and observed and that the tapes of these interviews are confidential and will not be available to me or anyone except the researcher and possibly a transcriber.

Children's interviews will be specifically oriented to age-appropriate levels. Some of the following concerns will be addressed:

1. Do they have friends or know of other lesbian families?
2. Who do they tell about their mom being a lesbian?
3. How do they view the step mother and step family situation?
4. How do they deal with homophobia from others?
5. What do they like about their family?
6. What do they fight about in their family?

I will allow my child(ren)_____

to participate in the research project.

_____   _____

Date   Name

Dear Youth Participant:

Your mother has given permission for you to participate in this research project on lesbian step families. She has agreed that you may be interviewed and the interview will be taped. No one except me (Janet Wright), and perhaps a person who will type the tapes, will listen to the tape of your interview without your permission. You do not have to answer any questions that you do not want to answer.

I will also be visiting your family and watching how you live together.

If you find that you do not want to continue to participate in this study at any time, you may stop without any problems for you. Your mother and step mother may also withdraw you from the study at any point.

If you have any questions or want to call me for any reason, my phone number is _____. If you have a complaint about me, your mother has the phone number of someone that you can call.

If you agree to participate in this study, please sign after the statement below.

Thank you for your very important help!

Janet M. Wright

_____

I have read the attached letter about the study with lesbian step families being done by Janet M. Wright and I have the phone numbers to call if I have any problems. I agree to participate in this study and give my permission to be audiotape recorded.

_____   _____

Date   Signature

Appendix B

Structured Interview Questions

General Questions

Who is in your family? Ages? Ethnicity?
Employment? Hours? Approximate income?
Religion?
Arrangement with other biological parent?
    Legal?
    Time?
    Financial?
    Emotional (how do you get along)?
Number of years that couple has been together?
Number of years since divorce/split-up of previous relationship?
How long in previous relationship?
Child(ren)'s age? School? Grade in school?
What are some of child's favorite things to do/interests/hobbies?
Family rules?
Family rituals and celebrations?

Mother/Unmother (Step)

What does child call step?
Who goes to school conferences?
Who goes to sports/music/theater events?
Who helps with homework? Reads bedtime stories/gives baths)?
What do step and child do together?
Tell me about a disagreement you (step and child) have had. How did
    you deal with it?
How do you divide household chores?
In the last two years, what is the most important decision you have had
    to make about (child)?

How did you handle that decision?

How has the relationship between (step) and (child) changed over the years?

Two Women as Parents

If (child) is upset about something, hurt, or sick, who does she/he turn to?

Are there special things (child) does with only his/her (step)? What are they?

Are there special things (child) does with only her/his mother? What are they?

Are there special things (child) does with only her/his father? What are they?

How do you divide household tasks?

Who takes child to dentist/doctor/haircuts/lessons, etc.?

How does (step) express affection to the child? Kiss? Hugs?

Heterosexual Supremacy

How does (child) explain his/her family to friends?

Does (child) have friends who know his/her parents are lesbian?

How did you decide to tell them? What happened?

Do (child's) schoolteachers/administrators know that you are a lesbian family?

Do people at your jobs know you are a lesbian family?

How do you handle health insurance?

Do you have a will in case one of you were to die?

Does (step) have power of attorney with child?

Can you get sick leave to be with a sick child or step child? Partner?

Do your families (of origin) know about your lesbian family? Would you be welcome to bring your partner and children home for a holiday visit?

Does (child) hear many antigay/lesbian jokes or comments? How do you handle it? Give an example.

What are the hardest parts of being a lesbian step family? Give examples.

What are the best parts of being a lesbian step family? Give examples.

Tell a story of how your family is unique.

If you could have three wishes to make life better for your family, what would they be?

Is there anything else you'd like to tell me about your family?

SECOND INTERVIEW—COUPLE

Tell me about how you two got together.

What kinds of relationships have you had before?

How is this relationship different?

Did you have any kind of commitment ritual?

Do you have any commitment agreements?

How has (step mom's) relationship with child changed over the years?

What did you fight about early in your relationship that you no longer fight about?

What would you say is your current most difficult struggle as a couple? Give examples.

If you could have a legal commitment to each other (such as marriage), would you? What would it look like ideally?

If (step mom) could have a legal commitment to the child, would you? What would it look like ideally?

What are some of your favorite things to do together? Tell me about one of your favorite times together.

If you could change one thing about (child), what would it be?

If you could change one thing about your relationship as a couple, what would it be?

Explain how you handle money?

Are you a feminist? What does that mean to you?

Explain family rules. Who enforces? How do you handle discipline?

Tell me about their reactions to your discipline.

How do you talk about sex with your kids?

Have you taught them any self-protective ways to cope with homophobia/heterosexism? Explain.

What do they/would they get from a dad that they don't get from you?

Do you think kids pull you out of the closet farther or push you in?

MOM INTERVIEW

When you first thought about (partner) joining this family, what did you envision? Has this vision changed? In what ways?

How would you describe (partner's) role in this family now?

Tell me about one of your lowest moments in your (this) family.

Tell me about one of your happiest moments in your (this) family.

Do you share mothering tasks with (partner)? If yes, what kinds of things does she do? What do you do? What does she never do? Why?

Is your family of origin supportive of (partner's) role as a step mom? In what ways, yes and no?

Give me examples of how you try to support your partner as a step mom.

Are there some kinds of mothering that you don't want to share with (your partner)? Explain.

If society were not homophobic, what would change for your family?

Do you get support from other lesbian parents? Explain.

What do you wish you had known before you formed a step family?

If you could change one thing about your partner's parenting style, what would it be?

What do you like best about (partner's) relationship with (step child)?

If you and your partner broke up, what role would you want her to have with (step child), if any?

How is being a mother different from being a step mother? Give examples.

How often do you talk with your child about oppression? Tell me about a discussion you have had.

Do you think lesbian parenting is unique in any way?

Do lesbian parents offer anything unique to kids?

Kids in lesbian families—are they different in any positive or negative ways?

Do kids need a father?

Discuss how you were parented and compare it to how you parent.

Do you think the biological tie of child/mom is unique? Or can it be achieved in other ways?

STEP MOM INTERVIEW

When you first thought about joining this family, what did you envision yourself doing/being with them? Has this vision changed? In what ways?

How would you describe your role in this family now?

Tell me about one of your lowest moments in your (this) family?

Tell me about one of your happiest times in your family.

What mothering tasks do you do?

What mothering tasks do you never do?

Is your family of origin supportive of your role as step mother? In what ways, yes and no?

Is your workplace supportive of your role as step mother? In what ways, yes and no?

Are your friends supportive of your role as step mother? In what ways, yes and no?

Tell me about ways in which (your partner) supports you as a step mother.

Tell me about ways in which (your partner) makes it difficult for you to be a step mother.

If society were not homophobic, how would your life as a lesbian mother change?

Do you get support from other lesbian step parents? Explain.

What do you wish you had known before you entered this family?

If you could change one thing about your partner's parenting style, what would it be?

If you and (your partner) broke up, what role would you hope to have with (step child), if any?

What do you like best about your relationship with (step child)? How often do you talk with step child about oppressions? Tell me about a discussion you have had with your step child about oppression/bigotry (if you have).

Have you always wanted kids?

How is your role different from a dad?

Discuss how you were parented and compare it to how you parent.

Do you think the biological tie to a child/mom is unique? Or can it be achieved in other ways?

CHILD INTERVIEW

Interviews with the children will have to be specifically oriented to age-appropriate levels. Some of the following concerns will be addressed:

What are some of your favorite things to do?

Do you have friends who are in lesbian families? If yes, what kinds of things do you do together? Do you ever talk about your moms being lesbian? If yes, what do you talk about?

Do any of your other friends know your mom is lesbian? Do you talk about it? What kinds of things?

What kinds of things do you do with (step mom)? What are things you do only with your mom?

Does your dad know your mom is lesbian? Do you ever talk with him about it?

Have you ever been teased about your mom being lesbian? Give some examples. What did you do?

What do you like about living with (step mom)? What is the hardest part abut living with (step mom)? or, Tell me about a time you really had fun with (step mom). Tell me about a fight you had with (step mom).

Do teachers at your school know your mom is lesbian? Have you talked with any of them about it?

Tell me about a time your family really had fun together.

What kinds of things do you like best about your family?

What do you wish you could change about your family?

Why do you think some people don't like lesbians?

Appendix C

Journal Instructions

ADULTS' JOURNAL

1. Give me an example from today of how you and your partner parent.
2. Give me an example from today of what it is like to be a step parent in this family.
3. Give me an example from today (if possible) of a challenge you faced because you are a lesbian family. How did you deal with it? How did you feel? Or something positive that occurred because you are a lesbian family?

CHILDREN'S JOURNAL

1. Tell me something about being with _____ today.
2. Tell me something about being with your mom today.
3. Did anything happen today that hurt your feelings or made you happy or made you think about what it is like being in a lesbian family? If so, can you describe what happened and what you did and how you felt?

Appendix D

Letters to Participants

January 8, 1996

Dear Participant Families:

Enclosed you will find the first of several pieces of information I will be sending you as I write my dissertation. This is a description of your family. I hope that when readers read this description they will get a real sense of who you are as a family, your own unique family "culture," and a taste of how you relate.

I would like your feedback on whether you think it paints a true picture of who your family is. Do you think I left something crucial out? Is there misinformation? Are you adequately disguised—or should I change more of the identifying information?

Please understand that I do not want to portray you as perfect. You are heroes to me because you persist in your families in spite of your human frailties, your imperfections, your challenges. Other lesbian families need to see attainable models, like yourselves, who overcome challenges and who work together with their imperfections. It would be discouraging to readers if I tried to make you look perfect. I hope you can see what a gift you have to offer others, simply by being yourselves.

If you really disagree with my portraits of your family, let's dialogue. I know that you are the experts on you. On the other hand, you might think of me as the artist who is painting a portrait of your family—you may not completely like my style or my interpretation—but it is my portrait of you. Another artist might paint a very different picture. My picture is simply one perspective of who you are—one little scene at a particular point of time. So I guess what I am saying is that I want to try to be true to you, but also true to myself. I am open to your feedback.

I tried to be somewhat true to your name—sticking with an old-fashioned name, if it was old-fashioned, for example, or trying to keep obviously ethnic names, or choosing an unusual name if yours is unusual.

I am open to your own ideas for names if you stay within those parameters.

I am on an extremely tight schedule now. Please call and give me feedback, if you have any, within two weeks of getting each mailing. Thanks again!

February 8, 1996

Dear Participant Family:

Enclosed you will find a copy of the first draft of Chapter 4—the chapter which I hope describes how the step family has created itself. I am interested in any feedback that you may have—particularly if you feel there is misinformation about your family or if you feel that I have included too much identifying information about your family. But I am also interested in your feedback on the chapter as a whole. Is it worthwhile? Do you think other lesbian step families would gain anything by having this information? Is it interesting to read? Does it go into enough or too much depth? Do you have any insights that might improve the analysis?

This chapter, as you can see, is on the family. I am working now on a chapter that looks at the couple relationship and its impact on the children. Chapter 6 will probably be on the impact of heterosexual supremacy on the family—or the interface of society with family, and Chapter 7 will be on implications and conclusions. For your information, Chapter 1 is a literature review; Chapter 2 is the methodology description; and Chapter 3 has the descriptions of each of your families. Of course, I will be giving each family a copy of the final dissertation whenever that is ready.

Give me a call after you get a chance to read this, or feel free to return it with your comments.

I hope you are well and surviving the winter OK!

Sincerely,

March 6, 1996

Dear Participant Family:

Here is Chapter 6. There will one more chapter—the conclusions and implications. After you receive that chapter, you won't get any further installments. However, I will send you a copy of the final dissertation.

I haven't received a lot of feedback from participants. I would like to hear from each of you before I finish the rewriting phase, which I hope will be by the end of May. Your feedback will improve the quality of my writing and of my analysis, I'm sure. I guess I'm also feeling a bit paranoid—wondering if you are all mad at me or thinking that this is just a bunch of garbage or what? Don't keep me in suspense!

Several of you have commented on how you don't like how you sound when it is transcribed—too many "likes" or "you knows" or hesitations. The standards for qualitative research require that I transcribe what you said as closely as possible. These hesitations in our speech often illuminate emotional and/or intellectual struggles. The truth is that we all talk this way—half sentences, misused words, fillers, etc. We just aren't used to seeing real speech in written form. I often found that when you said something very profound, it came out with lots of hesitations and missteps. I see this as how we struggle to convey what we are thinking and feeling. Speech is in imperfect form of communication. I never once thought of it as sounding "dumb," as one of you commented. I hope you don't think that that is what is conveyed to the reader.

Well, I am not waiting to hear from you, since I must plunge ahead. But I would love to hear any feedback that you may have. As soon as I finish Chapter 7 I will begin the arduous task of rewriting. My committee has made several (groan!) suggestions about what I need to do. So—why not get in your two cents worth, too?

I have incredible respect for each of you and your families and this respect continues to grow more and more as I sift through the data. Thank you again for this gift you have given me.

Sincerely,

March 27, 1996

Dear Participant Family:

This is the final chapter—the conclusion! The chapter numbers are off because I am probably going to divide a chapter. Now I begin the tedious task of rewriting. Sometime during the next month or two I will call you and ask if you have more feedback. I'd appreciate it if you could keep track of your suggestions for me. I am also willing to set up a time to meet with you and dialogue about some of these issues, if you have time. I really do want to hear your reactions!

I will be talking with you soon. I hope we really get spring soon—although the cold, gray weather has been good for helping me keep on task.

Sincerely,

Index

Simmel, G., 14-15
Skyles, A., 84,115
Slater, S., 98,100-101,198
Societal homophobia, 13
Socioeconomic resources, 13
Stacey, J., 20,26,30,211-212
Stack, C.B., 26,30,31,127
Stake, R.E., 27
Stark family, 60-67
Step Families Stepping Ahead, 207
Step family. *See* Lesbian step family
Step mother(s)
    African-American, 114
    and child(ren), relationship
        with, 122-126
    commitment to child, 117-119
    and discipline, 70-76
    as friend, 123,124
    gifts for, 87
    health of, concern for, 88
    helping, 86-87
    naming of, 86
    role of, defining, 127-141
    as teacher, 123,124
    vulnerability of, 115-116
Step mother stance, 133-137,199-200
Stress, 14-15,145. *See also*
        Homophobia, societal
    coping with, 12-13
    and heterosexual supremacy,
        172-173
    and oppression, 15
    reducing, 192
Study of lesbian step families
    data analysis, 23-24
    design of, 18-20
    ethical considerations, 28-34
    method, 16-18

Study of lesbian step families
    (continued)
    participant families, 21-23
    validity, 24-28
Supremacy, heterosexual, 145-146
    impact of, 201-203
    and stress in lesbians, 172-173

Teacher, step mother as, 123,124
Teasing, child's fear of, 146-150
Themes, comparison of, 23
Theoretical perspectives, 4-16
Theurer, S.L., 114
Thinking units, 23
Time, 39
Tolerance, 14
Triangulation, 25-26,27

Unmother, 5,7,11. *See also* Shared
        mothering
Upbringing. *See* Family of origin
Uphoff/Dillard family, 49-54

Validity, 24-28
Vaughn, J., 11,16,185
Violence, anti-gay, 154
Visher, E.B., 35,70,76,116
Visher, J.S., 35,70,76,116
Vulnerable, step mothers, 115-116

Wade-Lewis, M., 114
Walker, A.J., 26
Whitsett, D., 199
Witt, S.H., 6,7
Wright, J., 146,193

Order Your Own Copy of
This Important Book for Your Personal Library!

LESBIAN STEP FAMILIES
An Ethnography of Love

_____ in hardbound at $39.95 (ISBN: 0-7890-0436-4)

_____ in softbound at $19.95 (ISBN: 1-56023-928-X)

COST OF BOOKS_____

OUTSIDE USA/CANADA/
MEXICO: ADD 20%_____

POSTAGE & HANDLING_____
(US: $3.00 for first book & $1.25
for each additional book)
Outside US: $4.75 for first book
& $1.75 for each additional book)

SUBTOTAL_____

IN CANADA: ADD 7% GST_____

STATE TAX_____
(NY, OH & MN residents, please
add appropriate local sales tax)

FINAL TOTAL_____
(If paying in Canadian funds,
convert using the current
exchange rate. UNESCO
coupons welcome.)

☐ **BILL ME LATER:** ($5 service charge will be added)
(Bill-me option is good on US/Canada/Mexico orders only;
not good to jobbers, wholesalers, or subscription agencies.)

☐ Check here if billing address is different from
shipping address and attach purchase order and
billing address information.

Signature_____

☐ **PAYMENT ENCLOSED: $**_____

☐ **PLEASE CHARGE TO MY CREDIT CARD.**

☐ Visa   ☐ MasterCard   ☐ AmEx   ☐ Discover
☐ Diners Club
Account # _____

Exp. Date _____

Signature _____

Prices in US dollars and subject to change without notice.

NAME _____

INSTITUTION _____

ADDRESS _____

CITY _____

STATE/ZIP _____

COUNTRY _____ COUNTY (NY residents only) _____

TEL _____ FAX _____

E-MAIL_____
May we use your e-mail address for confirmations and other types of information? ☐ Yes   ☐ No

Order From Your Local Bookstore or Directly From
The Haworth Press, Inc.
10 Alice Street, Binghamton, New York 13904-1580 • USA
TELEPHONE: 1-800-HAWORTH (1-800-429-6784) / Outside US/Canada: (607) 722-5857
FAX: 1-800-895-0582 / Outside US/Canada: (607) 772-6362
E-mail: getinfo@haworthpressinc.com
PLEASE PHOTOCOPY THIS FORM FOR YOUR PERSONAL USE.

BOF96